What business leaders say about Building Wealth:

"*Building Wealth* is a commonsense, down-to-earth, no-nonsense guide to how anyone with real commitment can achieve financial independence."

> —Anthony Robbins, bestselling author of *Awaken the Giant Within* and *Unlimited Power*

"Russ Whitney is wealthy now, but he started with a lot less than the average person reading this book. He can—and will—show you how to create a fortune out of virtually nothing. In this fast-reading, easy-to-understand book, you'll learn a wealth-building system that you can start using tomorrow."

> —JIMMY CALANO, CEO, CareerTrack

"No fluff—just the specifics and inspiration needed on every page to help anyone achieve financial independence. Besides, while reading an advance copy it gave me an idea which made me $15,000 (no joke, Russ)."

> —VERNE C. HARNISH, Founder, Young Entrepreneurs Organizations (YEO)

"*Building Wealth* is a real winner. I have read dozens of 'how to' books, and even coauthored one, but this is one of the few books that, within weeks of purchasing it, shows you how to put cash back in your pocket."

> —Kevin Harrington, coauthor, *The Best 100 Spare-Time Business Opportunities Today*

"*Building Wealth* is great! Russ's principles for financial independence really excited me! This is not only interesting reading but valuable information to improve your life!"

> —ART WILLIAMS, Founder, A. L. Williams Insurance Corporation

"Russ Whitney is a terrific writer and a captivating speaker, but best of all he has experienced wealth-building for himself. For aspiring entrepreneurs, and anyone trying to maximize their personal profitability potential, Russ Whitney delivers the insights right here in *Building Wealth*."

> —GREG RENKER, Television Producer and Cofounder, Guthy-Renker Corporation

BUILDING WEALTH

HOW ANYONE CAN MAKE A PERSONAL FORTUNE WITHOUT MONEY, CREDIT, OR LUCK

BY

Russ Whitney

SIMON & SCHUSTER

New York   London   Toronto   Sydney   Tokyo   Singapore

SIMON & SCHUSTER
Rockefeller Center
1230 Avenue of the Americas
New York, New York 10020

Designed by Irving Perkins Associates
Manufactured in the United States of America

1   3   5   7   9   10   8   6   4   2

Library of Congress Cataloging-in-Publication Data

Whitney, Russ.
Building wealth : how anyone can make a personal fortune without
money, credit, or luck / by Russ Whitney.
p.   cm.
1. Finance, Personal.   2. Investments.   I. Title.
HG179.W5254   1994
332.024—dc20   93-35890
CIP

ISBN: 0-671-86617-6

Quote from *Think Like a Winner,* by Dr. Walter Doyle
Staples, copyright 1991 by Dr. Walter Doyle Staples, used by
permission of the publisher, Pelican Publishing Company, Inc.

To my wife, Ingrid; my daughter, Thea Renee; and my son, Russell. Your love, devotion, and support are the true wealth of my life.

Contents

Introduction

You're tired of being in debt. You're tired of watching a fortunate few live the good life while you're buried under a mountain of bills. You're tired of grinding away at your job with nothing to show for it.

Most people are looking for vehicles to provide them with more money, more freedom, and more quality time to spend with their families and friends. Yet most people are not financial geniuses, and very few of us have any significant amount of capital to begin building wealth with. That's why you need this book; in it you'll find a variety of conventional and unconventional methods to make money that no one but a street-smart, self-taught millionaire *could* teach you.

I wrote this book from my heart, and I made sure it was loaded with nuts-and-bolts information derived from my real-life experiences. I not only share my own personal story of how I became a millionaire, but I also tell you about dozens of regular, everyday people who have used my techniques successfully. You'll learn how we did it, and you'll learn how you can do it for yourself.

This book is so practical that you can read it quickly, immediately begin putting my strategies into action, and see instant results. These are not pie-in-the-sky ideas that work only in an ideal environment. You're not likely to find these strategies taught in any college course. Not one of them requires anything more than common sense and a basic knowledge of simple arithmetic to implement.

After reading this book, you can begin working toward financial independence right away, regardless of your circumstances. You will have enough information to enable you to move quickly toward a new and brighter future. You will know how to find capital, how to create part-time income and make it grow into financial independence, how to establish and repair credit, how banks really operate, how the government can help you become wealthy, and exactly what you have to do to build your personal fortune.

My motivation is simple. I became wealthy in part by reading and studying hundreds of self-help books. Though some of these books are quite good, the majority of them depend on capital, credit, or luck—or a combination of all three—for their methods to work: in short, an ideal world. The problem is, we don't live in an ideal world. I wanted to create a book with methods that have been proven in the real world, with practical advice you can always trust and believe in, and that will work for you regardless of your present position.

—Russell A. Whitney

CHAPTER 1

Light Your Internal Fire

Destiny is not a matter of chance; it's a matter of choice.

—UNKNOWN

When I was 20, I got the best job I thought I'd ever have: I was making $5 an hour killing hogs.

I worked in a slaughterhouse where, on a good day, 1,400 hogs were butchered. The process was very systematic. The 400-pound hogs were herded up a chute. At the top of the chute, they were stunned by an electric shock to the back of the neck, causing them to fall onto a conveyor belt. At that point, we could shackle their hind legs (that was my job) and they were flipped upside down so the man next to me could cut their jugular vein. Then they would bleed to death.

It was messy, disgusting work, and I believed I would be doing it for the rest of my life.

Then I noticed a magazine ad for a "get rich" program. I was wary and didn't respond to that ad; in fact, I studied a number of ads before I answered any of them. But just reading the first one set my thoughts in motion, and it wasn't long before I realized I didn't want "a job"—and certainly not a job in a slaughterhouse.

I wanted to be wealthy.

It was quite an ambition for a high school dropout with a bad attitude. And even though I knew what I wanted, I didn't know how to go about getting it. So I started answering some of those ads. I got replies about how to make mail-order millions, how to make $300,000 a year stuffing envelopes, the lazy way to riches, various franchises, and dozens of other responses that were probably a mix of legitimate opportunities and outright scams.

If you've ever responded to any of these ads, you've got a good idea of the kind of stuff that filled my mailbox. If you haven't, I'm going to save you a lot of disappointment, time, and money. I'm going to tell you how to find the real road to more money and security.

But first, it's important that you know how I did it. As I said, when I decided I wanted to become wealthy, I was a 20-year-old high school dropout working at a dead-end job. I easily could have used my lousy childhood as an excuse for never achieving anything significant. Also, I had to consider the fact that I was married and my wife was expecting our first child. I had obligations and bills, and I needed a steady income. I didn't have much, but I couldn't afford to risk what I had.

So there I was, accumulating a drawerful of money-making ideas that wouldn't work for me, primarily because they required large up-front investments. Then I saw an ad for a book on building wealth that did not brag about overnight success. I discussed it at length with my wife, because the book (long since out of print) was $10—a significant amount of money for us at the time. We debated, and since the publisher offered a money-back satisfaction guarantee, we finally agreed to give it a try. I mailed in my order, and when the book came, I started to read it.

I literally stayed up all night reading, taking notes, and making plans. I was young and naive, but I wasn't stupid. I immediately realized there was no magic to building wealth. It was definitely something I could do.

Three weeks later, I made $11,000.

Now that's not a tremendous amount of money, but it was more than I made in a year at the slaughterhouse—and I did it on a very part-time basis. I thought, if I could make that much money that quickly after reading one little book, imagine what I could do if I read a few more! I began building a library of these types of books, focusing on the fundamental principles, and selectively following the advice that sounded realistic and sensible.

By the time I turned 23, I was able to quit my job, because I had become financially independent. By the time I was 27, I had been written up in several publications as one of the youngest self-made millionaires in the United States!

The methods I used were not complicated. I've refined them slightly over the years, and they are still working for me today. They can be used by virtually anyone, anywhere, on a full- or part-time basis, and they don't necessarily require a lot of capital or credit. They do, however, require that you redirect your thinking and develop a game plan.

I've taken the fundamental principles—the ones that work—and figured out how anyone, regardless of their experience or education level, can use them to become wealthy, too. Basically I have cut out the pie-in-the-sky stuff, the empty promises, and put together a program that I know *works*—and I know it works because I've done it, and I've already taught countless others how to do it.

I can't tell you how wealthy you will eventually become, but I can tell you this: If you will follow the steps outlined in this book, you will see a very rapid improvement in your financial circumstances, and you will be on your way to building your own personal fortune.

Think like a High School Dropout

At the age of 20, it seemed as if my life had been just one hardship after another. My mother left my father and me when I was 3, and then he died when I was 14. Not only was I emotionally devastated, but I had to get a job to support myself and wound up quitting school in the eleventh grade. I was very naive, and I was desperate for something or someone to believe in. Everywhere I turned, I hit a wall.

But I kept on looking. I found my wife, and knew almost from the minute we were introduced that this was the woman I would spend the rest of my life with. We both came from working-class backgrounds where the accepted life pattern was to work at a job, save up enough to make a down payment on a house, work until you were 65, retire with a gold watch and a meager pension, and die a few years later. After we were married, we realized we wanted more for ourselves and our children. I began my search for financial security, and Ingrid provided the much-needed moral support. It wasn't easy, but we knew that America was full of rags-to-riches stories, and if it could happen for someone else, it could happen for us.

All we had to do was figure out a way.

In my own case, I went out and applied one idea—and made $11,000 in three weeks. I had faith in a system. Had I been a little more sophisticated, a little more educated, I might have questioned it, and I might not have tried it. But I was thinking like the high school dropout I was, and it worked.

As I travel around the country giving lectures, I frequently ask audiences for a show of hands of those who have gone to college. The usual response is about 90 percent. This means the vast majority of the people I speak to about wealth building have a college education—and they're coming to hear a high school dropout tell them how to make more money. And the real irony is that their education may well be the reason why they don't have more money than they do.

Let's be very clear on this: A college education does have value, but formal schooling will not teach you how to make money. You probably know some very well educated people who are living a life of financial failure, or at least economic mediocrity. You may be one of them. If you are, take heart: You can overcome your education.

The Paralysis of Analysis

I once had a business partner who held an MBA along with degrees in engineering and accounting. Every time I came up with a new idea, he would sit at his large, polished oak desk, making notes on a legal pad and coming at the idea from every angle possible to try and figure out why it wouldn't work. While he was doing that, I would be at the bank trying to get it financed.

Of course, there is merit to evaluating an idea carefully for the risk-and-reward ratio. But if you constantly focus on what could go wrong, you'll bury yourself under so much fear that you'll never accomplish anything. And the problem with most colleges is that they teach what I call the paralysis of analysis. They teach students how to figure out all the reasons why something won't work, instead of teaching them to go to work.

While I'm sure there are exceptions, it has generally been my experience that the more educated an individual is, the less likely it is that he or she will demonstrate the characteristics that lead to true financial independence. Business schools teach people how to get along in the corporate environment and do the nuts-and-bolts work of managing in a company. Engineering schools teach people how to be engineers. Journalism schools turn out reporters. Medical schools produce doctors.

Schools, whether at the primary, secondary, or post-secondary level, teach students how to perform at a job. That's okay if all you want out of life is a job, if you'll be content to go to work every day, struggling to put a little money aside so you can take a vacation every year, and hoping to have enough left over to support yourself in retirement. But if you want more, you must study the methods of wealthy people and learn how the rags-to-riches stories truly happened.

I talk to thousands and thousands of college graduates every year who tell me they bought into the "go to college, get a good job, and life will be rosy" idea, but today they're stuck in jobs they don't like and are worried about losing. They're struggling to pay bills, and they're searching for a way to get more out of life. These people and countless others have changed their lives by using just a few of the strategies you will learn in the following pages.

A point of clarification here: I am not advocating that we shut down our colleges and universities. Certainly when I'm sick I want a doctor who is highly trained in his specialty. I want an attorney who knows and understands the law. And I fully intend to send my own children to college. However, I have taught my children to think like high school dropouts, because I know that's the only way they will achieve their own financial security.

Remember, high school dropouts lack formal education, but they do not necessarily lack common sense. I am a high school dropout, but I'm also a national lecturer, I can converse articulately on a variety of subjects other than business and investing, I've written a number of books, and I am routinely called on by business and civic leaders when they need advice. Oh, yes, and I'm a multimillionaire.

There's a Bigger Reason for Wealth than the Money

I don't worship at the altar of the almighty dollar, and I'm not suggesting that you should, either. But having money makes your life easier, and having lots of money makes your life a lot easier.

As I look back, I can clearly see how I built the desire and belief that I should and could become wealthy. I can almost hear you groan, because most how-to books do the desire bit to death. You must have a *burning* desire, they say, a wrenching feeling in your gut that drives you to acquire wealth. It sounds as if you could eat a bowl of spicy chili and be on your way to your first million in a few hours.

Of course, we all want money and the niceties and freedoms having money provides. But just fantasizing about a bigger house, a sleeker car, and a membership at the country club won't get you those things. There's got to be a reason for the wealth that's bigger—much bigger—than the money itself.

Let me share how, for me, the desire for wealth grew from a tiny spark of an idea to a powerhouse of energy, determination, and the guts to get it done.

I've already mentioned that my mother left my father and me when I was three years old. Because he believed I needed a mother, my father remarried. Unfortunately, the woman he chose turned out to be the stereotypical wicked stepmother. She was sweet and loving until they were married, then her attitude toward my father became one of grudging accommodation. To me, she was negative and abusive. She told me repeatedly that I was no good, that I would never amount to anything, and that I would probably wind up spending most of my life in jail. She also physically abused me. I remember clearly how she held my hands over the flame of a gas stove to discipline me.

This type of treatment is not only difficult for a child to deal with, it's overwhelming. When you hear over and over that you are a bad person, you come to believe it. I tried to take my problems to my father, but my stepmother convinced him that I was either exaggerating or lying. And he worked long, exhausting hours as an elevator mechanic. I was miserable, but I didn't feel I could burden him when he would come home tired and dirty from his dead-end job. So I bottled up my frustration, anger, and confusion, and focused on surviving.

My father was 39 when he died of heart disease. I lived with an aunt for about a year, then ran away from her home and moved in with my 18-year-old half-sister. She couldn't afford to support me, so I quit school and went to work. I lied about my age to get a job as a short-order cook from five o'clock in the morning to three in the afternoon. I'd clean up from the restaurant and dash across the street to put in a few hours as a minimum-wage telemarketer. Then, using a fake driver's license, I drove a taxi until one or two in the morning. I needed all three jobs, because none by itself would pay enough to cover my share of our living expenses.

I lived this way, going from job to job, until I got the job in the slaughterhouse. I was working there when I met and married my wife, and she became my partner in our wealth-building strategies. Today one of our companies, the Whitney Leadership Group, employs nearly 100 people. Our corporate mission is to help people change their lives in a positive, productive way. In the process, I have made even more money, and I have helped others do the same. But I was never really motivated by the dollars.

Sure, I wanted to be wealthy. I wanted to be a millionaire. But it wasn't for the Rolex watch, although today I have one. It wasn't for the nice homes or expensive cars, although I have those, too. It took me years to understand what was driving me—and it wasn't positive thinking. For me, it was simply this: If I could become a millionaire, it would make all the pain from the past go away. I would be *somebody*. I could show all those people, like my stepmother, who said I would never amount to anything, that they were wrong. Most importantly, I could give my family all the security and safety that I had never had and I so badly wanted them to have.

To build the desire necessary to achieve wealth, you must unleash the energy of your own pain. Maybe your pain comes from someone telling you that you wouldn't ever succeed. Maybe your pain comes from imagining your children in a mediocre, financially deprived life. Whatever its source, you must find that pain, crystallize it, and understand what will make it go away.

Fortunately, somewhere along the way, my pain and animosity faded. I never gloated about my success to my stepmother. By the time I began achieving my financial goals, it wasn't necessary. And gradually the need to escape the pain of my unhappy childhood was replaced with the need to repeat the pleasure my achievements generated. The challenges and rewards of building wealth became my motivators.

Making Money Shouldn't Hurt

I am absolutely fascinated by wealthy people. I want to know how they got that way and what keeps them going. I found a study that tracked the fortunes and misfortunes of 12,000 wealthy people from across the United States. This study pointed out one significant common characteristic among people who are wealth builders: *They love what they do!*

Have you ever wondered why wealthy people keep on working? Why did Sam Walton continue to be actively involved in the running of Wal-Mart Stores, Inc., until his death—long after he had made more money than he would ever spend? Don't you think that Michael Eisner, chairman and CEO of the Walt Disney Company, made enough money while still in his 40s so that he could retire with a lifestyle most of us only dream about? Why does Bill Cosby keep doing television shows and Madonna keep recording music after they've become two of the richest entertainers in the world?

The answer is simple: They love what they do. Work is not a chore for them. They're eager to get up in the morning, to tackle new projects, to reach new goals. And because they love what they do, they are willing to do what it takes to succeed.

In my lectures, I frequently ask how many people do not like what they do to earn money. Some people find their jobs tolerable, but the vast majority do not like what they do to make a living. Most people have a job for which they're paid just enough not to quit, and they work just hard enough not to get fired. Only a very few really love the work they do. That being true, we have unwittingly associated the process of making money with something that's painful or, at best, not pleasurable.

Think about this. If for years you have associated making money with pain, your brain has built a wall between yourself and the pleasure wealth and prosperity brings. When you think about money, deep down you may be focusing on ideas like "not fun," "hard," "boring," "no future," "wasting time"—all things that are painful. And when you think about big money, your idea is "big pain." It's entirely possible that this thought process has caused you unknowingly to sabotage your dreams in the past.

But it doesn't have to be that way in the future. Making money can be fun. Becoming wealthy does not have to be all trials and tribulations. Once you find the right vehicle—one that will make money and be enjoyable at the same time—you'll see how this process works, and how it will keep on working for the rest of your life.

A friend of mine makes this point quite clearly. He's successful and he likes what he does, but he doesn't *love* it, and here's how I know that: He usually comes in to his office around nine or ten in the morning. He claims he's not a "morning person," so he chooses to come in late, and then stay late if necessary. But this guy loves to fish. Fishing is a passion with him. If I were to call him at any time and suggest we go fishing the following morning, he'd be up at 4:30 A.M., and have coffee brewed and the boat ready to go by 5:00. Interesting behavior from someone who claims he's not a "morning person."

Business and making money can be extremely pleasurable, as pleasurable as fishing is for my friend. I love what I do. Simply put, it's fun for me. When the stories of wealthy people are told, over and over the common thread of loving what they do clearly shows through. It doesn't matter if they are Bill Gates of Microsoft, a computer whiz kid who became one of America's richest men; or Wally "Famous" Amos, a black man from a Harlem ghetto who made a fortune selling chocolate chip cookies; or Mary Kay Ashe, who built her own empire and helped others become wealthy with Mary Kay Cosmetics; or any of the many others who have achieved their financial goals. They all loved what they were doing.

When making money becomes your hobby, getting up early is no longer a chore. Staying late doesn't matter, because you're enjoying yourself. In fact, you'll be having so much fun that you'll toss out the time clock. You won't need it. And when you find the right vehicle that lets making money become your hobby, you'll find yourself generating significantly more dollars in much less time than you're spending on your job right now. What's more, as you'll see in the pages of this book, locating that ideal wealth-building vehicle isn't difficult.

What Motivation Can't Do

I have attended countless motivational lectures over the years, including the one that concludes with the drama and excitement of a fire walk. At one such event, I was preparing to leave when I struck up a conversation with a young fellow who was all pumped up. He was pacing back and forth, breathing hard, his eyes flashing, on an incredible adrenaline high created by the session we had attended. I commented that it was great to see someone so excited, and then I asked what he was going to do.

"I don't know," he replied, "but, by God, when I find it, I'm going to really get going."

Obviously he was truly motivated. His problem was that he didn't have a clue as to what path he would follow to reach the goal he hadn't yet defined. He was excited, but just being excited and bursting with positive energy isn't enough to make you wealthy. That excitement, that adrenaline high, is only temporary, and without a plan, all the enthusiasm in the world is worthless. You need to know how you will acquire your money.

This book will provide you with a workable, step-by-step plan to build wealth that includes a variety of proven techniques. Some will appeal to you, others won't, but you will have plenty of choices. My point is this: Motivation alone isn't enough. Method alone isn't enough. But the combination of true motivation and proven method is a guaranteed winner.

CHAPTER 2

The 95 Percent Rule Will Make You Wealthy—or Keep You Broke

Things may come to those who wait, but only those things left by those who hustle.

—ABRAHAM LINCOLN

The first major milestone on the road to wealth is financial independence, and it's time to figure out how *you* are going to get there—and to understand why so many people never do. I call it the 95 Percent Rule, and it will either make you wealthy or keep you broke.

Most people are more negative than positive in their thinking and their perception of life. But if you ask successful people whether they believed their success was possible before it happened, they'll tell you they did. They believed it, they planned for it, they worked for it, and they achieved it.

Ask unsuccessful people whether they believe they will be successful, and they'll likely tell you no. They may not be so blunt about it, they may have excuses—"if I had more education," "if I hadn't married so young," "if I didn't have all these responsibilities," "if I just had a chance," etc.—but essentially their answer will be that they don't believe they will be successful. In other words, they have a negative attitude about themselves and their future. They may even convince themselves that they enjoy their failure.

I see this over and over in my seminars. In the average crowd of 1,000 people, a few will take the principles I teach, put them into action, and make big money. A slightly larger group will use my ideas to achieve some moderate success. The rest will listen attentively, take copious notes, purchase some of the more detailed home-study materials—and do absolutely nothing at all. Even more fascinating is this: If, during the course of the seminar, I ask the audience if they believe these percentages will apply to their group, they unanimously agree.

What's the message here? They're telling me that most people are negative, that they themselves are probably negative, and that they can't or won't do anything about it.

These people are victims of the 95 Percent Rule. They are the 95 percent of the population who will plod along, living their lives one day at a time, barely getting by and unable to plan for the future. Their dreams will never even come close to reality. They'll make wishes, but they'll never set goals or make plans to change their circumstances.

Their primary contact with success is secondary—that is, they're content to watch it happen to other people, either acquaintances or characters in movies, on television, or in books. But they know it will never happen to them. And because their belief is so strong, they are right.

What's different about the 5 percent who do achieve financial security?

Is it intelligence? No. I've known some extraordinarily brilliant people who can't seem to raise their income above the poverty level. I've also known some people with very average IQs who enjoy extremely above-average incomes.

Is it timing? No. We all live—physically, at least—in the present. Timing is a common denominator that can't be changed. At any particular moment, someone is getting wealthy, and a lot of other people are staying poor.

It is location? Not really. Certainly your opportunities will differ with your geography, but in any given community, small or large, at any place on the globe, you will find people who are successful and people who are not.

Is it the 95 Percent Rule? You bet!

Why Things Are Always Great

When you greet your co-workers in the morning, what kind of things do you hear? My guess is that when you say, "How are you today?" the responses you get are in the vein of "I'm getting by" or "Can't complain," spoken in a dull monotone. Sometimes the answers will be more articulate, like "I've got a touch of the flu" or "My car wouldn't start this morning, and the mechanic is estimating $1,200 for repairs." Sometimes they'll even say, "Just fine," in a tone that lets you know they're anything but fine. Then there's always the guy who sets the tone for the day by responding to your "Good morning" with a snarled "What's good about it?"

How often do you ask someone how they are and hear "Great, absolutely great!"—and you know it's a sincere answer?

Could it be, just maybe, about 5 percent of the time?

Could the 95 Percent Rule be at work here?

And when someone responds to you with something like *"Great!"* doesn't it lift you up just a bit? Of course it does. And I'll tell you something else: *It lifts them up, too.*

We believe what we say. When we respond to greetings with a mumbled "I'm doing okay" or "I can't complain," we will build a life that fits that description. And if all you want is a life where you're getting along without anything to gripe about, just keep on talking this way. If you want to make yourself sicker, talk about your aches and pains. If you want to have a bad day, talk about the negatives.

Are you getting the picture?

So make the word *great* an integral part of your vocabulary and use it when anyone asks how you are. When things are going exactly as you planned, that's great. If an important business deal just fell through, that's okay, *you* are still great. If you just broke your leg, make it the greatest broken leg you've ever had.

You can't control everything that happens, but you *can* control your attitude about it. If you give negativity control over your attitude, it will take control over your circumstances. Force positivity to control your attitude, and you will enrich not only your own life, but the lives of people around you.

If you do nothing else as a result of reading this book but change the way you respond to inquiries about your health and status, you will have made a major improvement in your life. And if you do that much, you'll find the remaining steps toward personal and financial wealth will come more simply than you ever thought possible.

Before you decide that I'm just another motivational preacher, let me stress that positive thinking alone won't make you wealthy. You won't make a fortune just by being enthusiastic and visualizing piles of cash. You need strategies, plans, and methods, and you're going to learn them in later chapters. But your attitude is a critical component of success.

You wouldn't want to enter into a business deal with someone whose outlook was consistently gloomy. A banker isn't going to lend you money for a project when your attitude is pessimistic. And who wants to be around someone who wears a consistently sour expression on his face?

Dr. Walter Doyle Staples said it best in his book, *Think Like a Winner:*

> When you change your thinking,
>   you change your beliefs;
> When you change your beliefs,
>   you change your expectations;
> When you change your expectations,
>   you change your attitude;
> When you change your attitude,
>   you change your behavior;
> When you change your behavior,
>   you change your performance;
> When you change your performance,
>   you change your life!

Once you start telling other people you and your life are *great,* you'll start to believe it yourself. You'll begin to see changes in your own aura. You'll see changes in the way others respond to you. Most importantly, you'll be constantly reminding yourself of the new "money-making you" we are about to build.

Why You've Been Fooled into Thinking Wealth Is Beyond You

If 95 percent of the population is more negative than positive, it's safe to say that's because we've spent our lives being exposed to more negatives than positives. That means we've heard over and over why we can't achieve certain things, why we shouldn't expect too much out of life, why we should just go to work every day, pay our bills, and raise our children to do the same.

A popular bumper sticker reads, "I owe, I owe, it's off to work I go." This isn't funny, it's a tragedy! And it's worse than depressing, it's devastating. The dream destroyers are everywhere, spreading their negativity like a cancer.

I routinely ask the people who attend my wealth-building seminars if they've told anyone what they were planning on doing that day. Then I ask if anyone they told tried to discourage them from coming. Without fail, more than half of the people who shared their plans with others had to deal with negativity.

Even more frightening is that people who don't know me, who don't have any idea what my programs are about, are not only passing judgment on what I do, but are also trying to kill someone else's dream of a better life. Why do people do that? Primarily because misery really does love company. For the most part, people who are unhappy with their lives really don't want to see anyone else do well. Rather than boost you up, they prefer to drag you down. I know that sounds harsh, and I genuinely don't believe they do it on purpose. But it's the reason that, whether you realize it or not, you have always believed wealth was beyond you and that "getting wealthy" was something other people did.

That's not true!

Wealth is available to anyone who is willing to go after it using sound, tested wealth-building techniques. That means wealth is possible for you, for the clerk at the convenience store, for anyone—even all the negative people who would try to stop you. And now you have a weapon to use against those dream destroyers: a simple, one-syllable word that's been in your vocabulary almost all your life: *Great!* It's like having a can of bug spray handy when a roach scampers across your kitchen floor. You'll get rid of the negativity that surrounds you by either chasing it away, or killing it completely.

People Are Happy to Help You Fail

Because there is no way to make money without interacting with others to varying degrees, you need a basic understanding of human nature. You already know that people are motivated by the need to experience pleasure and avoid pain. What you also need to know is that people love to talk about their problems, but they don't want to hear about yours. They might sound sympathetic as you talk, but they really don't want to hear it. More important, they probably don't care about your problems, so why bother telling them? And if they are willing to listen, it's usually with a smirk of internal satisfaction that somebody is worse off than they are. Or they might try to top your tale of woe with that age-old phrase "You think you've got problems? Wait until you hear mine!"

We all have problems, but wallowing in them won't make them go away. Of course, you can't ignore them, either. So resolve not to talk about them unless you are in a situation set up for problem solving.

You must come to terms with this reality: When you walk into the office in the morning and a co-worker says, "How are you today?" they don't want a health report or a financial statement. So don't give them one. Instead, say, "Great!"—no matter how things really are. They will be pleasantly surprised and may even allow some of your positive energy to rub off on them.

You might feel a little uncomfortable when you first start saying "Great!" That's understandable, because it probably goes strongly against the grain of the habits you've acquired over a lifetime. But no one ever got anywhere without great (there's that word again!) enthusiasm. This small word can literally change your life. If you keep saying "Great!" even when you don't quite mean it, you will come to believe it, and in less time than you might imagine, it will become true.

How to Reverse Lifelong Patterns

After I started my first business and had to hire people to work for me, I realized that my negativity affected my employees' productivity. I'd stop by the job site, scowling and snarling, and they'd slow down. Finally I decided that, since I had found books that told me how to make money, maybe I could find some on how to have a better attitude. I bought one of those "rah, rah" positive-attitude books and I hated every page of it. I thought it was the stupidest thing I'd ever read. Why? Because the author said that in order to become positive you had to go around saying things like "super" and "fantastic"—words that were not in my everyday vocabulary. Not only did the technique seem phony, but I wasn't about to embarrass myself or put my oversized ego on the line doing something I thought was silly.

But my desire to become a millionaire soon overcame my ego. I had to make the pain of my early years go away, and I knew reaching that million-dollar mark would do it. I had to make sure that my wife and children would never want for anything. And if being positive and saying dumb things would help me reach my goal, then I'd give it a try.

It was one of the hardest things I've ever done.

I began meeting with my employees and pumping them up by telling them how well things were going, what a great job they were doing, and how they were going to benefit when we had the project complete. I used words like "Great!" I smiled and put plenty of positive energy in my voice and gestures. In short, I put on a terrific show. And when I was finished, I'd scurry around the corner, out of their sight, and breathe a deep sigh of relief that my performance was over. I could go back to scowling and being negative until it was time to talk to my employees again.

Two very interesting things happened. First, worker productivity increased significantly. I was delighted, because that meant more profits. Second, and even more important, I began liking myself when I was wearing my positive mask. Some of my own medicine was working on me.

The more I pretended to be positive, the more I liked how I felt when I was doing it. The more I liked how I felt, the more I did it. Pretty soon, it wasn't uncomfortable anymore, and it wasn't long before I realized I had experienced a metamorphosis. I had unwittingly transformed myself from someone who was totally committed to negativity to someone who was positive, happy, and on a continuous search for bright things and the overall good in life.

People saw the change and thought it wouldn't last. In fact, my wife will tell you that I did a complete attitude turnaround in just a few days, and she sometimes found my new optimism irritating. But eventually it grew on her. Today, being positive is an integral part of both our natures. Being positive has enriched our lives in more ways than we can count. And being positive has helped us build our personal fortune.

The Magic of Conscious Change

People are not born either positive or negative. A positive attitude is not a magic ingredient some of us have and some of us don't. It's something we either develop—or we don't. We are shaped by our environment, and we tend to follow the path of least resistance. That means if we are exposed more to negative attitudes than positive ones, we will tend to be negative.

If you're thinking that it's easy to have a positive attitude once you've got a lot of money, you're right. But it's not easy to get wealthy without a positive attitude. I'm sure there are some wealthy negative people out there, but I've never met one of them—and I'd be willing to bet that their wealth was inherited, not earned. Let me also point out that money doesn't change people, it just makes you more of what you are. If you're a jerk when you're poor, you'll just be a bigger jerk if you become rich.

So what comes first—the attitude or the money?

There's no definitive rule that one has to come before the other. I was already well on my way to financial independence when I discovered how important it was to my ultimate success that I be more positive about life. And I was positive I wanted to be very wealthy. Today I can wholeheartedly agree with Sophie Tucker, who said, "I have been poor and I have been rich. Rich is better."

You'll find acquiring wealth is much easier once you've developed a wealthy attitude, and you do that through *conscious change*. To the casual observer, the results of your conscious change may look like magic, but there's nothing at all magical about the process. Conscious change is simply the tool you use to adjust your attitude so you feel deserving of wealth. Here's how it works:

When you do something—anything from scratching your ear to making a million-dollar business decision—you are acting either by design or from reflex. Most of our day-to-day activities are automatic; our actions and reactions are fairly predictable based on our life conditioning.

Picture this: You're relaxing in a chair, minding your own business, and you don't know me. All of a sudden, I burst into the room and throw a basketball at your chest. Within a split second, you'll throw your hands up to block the ball. Why? For the same reason you allow people to dump their negativity on you day in and day out. For the same reason you have convinced yourself you can't get wealthy. For the same reason you believe you'll be stuck in a workaday rut for the rest of your life.

You block the ball because your reflexes tell you to. In that split second it takes for your hands to go up, you will recall that if a large object strikes you, it will hurt. That reflex was plugged into your brain when you were a small child, it has been steadily reinforced over the years, and it works without any active thought on your part.

Let's change the scenario a little bit. You're still relaxing in a chair, but this time I enter a bit more slowly, and you know me and trust me. I tell you the basketball I'm carrying is made of foam, not rubber, and weighs only a few ounces. I say I'm going to toss it very gently so it will bounce off your chest and drop into your lap, and that when I do this, I want you to leave your hands at your side. You don't need to block the ball because you're not going to be hurt by it.

I toss the ball. It hits your chest and softly falls into your lap. Your arms don't move. Mission accomplished. We have just altered the way you think—for the moment, anyway.

If you try this experiment with a friend, you'll find the person sitting down will tense as they wait for the ball's impact. They know what's really happening, but they are rapidly searching their past for an appropriate response, one that is based on their life experiences. And their life experiences will tell them they must block the ball. But we have just proven that your ingrained responses can be changed. We were able to change years of programming simply by being aware of that programming and by believing that the change wouldn't hurt.

How to Feed Your Mind

How do you purge the negativity from your mind? The answer is a process called Mindfeed. I learned it by accident, and confirmed it during a period when I was working on understanding just exactly how

I managed to overcome my negative upbringing and become a millionaire. I needed to know how my attitude changed, how I kept my marriage together, how I learned enough about business without much formal education to make huge fortunes in several totally unrelated fields.

Why me? Because I learned to feed my mind with positive material. And why not you? There's absolutely no reason why you, too, cannot enjoy a life full of personal satisfaction and material comfort. You can begin by applying the process that will create the most dramatic change in the shortest time frame, and that process is Mindfeed.

We feed our bodies with liquid and solid foods every day. If we didn't, we would dehydrate and starve. Our minds operate on the same principle, but they need food of a different type. Just as a plant stretches toward light, our minds seek nourishment—and if that nourishment isn't healthy and positive, the only alternative is unhealthy and negative.

What do you get from reading most newspapers or watching television? Primarily rape, murder, car crashes, unpleasant economic news, and similar mental junk food. It's the mental equivalent of high-fat, high-calorie snacks—they may taste good on your tongue, but they are ultimately harmful to your body. I'm not suggesting that you cancel your newspaper subscription and sell your television. What I am suggesting is that you become as careful—or even more careful—about what you feed your mind as you are about what you feed your body.

When I bought my first get-rich book, I was searching for a new message. I didn't know about positive attitudes. I didn't know about success. All I knew was that I wanted to get rich. For me, rich was happy, because I didn't know any better. And I realized that if I wanted to get rich, I needed to listen to people who were rich. I needed to listen to people who were positive. I needed people to tell me it could be done and I could do it.

Belief is a powerful tool, and after I'd read a few books and listened to a few cassette tapes with good messages, I became a believer. But I didn't stop reading and listening. I continued to feed my mind with positive, productive information.

This is how Mindfeed works. It's the process of continually searching for good books and tapes with quality messages from people who have accomplished what we desire. It's the ability to sort and reject negativity, whether it comes from an individual or the media. It's the ammunition you need to offset the negatives you can't avoid. Amazingly easy and remarkably effective, Mindfeed is simply feeding your mind daily with nourishing material that will make you healthy, happy—and wealthy.

A Hobby That Will Make You a Fortune

Ninety-five Percenters are often scornful of Mindfeed. Many have shelves full of books and tapes that didn't work for them. You may even have some of them in your own home or office. This is your opportunity to revive that past investment and finally make it pay off. Books and tapes are nothing more than inanimate objects. They may hold valuable information, but results require action, and the action must come from you.

My personal library includes hundreds of books, tapes, and home-study courses. I've bought just about every self-help product that's come along in the past 15 years, from inexpensive paperbacks to audiotape and videotape sets costing hundreds of dollars. And I'm still buying them, because they have ideas that I can use to become a better person, to strengthen my relationships with family and friends, and to make more money.

My first financial success came from a technique I discovered in a "how to get rich" book. It came from feeding my mind. It just made sense to me that if I could get one idea and make $11,000 in three weeks, then feeding my mind with more ideas would help me make more money. But had I not *tried* that first technique, it wouldn't have been the technique's fault. And if I wasn't willing to try, all the books and tapes in the world would be worthless to me.

Essentially, I have made self-help my hobby, and it's a hobby that has made me wealthy. I look for information on how to improve myself, and I want to learn how other people have done so. Then I take what I consider to be the best ideas and apply them in my own life and business. And I'm not alone in this practice. Ask any self-made wealthy person if they routinely study a variety of self-help and self-improvement methods. I think you'll find that they all have extensive libraries and enjoy learning how to make themselves better and wealthier. Virtually all of them share my passion for Mindfeed in one form or another. They all understand that being wealthy is a way of life, not just the balance in your bankbook.

This is not just a lot of psychological claptrap—it's common sense. And common sense existed a long time before psychology ever did. So make self-help *your* hobby. Use these five simple steps:

1. Haul down all the books and tapes you already have and dust them off. Take inventory; you need to know what you have so you know where to look when you need information.

2. Look for an idea you can apply today that will help you make money or improve some other area of your life. (By the way, you'll find plenty of them in this book.)

3. Put the idea into play, and watch what happens.

4. Do step number three again—and again.

5. Continue feeding your mind and building your library until self-help becomes a way of life for you.

CHAPTER 3

You Can Get Wealthy Only if You Know What Wealth Is

Genius is the ability to simplify those things we perceive as complicated.

—C. W. GRAN

Picture this scenario: You've found a method of generating $3,000 to $5,000 of steady, reliable monthly income. It's a fairly simple method, something you could put into action within the next 90 to 120 days. And the income is passive, which means you don't have to spend eight hours a day at the plant or the office to earn it.

Would you quit your job?

I hope you saw yourself handing in your resignation.

Of course, $3,000 to $5,000 a month is not a fortune, but for most people it's enough to cover basic living expenses, allow for reasonable recreation and entertainment, and provide the freedom to begin building wealth. This is what financial independence is. It's the first step in becoming wealthy; it's the ability to break free of the shackles of a workaday job; it's the recognition that money rarely comes in windfalls but rather in steady, planned, increasingly larger increments.

When most of us think about becoming millionaires, our minds automatically reject the picture. Why? First, because we associate making money with pain. Second, because the idea of a million dollars is so far outside the realm of our day-to-day experience that we feel it is unattainable. And third, because becoming wealthy means a lot of work and responsibility, and it's definitely something that only happens to other people.

The result is almost guaranteed failure.

So what should you do to change the pattern?

First, as we've already discussed, do what other wealthy people have done and find something you love, so that making money is not painful. In later chapters, we'll take a look at various ways you can accomplish this.

Second, you need to learn how to set up short-term and mid-range goals and make them work for you. It's not necessary to start with a goal of $1 million; you just have to start with enough income to allow you to quit your job. Then you move on to $250,000, then $500,000, and then $1 million.

Third, take action and don't let anything deter you.

If you're doing something you enjoy, the work and responsibility are easy to accept, and the idea of being wealthy is even more natural than being poor ever was.

What *Not* to Do with Financial Independence

When I tell people I was financially independent at age 23, their reaction is usually one of awe. They make comments about my good fortune or my "Midas touch." They tell me I must be a genius, or that I have incredible luck.

That's all totally absurd. I don't have a Midas touch, I'm not a genius, and there wasn't much luck involved in what I did.

What was financial independence for me was still poverty for most people. After three years at the slaughterhouse, I was earning $6 an hour, or about $1,000 a month. I was able to meet all my personal bills with that salary, which meant that if I had $1,000 a month from another source, I could safely quit my job.

Financial independence for me was only $1,000 a month. When I had created a passive income of $1,400 a month, I knew I could leave the slaughterhouse and concentrate all my efforts on becoming wealthy. The vehicle I was using is one I still use today, and I will share it with you later. But the point here is not that I had managed to build an income independent of my job—an income that actually paid more than my job—but how I used that income.

First, here's what I did *not* do. I did not use any of that extra passive money on consumable items, such as cars, jewelry, or clothing, that would depreciate in value and create debt. While I was still working at the slaughterhouse, I plowed those passive dollars back into my hobby of money making to get the income up to a level that would cover my basic monthly bills: my mortgage, my car payment, and necessities for my family. Once I had enough money coming in to do that, I quit my job, and invested all of my time in my hobby.

And this is the most pleasurable hobby I've ever had: The hobby of accumulating wealth and security for myself and my family. My success at this hobby has given me the freedom to pursue other interests, such as boating, fishing, tennis, and enjoying time with my wife, children, and friends. And since I was willing to forgo luxuries early on, I can now afford expensive cars, elegant jewelry and clothes for myself and my family, and an assortment of other consumer items that were once only dreams.

You see, the first step toward financial independence is a very small one. It's creating just enough regular income to allow you to quit your job so you can focus your energies on the various vehicles that can and will make you a millionaire. When you look at financial independence from this angle, it's not overwhelming; in fact, it's quite manageable. And you'll never again fall victim to the idea that success is beyond you.

What You Must Have in Common with the Wealthy and the Superwealthy

The business of getting wealthy in America has changed over the past decade or so, and successful wealth seekers have adjusted their strategies accordingly. One of the fastest-growing methods of making money in America today is being in business for yourself.

More people will start their own part-time or full-time businesses in the next decade than have done so in any other decade in our history. And not just in the United States. The spirit of entrepreneurship is thriving around the world. Traditionally socialist countries like Sweden are seeing the wisdom of private enterprise. Throughout the various republics that were formerly the Soviet Union, individuals are seizing the opportunity to be in business for themselves and to control their own destinies.

There is, however, a difference between people who start a business just to make a living and people who start a business to become wealthy. The people in the second category all have something in common with each other and with high-dollar-earning corporations: With few exceptions, they all own real estate. Certainly, they all make money in a variety of ways, but their portfolios have a solid foundation of real estate investments. In many cases, the superwealthy receive a high percentage of their long-range money—that is, steady yields from assets that regularly increase in value—from real estate.

I have always believed that intelligence means you can learn from your mistakes, but true genius means you also learn from the mistakes and experience of others. So if there is a clear pattern of wealthy individuals investing in real estate, and you want to become wealthy, does it make sense for you to follow their example? Of course it does.

Consider Arnold Schwarzenegger. He's made millions on movies, but he's also an extremely savvy real estate investor. He was buying and fixing up run-down properties in California while he was still an obscure body builder. In fact, he did that while he was training for the competitions that would ultimately make him famous. For Schwarzenegger, real estate was the initial stepping-stone toward financial independence and the freedom it would provide him to pursue his acting career and other wealth-building opportunities.

Actress Jane Seymour is a multimillionaire, and she didn't earn it all from television miniseries. A major portion of Seymour's fortune came from buying California real estate, restoring houses, and reselling them for a considerable profit. Ted Turner owns 57.7 percent of Turner Broadcasting System but receives a substantial portion of his income from real estate. Swiss shipping magnate Basil P. Goulandris shrank his fleet in 1987 and invested in real estate. German billionaire Josef Schorghuber bought a sheep pasture in 1954 and turned it into the first of thousands of office and housing developments in Munich. He has since diversified into other businesses, including breweries and travel agencies, but real estate remains a strong portion of his wealth portfolio. When Taikichiro Mori died in January 1993, at the age of

88, he was known as the richest private citizen in the world. He made his $13 billion fortune in Tokyo real estate.

The Hunt family of Texas is best known for oil money, but their real estate holdings are major. When billionaire Ross Perot disclosed his financial holdings during the 1992 presidential campaign, his portfolio included a significant amount of real estate in addition to tax-free state and municipal bonds and other relatively risk-free investments. And since these wealthy individuals recognize the value of real estate, it naturally follows that the corporations they influence also invest in real estate. If you check the holdings of the world's major corporations, you'll find they include real estate.

Let's bring the idea of real estate investment closer to home: The largest single purchase most people will ever make will be their home, and the largest single sum of money they will ever receive will come from the sale of that house. For that reason alone, you need a solid understanding of the various ways real estate can contribute to your bottom line.

Simple but Not Easy

Are you ready for a simple plan to reach financial independence? Great!

But first, note that I used the word *simple*, but I didn't use the word *easy*. Becoming financially independent is simple, but it's not necessarily easy.

Simple means anyone can do it.

Simple means it does not take complex formulas to figure it out.

Simple means anyone with common sense can go out and do it if he has any initiative at all.

Not easy, on the other hand, means you may have to make some phone calls. You might have to get up early. You might even have to do some paperwork.

Not easy means that anything worthwhile in life is not going to be tossed in your lap because you just happen to be a nice person.

What simple and not easy *does* mean, though, is that you can achieve financial independence if you want it badly enough. My wife and I have done it. Arnold Schwarzenegger did it. Mike Bartlett and

Jim Avisa did it; they started out as construction workers and today they're millionaires. I offer these examples to prove that no matter who you are, no matter what your present circumstances are, no matter what your background is, financial independence is within your grasp.

Reaching Financial Independence in 180 Days or Less

Imagine a typical house in Any City, USA. In places like Detroit or Florida, this house might sell for $50,000. In Los Angeles, the price might be $150,000. For the purpose of explanation, the actual price doesn't matter, but we will assume that every house in the neighborhood sells for a comparable amount.

The problem with purchasing such a house to rent as an investment is that in most cases the rent won't cover the mortgage payment.

Or could it?

If you take the conventional viewpoint, the answer is no. But by changing your perception you'll see that buying a house like this one is just one of many ways you can put yourself on the fast track toward financial independence. Here's one technique I used.

After I moved to Florida, I found a house listed in the real estate classifieds of the local paper in Fort Myers. The owner was very motivated to sell the property because she wanted to move closer to her children, who lived in another city. She was more interested in a steady income than a large, lump-sum payment that would have cost her thousands in capital gains taxes, so she agreed to take a small down payment and hold the mortgage. This was perfect for me, since I didn't have to go through the hassle of getting a bank loan or the expense of paying points.

The house had five bedrooms upstairs. Downstairs there was a parlor, a dining room, and another large room. I left the parlor alone but hired a carpenter to turn the other large room and the dining room into four rooms. It cost me $500 and the price of plywood and pre-hung doors from the local building supply store. Then I put the following ad in the newspaper:

Cozy rooms for rent—$55 per week.

Now, $55 was about $10 below what other rooms in the area were renting for, but everything else was comparable—size, furnishings, the number of bathrooms (this house had three the tenants shared), etc.—so it took me less than two weeks to achieve 100 percent occupancy. I had 10 rooms to rent out, which meant each week I was bringing in almost as much as I would have in a month if I had rented the house to a single family.

Here's how the numbers stacked up:

Rental income
10 rooms @ $55 each per week = $550 per week
$550 per week × 4.3 weeks = $2,365 per month
$2,365 per month × 12 = $28,380 per year

Monthly expenses
Mortgage = $676.81
Other expenses* = $322.00
* Insurance, taxes, utilities, garbage collection

Summary
Total rents = $2,365
Less mortgage = $676.81
Less expenses = $322.00
Net monthly profit = $1,366.19

My profit, or net positive cash flow on this house, was more than $16,000 per year. Even after subtracting my initial costs, this is a tidy sum to earn by doing little more than making bank deposits.

So I did it again. My next property was a larger house that I was able to convert into 13 rooms. Of course, my expenses were higher—about $1,500 per month—but that still left me with a net positive cash flow of $1,500 per month. In a very short period of time, some creative thinking and those two little rooming houses were earning me $2,800 a month. That's over $33,000 a year net income—more money than most people earn at their jobs, working eight or more hours a day doing something they hate.

If you had a little more information on the details and put a little pressure on yourself, could you make one small rooming house deal in the next 90 to 120 days? Sure you could. You might even stretch it to two deals, because that will give you your first taste of financial independence—and believe me, nothing tastes sweeter.

Does this mean your destiny is running rooming houses? No, not unless you want to do so. But consider this: Conrad Hilton, who founded the Hilton hotel chain, got his start by renting rooms in his family's New Mexico home. In Chapter Eight, I'll explain rooming houses in complete detail, so you'll have the information you need to use this wealth-building vehicle.

Are rooming houses the only way to gain financial independence? Of course not. Rooming houses are a possible, simple, manageable first step, and they will buy you the freedom to pursue your dreams. However, they are just one way, not the only way.

Since I bought my first two rooming houses, I have owned or been involved in at least two dozen other businesses that earned varying amounts of money and increased my wealth. More than half of these were started with little or no money. The point is, I was able to get involved in those other businesses because I had financial independence, not necessarily a lot of capital, and because I had taught myself to see things other people didn't.

CHAPTER 4

How to Turn $1,000 into $4.7 Million in 18 Months

People are always blaming their circumstances for what they are. I don't believe in circumstances. The people who get on in this world are the people who get up and look for the circumstances they want, and, if they can't find them, make them.

—GEORGE BERNARD SHAW

Once you know how great it feels to have your own personal fortune, you'll never again be satisfied with just getting by. When a series of circumstances tied up most of my money and resources for an extended period of time, I had to figure out how to rebuild my fortune—and do it quickly. This is how I took $1,000 and turned it into $4.7 million in just 18 months, and how you can do it, too.

But first, a brief history.

I made my first fortune in real estate in upstate New York. I bought run-down properties, fixed them up, and turned them into steady money-makers. By the time I was 25, I owned well over $1 million in real estate and was an owner or partner in several other businesses. I was financially independent because of the income my properties and businesses generated, so I decided it was time to investigate investment opportunities in other parts of the country. I chose Florida for a number of reasons.

The most obvious was the climate. I was tired of six months a year
of freezing temperatures and snow. It's harder to do exterior maintenance in the winter, and the heating bills were an expense I thought it
would be nice to get rid of. Properties in a more attractive climate
should be easier to maintain and therefore more profitable, I reasoned.

Another important consideration was that New York was losing population at the rate of about 4 percent per year, but Florida was growing
by leaps and bounds. Property values in New York were fairly stagnant,
but they were rapidly increasing in Florida. Though I could have continued to increase my personal wealth in New York, I decided that if I
was going to continue investing in real estate, I wanted to do it in a
growing area.

Before I tell you what happened when I moved, let me emphasize
that just because you might live in a northern climate, you aren't
automatically excluded from using my methods to make money with
real estate or other businesses. Every geographic region has its advantages and disadvantages, and I'll explain more about how to recognize and capitalize on various circumstances as we go along. For
now, let me reassure you that older northern and midwestern cities are
great places to begin investing in real estate because the properties are
affordable and they generate decent cash flow. In addition, older cities
have a variety of government programs that offer incentives to people
who are willing to invest in disadvantaged areas.

I have used those programs and made money while I provided a
valuable service to the community. But I was ready to move on, so I
took a trip to Florida. I had been there before on vacations, but now
I was looking with an eye to investing. I had to find an established city
with distressed and older properties that I could rehabilitate, but I also
wanted a vibrant and growing area for other business opportunities. I
found the ideal situation in southwest Florida with two neighboring
communities, Fort Myers and Cape Coral.

Fort Myers is an older city. It was the site of Thomas Edison's
winter home and laboratory, and Henry Ford had a home there for
many years. I would have no trouble finding older properties to fix up.
The adjacent city, Cape Coral, began as 100 square miles of scrub
land on the Gulf of Mexico in 1958. The second-largest city in land
area in the state (the largest is Jacksonville), it is an excellent example
of foresight on the part of its developers. They dug more than 400

miles of navigable canals that will take a boater from his backyard right out to the Gulf of Mexico. Thanks to those canals, waterfront property—which almost always goes for a premium price—is plentiful in Cape Coral. The town was planned for an eventual population of 500,000. When I first saw it, only 37,000 people made their homes there; today it has grown to approximately 85,000. Talk about an embryo opportunity!

A realtor I met with had been working in the area for about 16 years, and he had long since achieved millionaire status thanks to Cape Coral real estate. He had a deal on 12 lots for $24,000 that sounded good, so I gave him a deposit and listened attentively as he tried to sell me on the idea of moving to Cape Coral.

I investigated a few more cities before heading back to New York. I was still debating the idea of moving when I drove through North Carolina and had to turn the heat on in the car because it was getting colder outside. That clinched it: I wanted to move. All I had to do was convince my wife to give up the familiarity and security of the family, friends, and community she had lived with all her life and move 1,500 miles away to a place where she didn't know a soul. I thought it would take every ounce of persuasion I could find.

Wrong Decisions Give You Right Experiences

The temperature was below freezing and it was snowing when I got home. I presented my idea to Ingrid and, to my surprise, she was immediately enthusiastic. We decided our best strategy would be to dissolve our New York holdings. We thought we could do that in six months, so we set a goal of moving the following September.

I put our properties on the market. Because of our circumstances, I was now in the position of being a motivated seller. This is good from a buyer's point of view, and I'll explain more about it in Chapter Six, but for now suffice it to say that I was at a definite disadvantage, particularly in a stagnant market. I received several ridiculously low offers, but I had already decided on my bottom line and I was determined to get it.

Though I was charging forward at full speed with our plans to move, I decided to back out of the lot purchase in Cape Coral. Up until that point, all of my successes had occurred when I controlled my own investment—that is, when I saw the property, knew the market, and negotiated the deal either by myself or with a real estate agent. Even though the realtor in Cape Coral had been introduced to me with a strong referral from a close friend, the fact was that *I* barely knew him, and I was getting ready to send him a sizeable down payment on lots I had never seen that were very far away. Another factor was that although I had plenty of cash flow, I didn't have much ready cash at the moment to use as working capital; my assets were tied up in the real estate I was trying to sell.

I decided the Cape Coral lots were just too risky, so I forfeited my deposit and canceled the deal. It turned out to be an expensive mistake, because the broker found another investor for those lots, who sold them again nine months later for $60,000—a $36,000 profit. I may have made a bad decision, but it was obvious there was plenty of money to be made in Florida. Notice what I just said. I missed a $36,000 opportunity and thought it was great because now I knew for sure there was plenty of money to be made in Florida.

I'm telling you this part of my story so you know that successful people make mistakes, too. The difference is that they don't quit because they make a mistake; they learn and keep going, and that's what you have to do. I have studied the life stories of many successful people, and they've all made their share of mistakes. They are proof that making a mistake doesn't mean you've failed; it just means you have to find another way, take a different action, and produce a different result. Mistakes give you the experience you need to make better decisions the next time. Never let the possibility of making a mistake keep you from pursuing your dreams.

Gail Borden's first attempts to concentrate foods resulted in a "meat biscuit" that consumers denounced as an inedible failure. When he later tried to condense milk, he was happily unaware that scientists of the day said the process was impossible. Early efforts at condensing milk produced burned, foul-tasting broths, but Borden finally found a technique that worked. His first condensed milk company failed when consumers were slow to buy the product. His second company was better financed and also benefited from a growing public awareness of the need for food cleanliness and quality standards. That plant grew into one of the world's food giants. Gail Borden died in 1874 and is buried in New York's Woodlawn Cemetery. On his tombstone are the words: "I tried and failed; I tried again and again, and succeeded."

Fred Smith came from a monied background and was a student at Yale when he presented a then-unique concept for an air freight operation in a business term paper. One can only imagine the chagrin of the professor who gave the paper a grade of C, because Smith would make the concept it outlined one of the greatest entrepreneurial success stories of our time: Federal Express Corporation.

Missing that Florida deal wasn't the only error I made during this period. I was working hard at marketing my properties, but I couldn't find anyone who was willing to pay my asking price. We had to push our moving goal from September to January. But we were still determined to go, and Ingrid and I made a trip to Cape Coral together in November. We bought a six-unit apartment building there with about $4,000 cash by assuming three existing mortgages and arranging for seller financing on a fourth mortgage. (I'll explain how to use these and other creative financing techniques in later chapters.) We planned to live in one unit and rent the others while we built up our real estate portfolio in Florida.

On the surface, moving from a nice house in New York to a much smaller apartment in Florida might look like a step backward, but we didn't think so. It was what we had to do to reach our ultimate goal, and we were willing to make what some people might think of as a sacrifice. But we knew it would be just a temporary lifestyle change while we worked on getting to where we really wanted to be.

Back in New York, I met a young investor at a bank foreclosure auction. He had bought several run-down properties and was fixing them up nicely. He had also arranged for some government rehabilitation loans, and it seemed as if he knew what he was doing. Since I was going to hold the mortgage on the properties, this was an important consideration. We spent months negotiating, and at least ten times I thought we'd settled on a deal only to have him come back a day or two later with a totally different proposal. This bugged me, but I was a motivated seller, and I was trying hard to stay on schedule with my goal of moving to Florida. Of course, today I know the difference between being goal-oriented and just plain stubborn, but then I was determined not to let anything get in my way.

I sold a few of my properties to a couple of investors I had worked with before, and finally agreed on the purchase terms for the rest with the young investor I had been negotiating with for so long. He was getting a great deal, and we set the closing for January 29. I planned to close on the deal in the morning and be in my car with my family heading to Florida by lunchtime.

When I arrived at my attorney's office, thinking all I had to do was sign a few papers, I was slapped with the news that the buyer wasn't ready to close. In an obvious stall, he claimed there were some points in the contract his attorney still had to review. But he generously assured me it was a minor detail, and he would manage the properties until we closed.

I had a bad gut feeling about the deal, but everything was packed, we had the apartment building in Florida and we were ready to go. So I arranged for my accountant and attorney to handle the money. The buyer was to collect the rents and turn them over to my accountant for deposit, and to submit any request for maintenance monies to my accountant.

Six months later, we still hadn't closed. Worse yet, the properties that had showed such a handsome profit when I managed them were now operating almost at a break-even point. I flew back to New York to find that my so-called buyer was ripping me off royally. He had arranged for unnecessary maintenance at absurdly high prices. He wasn't responding to legitimate maintenance requests from tenants. He wasn't bothering to turn over utility bills to the accountant, so they were going unpaid. He was also reporting rented apartments as vacant and pocketing the money himself.

I have no idea how much money he made from my properties during that time with his own unique brand of management, and even today I don't like to think about it. However, I did learn a very valuable lesson about absentee management of low- and moderate-income properties. It's very difficult to manage these properties from a distance. Today I own all types of real estate in just about every income range, and I'm comfortable using management companies for commercial and upper-income residential properties, but low- and moderate-income units need an owner or managing partner nearby.

So I formally advised my "buyer" that I was backing out of our deal, and I went to work correcting the damage he'd done and looking for legitimate buyers. It took another six months—a year after we'd moved—before I sold all my New York properties and was able to realize the cash flow from holding the mortgages that I had originally anticipated. This was a serious setback, but I don't consider it a failure. It was a learning experience for me—and I hope for you, too.

While all of this was going on in New York, I was figuring out how to survive and prosper in sunny Florida. My money was tied up in New York, and I didn't have a lot of cash. The market was different from what I was used to. Even more critical is that Florida, because of the transient nature of its population, is a difficult place to establish banking relationships. Let me tell you, going in a matter of weeks from comfortable financial independence to worrying about how I was going to support my family was emotionally devastating. I felt as if I didn't have a choice, so I started looking for a job.

The job I found was selling vending equipment on commission. I had to travel around the state, and I spent about three months getting nowhere fast. I quit that job and got a real estate license. My logic was that I would have an "in" in the local market and I could present my own offers. I would also have the opportunity to try to sell some properties for the commission.

My low and no-money-down offers were being rejected as fast as I could make them. The properties I was trying to represent as a real estate agent were vacant lots—not an area in which I had much expertise. I wasn't very successful there, either. I was discouraged and frustrated. I had been so successful in New York; why couldn't I repeat that performance in Florida?

Learning from Getting Off Track

I finally got fed up enough to figure out what my problem was. I had been flailing away at things I didn't know much about and that hadn't made me much money. My success in New York had been built on income properties; it was a comfortable and natural environment for me. So why was I messing around with all this other stuff?

The answer was that I had allowed myself to get off track. I knew where I wanted to be and I knew what I had to do to get there, but I wasn't heading in the right direction. And I wasn't really sure how I'd gotten turned around.

When people get off track, they rarely do it a mile at a time. If they did, their mistakes would be very noticeable and easy to correct. People get off track an inch at a time. Then, inch by inch, they get farther away from the track until they're off a mile, but because they did it so gradually they don't realize what's happened. All they know is that they're lost.

I had gotten off track because I'd refused to recognize the difference in the market and the bankers in Florida. It would have been the same if I'd gone to any other part of the country; every area has its own business personality, and you have to learn that personality before you can successfully do business there. I had gotten farther off track by focusing too much time and energy on areas I didn't know enough about. Once I realized this, I was able to get myself back on track in a hurry. I made a decision to get back to the basics of what I knew would work, and that was dealing in various aspects of income properties.

If It Worked the First Time, It Can Work Even Better the Second Time

I sat down and reviewed the things I had done in New York that had worked and mapped out a plan to make the most money in the least amount of time. I set long-term goals, and then broke them down into monthly increments. I made detailed "to do" lists outlining the daily and weekly tasks that were necessary to reach those goals. I developed a plan that would turn $1,000 into $4.7 million in just 18 months. As I go along, you'll see how you can follow the same plan, regardless of where you are, and start building your own personal fortune immediately.

Make a Passbook/Signature Loan Your Passport to Wealth

This is the technique I used to build my line of credit when I was 20, and it made sense to use it again to become established with bankers in Florida. Since the six-plex I initially bought was purchased by a combination of assuming mortgages and seller financing (something

I'll explain later), I had no local banking relationships at all, other than my checking account. So I deposited $1,000 in a local community bank, and then asked for a short-term loan using that money as collateral. I took the loan money, deposited it in a second bank, and took out another loan. I used that money to repay the first loan early. Then I went back to the first banker and asked for another loan. I used that money to pay off the second loan, also early. I was using this process to establish myself with local bankers as trustworthy and reliable so they would feel comfortable with me when I applied for a larger loan to buy real estate.

This is an important step, even if you have credit and especially if you don't. If your credit rating is good, chances are it's focused on the consumer side—bank credit cards, store charge accounts, personal home mortgage, etc.—and not the commercial side. You need to build a relationship with several bankers as a commercial borrower. If you don't have credit, or if you have poor credit, this will help you overcome that disadvantage. We'll talk about credit in detail in Chapter Sixteen; right now, I want to explain how you can use a passbook/signature loan to build access to seed capital for real estate and other business ventures.

Start with $1,000, or more if you have it. If you don't have that much in savings, borrow it from a relative or take an advance on a credit card. If you have any credit record at all, you'll be able to come up with $1,000 to begin this process. Just be creative and determined. And don't be overly concerned about interest; if you borrow $1,000 at 10 percent, you'll only pay $8.30 a month in interest—a wise investment for the returns you'll gain.

Take that $1,000 and open a savings account with a community bank. Stay away from the largest banks; they tend to be impersonal and inflexible in their loan policies, especially when dealing with smaller depositors. Community banks are almost always more aggressive in trying to acquire customers, and they offer more personalized service.

About a week after your account has been set up, call and request an appointment with the branch manager. Bankers are very open to this type of meeting; they like contact with the community. Just don't barge in unannounced and expect them to drop what they're doing to chat with you. Go in as scheduled in a businesslike manner and ask about the different services the bank offers, what types of loans it makes, what types of customers it's looking for, even what the goals of the bank are. At the end of the meeting ask for a short-term pass-book loan of $1,000, which is, by happy coincidence, the amount of money you have on deposit with the bank. Since this is your first meeting and you don't have an established relationship with the bank, the banker will probably lend you the money but will want to put a lien on your savings account. This way the loan is 100 percent secured, which is a very safe loan. When you repay the loan, the lien will be released.

By short term, I mean a period of six months or a year, which is standard for a passbook/signature loan. You can pay it back sooner, of course—and, if you follow my plan, you probably will. "Passbook loan" is a generic term, and different banks may have different names for this type of loan, but any experienced banker will understand what you mean. You won't make installment payments on this loan; you'll make scheduled interest payments once or twice a year, and pay the amount of the loan in full at the end of the term.

Chances are the banker will want to know why you want the loan. Your answer could be that you want to consolidate some bills, pay off a charge card, or something of that nature. There's an endless list of reasons why someone would want a short-term loan. Explain that you have a commission check, tax refund, or family gift due in the next 60 days, and you'll be using those funds to repay the loan.

Will the banker wonder why you don't just use your savings? Probably not, because borrowing against savings is a common and smart thing to do. If the subject comes up, point out that you want to keep your savings safely in the bank, earning interest, and that it's a lot easier to repay a loan than it is to replace spent savings. That's just a fact of human nature, and an experienced banker will understand and probably like your reasoning.

Once you've received the proceeds of your passbook loan, take that $1,000 to another community bank, open another savings account with it, and go through the same procedure. Then use the money from the second loan to pay back your first passbook loan early. Give the first banker a call, tell him you've enjoyed doing business with him and you're looking forward to building a long-term relationship with him and his bank. Leave your initial deposit in the bank, and wait a few weeks.

Then go back in, with an appointment, and ask for another loan. The second or third time you do this, the banker usually will not put a lien on your savings account. That means you've now gotten a signature loan, which is an unsecured loan guaranteed only by your signature. But even though your savings account may not have a lien on it, leave the money where it is. Don't shake the banker up by pulling your money out. Use your loan money to pay back the pass-book loan at the second bank. Then, as you've already done, call the second banker, thank him for the excellent service, wait a few weeks, and apply for a signature loan at that bank also.

Now, though you haven't bought a business or property or made any money, you have accomplished something significant: You have established a line of credit at two banks where you can go in and sign for $1,000 (or more) at each, for a total of $2,000 any time you need it, without having to come up with collateral. After you've established a few $1,000 lines of credit, you can begin building them to $2,500, then $5,000, then $10,000, and on up.

It's possible you may have to do several guaranteed loans before you get the signature loan, depending on your overall financial status and the bank's policies. That's okay, because the cost to you is a little bit of time and a very nominal amount of interest; the benefits are that you've begun laying the foundation of your wealth.

After you've paid back both signature loans, take $500 from each savings account, go to a third bank, and repeat the entire procedure. When I did this the first time, I went to five different banks and deposited and then borrowed $1,000 from each of them. After I was finished, I had a $5,000 line of credit—money available to me on my signature alone.

Scott Ames of Utah, one of my early students of this technique, did this with $750 he borrowed on a credit card. He was amazed at how easy it was to get a passbook loan just two weeks after opening a savings account, and then to move to unsecured loans a short time later. In another case, a young New York attorney who was just starting out and had no credit used this same technique over the span of a year to build a line of credit at several banks totaling $1 million. Once he established his reputation, he was able to use his credit line to invest in Manhattan real estate and become a multimillionaire.

If you're thinking that you couldn't get an unsecured signature loan, think again. Credit cards are essentially unsecured loans, and if you have one in your wallet, you have access to almost instant cash up to your credit limit. If you can get unsecured money from one source, why shouldn't you be able to get it from another?

After I had successfully negotiated and paid back two or three passbook/signature loans, I began receiving offers for more lines of credit from other banks. You've probably gotten plenty of these, too: a direct-mail marketing promotion that tells you you've been pre-approved for a credit card, a loan, or a line of credit of $1,000, $5,000, or more, and all you have to do is sign the application to open your account. I received one that was a book of checks; when I wrote a check, I was actually writing myself a loan. A word of caution on unsolicited credit: Some companies that market credit cards by mail ask for an up-front fee to establish your account. Don't pay it. Legitimate lenders don't need you to give them money before they can lend you money.

You may not realize how valuable even small lines of signature credit can be. Most people see themselves spending their borrowed money on consumer items and building debt, and they feel quite noble when they decline an offer for more credit. But as you read on and start to change your relationship with money, you'll see that you can use these borrowed monies to buy *appreciating* assets that will build wealth.

Once I had established a few very small credit lines and signature loans (several were as low as $1,000), plenty of institutions were happy to lend me money. And I was happy to take it, then use their funds as my springboard to financial independence and wealth both in New York and again in Florida. You can do the same thing.

Getting on Track Can Make You $33,000 in Less than Two Months

While I was building my banking relationships, I was also busy looking for property. I found a run-down four-unit apartment building with an asking price of $75,000. Other similar properties nearby were appraised much higher, so this was clearly a good investment.

I bought the building with a 10 percent down payment. I was able to make the purchase with this relatively small down payment because the seller was willing to hold the mortgage, and sellers typically don't require as high a down payment as a conventional lender does. Then I immediately had the property cleaned up and painted, and some minor repairs done. A little bit of new landscaping provided a finishing touch. I paid for this work using the line of unsecured credit I had established with the passbook/signature loan technique.

A month later, I had the property appraised at $130,000. I applied for a new mortgage based on the improved value. At the time, banks were willing to lend only 75 to 80 percent of a property's appraised value, so I was able to get a loan for $106,000 (81 percent of the appraised value). I used that money to pay off the original mortgage of $68,000 (which was the asking price of $75,000 less my down payment and the credits I received at closing) plus the $5,000 in signature loans that paid for the fix-up.

My new mortgage payments were $815.04; my rental income was $2,000 a month. Even after paying the additional expenses of taxes, insurance, water and sewer, trash collection, and so forth, the building produced a positive cash flow. The bottom line was that I had now had some passive income—income that would come in month after month without me having to go to the office every day—and I had more than $33,000 in tax-free cash to use as I pleased. I used that run-down property that plenty of other people had overlooked to achieve a financial goal and provide the capital to do more, and it was easy to do.

I was definitely back on track.

How to Get a Banker to Give You a House Plus $3,000 in Cash

You've probably heard over and over that the best form of advertising is word of mouth. That's true in every business, especially real estate. When you provide a service that people need and you do a good job, deals will come to you. That's what was now happening to me, I've since seen it happen to my students, and it will happen to you if you follow my plan.

A fellow I met through the real estate office I worked in approached me one day with a deal he thought I might be interested in. He told me about a lady who owned a home in Cape Coral that was being foreclosed. She had lived in the house with her husband, who had abandoned her and disappeared without a trace a year or so earlier. The memories she associated with the house were pretty horrible, so she moved out. Her son moved in with several other guys and a pack of dogs and cats. They made payments for a while, but eventually stopped and then moved out.

I went to look at the property immediately. It had three bedrooms, two baths, a Florida room, and a den that would also work as a home office. But the condition it was in was a classic example of cosmetic distress. There was animal excrement on every bit of carpeting, garbage was strewn everywhere, the rooms were still full of discarded junk and clutter, and the lawn was overgrown and out of control. It was perfect!

The next step was to meet the owner. She was very open with me. She had bought the house new nine years before. Her parents had loaned her $14,000 for the down payment, and she currently owed $22,000 on the mortgage, which was held by a local savings and loan. They were about six months into foreclosing, so it wouldn't be long before she lost her entire interest in the property There were some other legal complications because her former husband's name was on the deed, and she had put the house in the hands of the court, which had appointed a court master to act in good faith for her.

Her primary concern was recouping the $14,000 her parents had loaned her, and she didn't care how it was paid. So I made an offer to take care of the $22,000 existing mortgage either by assuming the old one or getting new financing, which would stop the foreclosure. I would also pay her $14,000 in the form of a second mortgage over 20 years at 11 percent. On the second mortgage, there would be no payments due for two years, and no interest would accrue during that time. I explained that I needed those two years of freedom from payments to be able to take care of the repairs and improvements the house obviously needed to make it livable.

The owner accepted the offer, so I submitted it to the court master and judge, who also approved the deal. While I was waiting for their decision, I went to the savings and loan that held the mortgage to see what it could do. Several things were working in my favor. It would save the bank money if the house was sold before foreclosure. Also, the house was in such disgusting condition that the bank would have to sink about $10,000 into it before it could reasonably expect to put it on the market. The market was slow at that time, so the bank would probably have to hold it for quite a while before it sold.

Here is something very important you need to know about banks and other lending institutions: They are not in business to foreclose on property. They don't want to foreclose, and they will usually work with just about anyone in a good-faith effort to avoid a foreclosure. They know, and you need to realize, that their business is lending money, not managing or marketing property. So when you offer a banker who is facing a foreclosure an opportunity to avoid it, you'll get his attention and probably his cooperation. And that's what happened to me in this situation.

After several meetings, the bank's branch manager and I made a deal. He would give me a new $30,000 mortgage. With the proceeds, I would satisfy the old $22,000 mortgage and pay $5,000 toward the legal fees and costs they had incurred. The branch manager and I had agreed I would need some money to get the house into shape, so at the closing I received $3,000 from the loan proceeds. I used that money to clean, paint, and put in new carpet. When I was finished, the house was appraised for $63,000—a ready-made equity of $19,000. It was so nice that Ingrid and I moved into the house ourselves and put tenants in our apartment.

It may seem odd to you that a bank would agree to this kind of financing deal, where the buyer walks away with cash from the loan. This is actually very common. The key was that I figured out the numbers ahead of time. I knew what the house was worth in its present state, what it would be worth after I fixed it up, how much those repairs would cost, and how the monthly mortgage payments would fit with my debt-to-income ratio. When I went in to talk to the banker, I was able to give him all this information before he asked and show him why this was a good deal for everyone.

I now had two bank mortgages in Florida, which helped establish my credibility with other lending institutions and gave me some borrowing power. I also positioned myself as an outlet for that bank with other foreclosed properties. The loan officers recognized the favor I was doing them by taking these run-down properties off their hands, and that motivated them to be a little more lenient with me in terms of financing.

I was geared up for a new surge of success. While I continued looking for more income properties, I went to work putting the other elements of my money-making plan into action.

How to Cash In Twice on One Smart Buy

I've already mentioned that the first building I bought in Cape Coral was a six-plex we purchased by assuming the existing mortgages and asking the owner to hold a mortgage. The purchase price was $198,000; I put up approximately $4,000 in cash and got credited for $12,000 down (an easy technique I'll show you later); assumed a first mortgage of $42,000, a second mortgage of $67,000, and a third mortgage of $45,000; the seller held a fourth mortgage of $32,000. It was a good deal, but I wasn't altogether happy with the terms of that fourth mortgage, which required semiannual payments of $5,000 each. As the due date of the first payment on that mortgage approached, I was strapped for cash because of the problems I was having with my New York properties. I put the building on the market, but there were no takers.

I approached the bank that held the first mortgage about refinancing the entire $186,000 I owed, but it was willing to lend me only $145,000. The second mortgage holder was a fellow in his sixties, and there were 22 years left on his note. I offered him $45,000 in cash to settle the $67,000 debt. While he was considering the deal, I offered the third mortgage holder $30,000 to cancel the $45,000 debt, and the fourth mortgage holder $18,000 cash for his $32,000 mortgage. I really didn't think they would all agree to my proposals, but if one or two of them did, I could take the new first mortgage, use the borrowed $145,000 to get rid of that fourth mortgage with its large payments, and comfortably keep the building.

To my surprise, they all agreed to discount their mortgages for cash rather than taking the payments over the next 20 to 30 years. I took the new mortgage, paid off the three junior mortgages, and immediately made $41,000 profit in equity just by asking for discounts. I also appreciated the bonus of improving my cash flow by $620 a month, since my payments on the four loans totaled $2,200, and after the refinancing, the payment on the new loan was only $1,600. When I later sold the property for $209,000, my profit was $64,000 instead of $11,000, thanks to those discounts.

This technique is called discounting mortgages, which simply means the mortgage holder is willing to accept a cash payment of less than the total mortgage to settle the debt in full. Many sellers—especially those middle-aged and older—do not really want to be long-term mortgage holders. In many cases, after a year or so of receiving payments, they're happy to "take the money and run." You get the cash to pay them off by refinancing the property with conventional mortgage money, which you'll obtain either after improving the property if it was distressed or after other loan money becomes available.

I use seller financing and discount mortgages as a strategy when I buy, especially during down market cycles. When the market is slow, sellers are motivated to hold mortgages to sell their property. When the market loosens up, they often would rather have a lump sum of cash than payments over the years. Whenever I purchase a property with seller financing, I make a note in my calendar to follow up in a year or so and offer a discount.

You'll generally have more success with discounting mortgages when dealing with a private or individual lender, but don't automatically assume this technique won't work with a commercial lending institution. Though most do not routinely discount mortgages, many will consider it, especially if the loan is shaky and the property is at risk of being foreclosed. You'll never know unless you ask, and the worst that can happen is you'll be turned down. The best, of course, is that you'll make a handsome contribution to your personal fortune.

CHAPTER 5

Turn an Idea into a $1 Million Business

Success is simply a matter of luck. Ask any failure.

—EARL

As I was laying out my personal wealth-building strategy, I was guided by a philosophy I hope you'll take to heart, too. It's this: You make a living with your hands, but you become wealthy with your mind.

As I mentioned in the last chapter, I have made a lot of money buying run-down properties and fixing them up. In the beginning, I did a lot of the labor myself, but now I realize that my time is better spent on negotiating deals, planning future investments, and managing the various stages of my projects. I tell my students that there are plenty of people around who are looking for part-time work, either students or other people who want to supplement their regular jobs and will do painting and other fix-up work on the weekends at very affordable rates. You don't have to pay a painting contractor $20 or $30 or more an hour when you can get a teenager to do the same work for $8 an hour.

What distresses me at seminars is when I ask how many people in the crowd would be willing to spend a Saturday painting a house for $100, and more than half the hands in the room go up. Earning $100 a day may be a reasonable living, but it's not, and never will be, wealth.

I'm not saying you should never do any of the work yourself on your properties. What I'm saying is that you need to think about whether or not slinging a paintbrush or hauling trash is the best use of your time if you want to become wealthy.

A Small Business That Can Really Make You Money

When I began accumulating properties in Florida, I formed a separate corporation to operate as the management company. The properties paid the management company for its services, which included maintenance, repairs, and rent collection. I hired two people to handle the routine maintenance—changing locks on doors, cutting the grass, painting, or whatever needed to be done—but they weren't always busy. Rather than shortening their hours, laying them off, or paying them to do nothing, I approached other owners of moderate-income properties and negotiated contracts to provide management services for them.

To understand the tremendous opportunity here, you should know that most management companies don't do a particularly good job, especially if property management is just a sideline business for them. Most real estate companies have a property management department, but it doesn't mean they know what they're doing; often it's just a service they offer to help them get listings. It probably works fairly well, too, because if the property is poorly managed, it may not be profitable, and eventually the owner may be glad to give the real estate office the listing to get rid of what has become a headache.

An independent property management company just doesn't have the interest an owner does. Also, many management companies, especially those associated with real estate offices, are geared more to middle- and upper-income properties. If you can offer quality management, particularly on low- and moderate-income properties, you'll find it fairly easy to get contracts from other owners.

For their services, management companies generally receive a percentage of the collected rents. The range is 10 to 15 percent, with harder-to-manage properties commanding a higher fee. This fee covers keeping tenants in the units, accounting for rents, and arranging for necessary maintenance. Actual maintenance and repair expenses are billed back to the owner and have the potential to be even more profitable than your basic management fee.

One of my first management contracts was for a 34-unit building. The rent averaged $400 per apartment, which meant the building generated $13,600 in gross revenue each month. The property was not in the best shape when I got the contract, so I negotiated a 15 percent management fee. That meant I had the potential to earn more than $24,000 a year on this building alone. It only took a few more properties to build a $100,000-a-year business.

I used the maintenance workers I already had on my payroll to handle the work needed on my contract properties. The first few times I sent them out to do maintenance, I simply billed the owner my actual cost. But then I found out how many other management companies and even the owners themselves handled problems: They looked in the telephone directory for companies that provided whatever type of repair they needed—and they paid top retail dollar for the service. To replace the washer in a leaky faucet, for example, they called a plumbing company that sent out a licensed plumber and charged $35 for the service call and another $35 an hour for labor, plus retail price on parts. I was charging $7 for my hourly worker, plus my actual cost for parts, which I bought with my contractor's discount.

I decided to start billing maintenance and repairs as though I had to hire out the work instead of using my own employees. I still gave my clients a better deal than they would get going through the telephone book, so it was a win-win situation for both of us. For example, my trip charge was only $15 to $20 and my hourly rate was less than half of what they might otherwise have to pay, but my markup was at least double my cost. I also started charging the owners retail for parts, even though I had gotten a discount; if they had bought the parts themselves, they would have paid the full price, so they were still saving some money. This is the capitalist system at work, it's what makes the United States such a great country, and it's why anyone who is willing to do what it takes can become a millionaire.

The bottom line was that my clients were getting a better deal with me than they'd ever gotten before, and I was making more on maintenance than I made on the management. And in a matter of months, I had created a management and maintenance company that was showing profits of hundreds of thousands of dollars a year.

When I started my property management company, I owned 10 rental units in Florida—a four-plex and a six-plex—plus the house I lived in. Managing them was easy and didn't take much time. But they, and the knowledge I had gained over the years, gave me the credibility I needed to contact other property owners about managing their buildings. To find prospective clients, all I did was look around. When I saw buildings in less-than-top condition, I made a note of the address. Once or twice a month I went to the courthouse and looked up the owners in the public records. I wrote them a letter offering my services, and then followed up with a telephone call. Some weren't interested, but enough were that I was able to quickly build a business generating more than enough cash flow to support my family and finance other investments.

Another advantage of being a property manager is that I was almost always first in line as a prospective buyer if the owner decided to sell. Since I had already proved how well I could manage their properties, negotiating seller financing was easier. Starting a property management business is not only great for immediate cash flow, it also provides you with tremendous long-term investment potential.

This is just one reason I strongly recommend that any real estate investor, especially in the early stages, should manage his or her own properties. The experience will give you the knowledge you need either to start your own property management firm, or to protect yourself if you should decide to hire such a firm later on. This theory should apply to any business; after all, you wouldn't buy a restaurant franchise unless you knew how to run the place.

A technical note: Some states require property management companies to have specific licenses if they are going to be managing property for other people. You don't need a management license for your own properties. Other states don't have any licensing requirements at all; you can check with your state to determine what you will need. And don't worry about not being "handy." You don't have to be able to perform any of the maintenance chores yourself, you just have to be able to make sure they get done and take the checks to the bank.

Become a Highly Paid Contractor Without a License or Ever Hammering a Nail—Even if You Don't Know Anything about Construction

Another important part of my wealth-building plan was to start my own contracting company to handle the repairs and renovations on my properties. This is a technique I learned by accident, but it allowed me to make $117,000 of tax-free money during my first year in real estate. It made sense to use it again in Florida, particularly when I was in circumstances that required me to accumulate as much money as possible in a short amount of time.

You probably know that most general contractors are essentially project coordinators. When a general contractor is hired to build a house or add a room or do a major repair, he or she doesn't actually do any of the physical work. Contractors simply hire subcontractors (electricians, plumbers, roofers, painters, drywall installers, and so on) who come in and do all of the work for them. The general contractor determines the specifications (what needs to be done and who needs to do it) for the job and makes sure the work is progressing satisfactorily and on schedule. And he makes a healthy profit for doing so.

I figured this out the first time I applied for a home-improvement loan. I had a property that needed repairs, but I didn't have the cash. The bank said a loan was no problem—just bring in the contractor's estimates and it would cut the contractor a check. On the surface, that sounded pretty good, but then I started thinking about it. I did all the work finding the property, figuring out what needed to be done to improve it, finding a contractor, and then dealing with the bank. The contractor would make money on the work and the bank would make money on the loan. The only person in this deal who wasn't making money was me.

Then I realized that anybody can act as his own contractor without a license as long as he owns the property. If you own your home right now and something goes wrong with the plumbing, you can call a plumber to come and fix the problem. You don't have to go through a general contractor; essentially, *you* are the general contractor who is contracting with the subcontractor to get the needed work done. The plumber has to have a license, but you don't. The same thing is true with any rental property you may own. You can call a roofer, a plumber, a painter, an electrician—any subcontractor you need to get the work done. And you can contract with them directly without being a licensed general contractor as long as you are the owner of the property involved. (You can also do this if you are a co-owner in partnership with other investors.) You pay the subcontractor directly, just as any general contractor would, but you don't have to pay the general contractor's markup, which can be anywhere from 25 to 400 percent, and more.

Acting as your own contractor, especially with investment property, will do more than just save you money—it can make you huge sums of tax-free cash. When I formed my own contracting company, I continued to apply for loans as though I was using a general contractor, so the estimates for the work I planned to do were in line with what the banks were used to seeing. By hiring the subcontractors directly, I was able to keep the contractor's profit, and since I was doing the contractor's work, everything was perfectly legitimate.

Can you do that? Sure you can. And you don't need a lot of training. I'm going to tell you what you need to know to get started, and you'll get better as you go along.

As long as you are working exclusively on your own properties or properties you co-own in a partnership or joint venture, it isn't necessary to formalize your business by filing a company name or a "doing business as" (DBA) with your local county courthouse. However, you can do so for a nominal filing fee; just check with your city or county occupational license department for details on local regulations. All you really need are some business cards and estimate forms. Generic estimate forms are available at most office-supply stores, or you can have your own printed with a company name on them for a small fee.

How to Make a 500 Percent Profit Using the Bank's Money

When you approach potential lenders for a home-improvement loan, you'll need to show them what you plan to do and how much it will cost. That is done by including copies of your contractor's estimates with your loan application. If those estimates are reasonable, they will rarely be questioned.

Let's say you've bought a cosmetically distressed duplex and you want to act as your own contractor to fix it up. Here's how you would do it and pocket some of the easiest money you'll ever make. (This example is drawn from my personal experience with numerous home improvement loans.)

Begin by making an inventory of the work you need done. We'll say you need some light fixtures replaced, new carpet, interior and exterior painting, and some landscaping. None of these projects requires a license; they are simple to do, yet they make a major cosmetic improvement.

Your next step is to get estimates on the work. For the lighting fixtures, check with building-supply stores and ask for their contractor's prices. Your estimate will show the retail price, but you'll actually pay less. Find out what an electrician would charge to do the work. Get several quotes on carpet, and be sure to ask for a contractor or commercial discount. Ask a few painting and landscaping contractors for quotes on those jobs.

Then take the estimates you received, mark them up 100 percent or more—which, by the way, isn't considered at all excessive in the industry—and transfer them to your own estimate form. I have marked up $3,000 worth of work to a retail price of $17,000 on a consistent basis, and never had a lender question the figures. That means I'm able to pay myself as much as $14,000 to get the work done on my own property. Remember, when you form your own contracting company, you're taking the markup yourself instead of giving it to someone else. Yes, the money will have to be repaid, but it will be repaid from the rental income, while you're using the tax-free lump sum of cash for other investments. Or you could sell the property, have the new buyer assume both your first mortgage and the home improvement loan, and walk away with the cash.

Let's say the electrician gave you an estimate of $400 to replace the light fixtures; the retail cost of the fixtures is $900; the highest carpet quote you got was $2,000 installed; the painters quoted $3,000; and the landscapers came in at $700. You now have a total of $7,000 in quotes. Mark that figure up by 100 percent and transfer it to your own estimate form, which means you'll take an estimate of $14,000 to the bank.

At 9 percent for 20 years, your monthly payments on a loan of $14,000 will be $125.96 and should be covered by the property's positive cash flow. The terms of home-improvement loans will vary; shop around for the best deal.

Once you get your money, have the work done—but do as much as you can yourself, or hire the contractors who gave you the lowest estimates. Purchase your own light fixtures; with your contractor's discount, you shouldn't pay more than $600. Either install them your-self or hire a handyman to do the job; there's no reason to use a licensed electrician. Purchase the carpet with your contractor's dis-count and use your handyman for this job, too. Or you might find carpet installers who are willing to moonlight and install carpet for a fraction of what you'd pay a carpet retailer. Figure out how much paint you need and buy it with your discount; you'll probably spend $200 to $250. If you have the time and are so inclined, do the painting yourself or hire students. For the landscaping, use your discount again, and either do the work yourself or hire someone at a reasonable hourly rate.

Depending on how much of the work you do yourself, the actual costs of the improvements could be as low as $3,000 to $7,000, which leaves you with as much as $7,000 in cash as your general contractor profit.

By the way, be sure to take several good-quality photographs of the property both before and after the work. Include these pictures in your portfolio to show future lenders what you do with your investment properties.

How Everyone Involved Makes a Profit

Especially in recessionary times, it's much easier to get home-equity and home-improvement loans on property you already own than to get mortgages to buy new properties. In fact, due primarily to the eco-nomic cycle of the early 1990s, we are seeing a growing abundance of funds available for existing property repair and renovation. Take ad-vantage of this tremendous opportunity. By fixing up your own prop-erties as a general contractor, you'll be increasing their value and making big money for yourself and creating a profitable, secure loan for the bank.

A bonus that comes with creating your own contracting company is that you become eligible for contractor's discounts at building-supply stores, both independently owned stores and large chains such as Home Depot and Builder's Square. As you accumulate properties, your contractor discounts can become sizeable, so call the stores you'll be buying from and find out how their discount program works before you start your first improvement project. What's more, you can use your discount for anything you purchase, even items for your own home. Do you see how even this small, informal business can both save you money and make you money on many fronts? It's not any one big deal that will make you rich; it's a series of deals and the small things that both save and make you money that will eventually add up to wealth.

Always be sure the property you are borrowing against will generate enough cash flow so that you cover your debt service and ideally have money left over. For example, let's say you have a four-unit building generating $1,200 a month in revenue. Your mortgage payment is $600, your monthly expenses (taxes, insurance, utilities, etc.) are $300. You have a $300 per month positive cash flow, so you can afford to take out a home-improvement loan as long as your monthly payments are less than $300. And it's possible your improvements may allow you to raise the rents and even increase your cash flow.

On the other hand, if for this same apartment building, your mortgage payment is $900, with monthly expenses of $300, you're breaking even, and you can't afford to increase your monthly expenses on the property. In this case, consider a home-improvement loan only if you are convinced you will be able to raise your rents enough to cover the debt.

You can take as many home-improvement loans as you have properties to borrow against and can qualify for. Even if you do only one or two a year, you'll turn a handsome profit with little effort, so make this technique a part of your wealth-building strategy.

If for some reason you're having difficulty qualifying for a loan, find a partner who can. Show him or her how much cash will come out of the deal, and how the property will take care of repaying the loan. You'll both be winners.

Remember, I made $117,000 in spendable cash in my first year of real estate investing by acting as my own general contractor and securing home-improvement loans on my properties. It's a very simple, nonintimidating, cost-you-nothing-to-start business that has the potential for huge profits.

How to Make $200 to $5,000 an Hour

Once you get started on a wealth-building program, you'll find that more opportunities than you can handle will drop in your lap. When

I got back on track and started prospecting properties, I was running into more good deals than I could buy. Once you train your eye and mind to see what the 95 percenters overlook, you'll realize there are many great deals out there.

As you begin buying properties, you'll be excited and you'll talk about it to people you know. As they see you accumulating real estate—and wealth—they'll want to know more about what you're doing and how you're doing it. And that can make you even more money.

My first experience with making money from my market knowledge was in New York when an insurance agent I'd known for a while came to talk to me about buying a policy from him. He asked me what I did and how I did it. I told him I invested in real estate and earned anywhere from 30 to 100 percent return on my money. I explained the process to him the same way I'll show it to you in Chapter Seven. He got excited and wanted to know how he could do it, too.

At the time, I had several property deals I was working on, but I knew I didn't have the cash to buy them all. So I offered to pass one or two of the deals along to him—for a small fee, of course. There are two ways to do this. If you have a real estate license and the properties are listed, you can simply sell them as an agent and make a commission that way. If you don't have a real estate license and/or the properties aren't listed, but you have negotiated a good deal someone else would like to get in on, offer to turn it over to him for a fee. You can either mark the property up or charge an hourly rate for your consulting time.

If you go the hourly route, charge at least $100 per hour; even $200 is not unreasonable for the service you're providing. I found it more profitable and easier just to add a premium of $3,000 to $5,000 to the price of the property. Even with that, everyone can win.

One of my first clients as an investment adviser was a church pastor I knew who told me he was interested in doing some investing to supplement his income. I had several deals in various stages of negotiation, but I knew I wasn't going to be able to complete them all. (It's always a good idea to have more deals in the works than you think you can do; you never know if one of them might not go through, and you always want other deals to fall back on.) One particular deal fit the pastor's parameters exactly, so I showed it to him. He bought it and paid me a $5,000 consulting fee. Five years later, he still owns the property, has more than doubled his investment in equity alone, gets a good tax write-off every year, and enjoys a few thousand dollars a month in positive cash flow. It was a great deal for both of us.

What's especially great about this type of investment advising is that it is a truly part-time activity. Just a few hours of your time can be worth several thousand dollars. Or you can approach other investors and offer your advice and management skill for a part ownership. In my early days of investing, I had many profitable deals where someone else put up the money, I did the work, and we split the profits.

Partners Can Be Worth Their Weight in Gold

In one case, a fellow I had bought a property from had another rundown building he wanted to sell. He saw how well I'd taken care of the first property, so I had his confidence. The only problem was that I couldn't get a loan because all the bankers in town thought I'd been borrowing too much. We decided that I would take half ownership in the property for overseeing the rehab. He qualified for a home-improvement loan, and I used the money to get the building in great shape. It wasn't long before it was generating positive cash flow, and thanks to my half ownership, I made a nice profit when we sold the property a short time later.

So don't stop prospecting when your personal investment plate is temporarily full. Instead, let these skills continue working for you by expanding your prospecting to other investors and helping them build wealth, too.

Simultaneous Closings Will Net You Thousands

As an alternative to just turning a deal over to another investor, you can buy the property yourself and immediately sell it at a higher price. It's called a simultaneous closing, and here's how I do it.

I make an offer to purchase a good piece of property but make it contingent on financing and closing in 90 days. This contingency, which is included in the contract to purchase, means that I don't have to buy if I can't get financing, and I've given myself three months to find the money. Then I talk it up to the people I know, and sometimes even advertise it. If I can find a buyer, I arrange for the two closings to be held simultaneously. The property is transferred briefly to me, then to the new owner. I don't have to come up with any cash, and I walk away with a nice profit for my efforts.

I used this technique on my first deal with Mike Bartlett and Jim Avisa, two construction workers I knew in New York who became millionaires through real estate. I had signed a contract to purchase a duplex and was preparing to close in about a month. Mike and Jim wanted to get into real estate, but they were afraid. I knew I could give them the little bit of help they needed to overcome their fear by working with them on their first purchase. So I showed them the duplex and offered to build in a profit for me and transfer the deal to them. We added $5,000 to my contracted purchase price and calculated the numbers. Mike and Jim would still net a 100 percent return on their investment the first year, so we agreed to do the deal. At the closing, Mike and Jim gave me the cash I needed for the seller, then I immediately signed the property over to them. I literally owned that duplex for less than an hour, and made $5,000 on it.

I hope you are starting to see the multitude of ways you can begin creating your own personal fortune, regardless of where in life you are right now or where you've been.

CHAPTER 6

The Quickest Way to Build a Money Machine

Opportunity is missed by many because it is dressed in overalls and looks like work.

—THOMAS EDISON

I've made fortunes in a number of businesses, but I know from personal experience that real estate is the simplest, fastest, and most productive way to generate significant sums of immediate cash, and it can help you lay the groundwork for even greater profits in the future. This is especially true for beginning investors.

Take a look around the area where you live right now. Is real estate more expensive than it was 15 years ago? The answer is yes. Is real estate more expensive than it was 25 years ago? Yes again. And is real estate more expensive than it was 200 years ago? Definitely yes. In fact, America's Founding Fathers valued real estate ownership so highly that in the country's early days, the legal right to vote was limited, with few exceptions, to landowners.

The story is the same virtually all over the world. Real estate has steadily and consistently increased in value. If you want to build wealth, you simply cannot ignore an investment with this kind of track record. Of course, there have been cycles when the value of real estate has leveled out or even dipped slightly. But it always comes back, and comes back stronger than before.

One more question: If you had some money to bet right now, would you wager that in 10 years real estate where you live will be more valuable than it is today? I'm not a gambler, but this is a bet I'd be willing to make.

A home is the largest single investment most people ever make in their entire lifetime, but I have found through talking with hundreds of people that most homeowners don't have any idea why or how they bought their house. Maybe somebody told them owning is better than renting, or they just decided they should do what other people do and buy a house. So they go out, maybe with a real estate agent, shop around, find a house or condominium they like, figure out how to get a loan and handle the closing, and suddenly they own a home.

The same process can apply to your second property, your third property, or even a business you might want to buy. You shop, you do research, you make commonsense decisions, you figure it out and get it done. It's that simple.

Think about this: If your home is the largest single investment you're likely to make in your life, doesn't it make sense that buying two or three other houses could, over time, have a significant and positive impact on your financial security? And if you could buy one house, don't you think buying a second one would be easier than the first? By the time you get to the third or fourth, you'll have plenty of confidence and expertise. Even if you don't net any positive cash flow and just let tenants pay the mortgages off, in 20 or 30 years you'll have a substantial net worth and assets you can sell if you want to.

I became a millionaire in my early twenties in New York. I did it all over again when I moved to Florida. And if I had to do it again, I would do it the same way. I have studied the techniques used by some of the world's wealthiest people, especially things they did to become wealthy, and I am convinced that my program is a "best of the best" combination of methods to build financial security.

Rich people who are also famous are the exception, not the rule. There are millionaires all over the world you've never heard of, and when you meet them, you wouldn't think they are wealthy. Most of them made their money with a combination of their own businesses and real estate. Here's what you need to know to make real estate your initial wealth-building vehicle.

How Economic Cycles Can Make You Wealthy

Our economy moves in fairly predictable cycles, which include a period of high prosperity and growth, a slowdown, a recession, a gradual increase in activity, and then high prosperity again. We run through this cycle every 7 to 10 years. Learning to recognize these cycles and adjusting my strategies accordingly provided a major boost to my wealth-building plan. If you're going to become wealthy, you need to learn this, too.

You've probably heard that, especially during a recession, rich people get richer—and it's true. When the economy hits a downswing, most people tighten their belts and prepare to ride out the tough times by not doing anything. But wealthy people have the cash to take advantage of the bargains a recession offers. They buy up real estate and other assets at rock-bottom prices. And because they have money to start with, they can afford to hang onto those assets until the market comes around. And the market *will* come around—it always does.

Another point about economic cycles is that when times are good, banks are willing to lend more. It's easier to borrow 80 to 95 percent of the value of a property. When times get tough, you'll have to search for even an 80 percent mortgage. On the surface, that looks as if you need tremendous amounts of cash to take advantage of a recession, but that's not necessarily true. During lean times, more sellers are willing to hold mortgages (that is, let you make the payments to them rather than to a conventional lender) because it's the only way they can get rid of the properties—especially ones that are run-down. And seller financing can be much more flexible than most conventional loans will ever be. With seller financing, you don't pay points or other loan-origination fees, there is rarely a credit check, and the closing can usually occur much faster than with a bank or mortgage company. There's also the opportunity to profit by discounting the mortgage later on.

By understanding economic cycles and using creative techniques, you can consistently build wealth in good and bad times. The object is to not fear economic cycles and to recognize that each stage of a cycle has its own special benefits. The wealth-building techniques I'm sharing with you are timeless. They can be adapted to work in good times and bad.

The Buy-Low, Sell-High Myth

Most people think the best real estate strategy is to buy in a down cycle and sell in an up cycle. Though that is a good strategy, it's limited, because those cycles come around only every 7 to 10 years. If your plan is to buy low and sell high, it can take you a long time to make any money.

When I began investing in real estate back in the early 1980s, I wasn't buying because we were in a recession and it was a good time to buy—though certainly that was true. I understand that now, but at the time I was buying because I'd learned a technique to buy run-down properties, fix them up, and rent them out to build a positive cash flow that would cover my debt. The theory was that as my equity increased, so would the value of the properties, and maybe in 20 years I'd be wealthy.

I have since learned how to make money *right now* on real estate, regardless of the cycle. In fact, I have personally made more money in the down cycles than I have in the up cycles. I used techniques like seller financing, discount mortgages, home-improvement loans, and several others that I'll explain as we go along.

People tell me I was lucky, and to a degree I was. I had accumulated quite a few properties, and when the economy picked up, I was able to quadruple my money on many of them. But let me make two very important points: First, I was "lucky" only because I took action. If I hadn't bought that first investment property, I would probably still be working at some menial job for slightly more than minimum wage. Second, I would have made money doing what I did at any point in the economic cycle because I bought run-down properties and fixed them up to create value. I also chose properties that could support themselves while they made money for me.

Once you understand economic cycles, and have either lived through one or two of them or studied their patterns, you'll see that they don't present obstacles to wealth building. Instead, economic cycles are tremendous opportunities. All you have to do is take advantage of them.

I'm not advocating that you run out and buy every piece of real estate you can find as soon as the economy shows signs of slowing down. In fact, I don't recommend buying a property that must be sold immediately to produce profits. If we are in a down or flat cycle, and you buy and must sell right away to make a profit, you could lose your shirt. But if you buy properties that have enough cash flow to pay the expenses and have a little left over, you can afford to wait until the cycle comes around. So look for properties that can support themselves (and you) with positive cash flow, and ones that will make money for you whether you keep them or sell them. We'll talk about how to choose the right properties a little later on in this chapter.

What's important now is that you understand that every recession has been followed by a period of prosperity, every period of prosperity has been followed by a recession, and there's no reason to expect that pattern will change. It's one of the natural laws of our economic system, so don't sweat the tough times. Recognize and take advantage of the fact that tough times create great opportunities. In fact, it's during the tough times that wealthy people set themselves up to hit major financial home runs when things turn around.

The Three Types of Properties

There are only three types of properties you can buy. The first is low-income property. The second is middle-income property. The third is upper-income property. I figured this out early in my investing career. It doesn't matter if you're buying a single-family home, a duplex, a multi-unit apartment building, or even commercial real estate—the property will fall into one of those three categories.

When you go into the low- or even moderate-income areas, you'll find the price of real estate is lower than in other areas. And if the property is cosmetically run-down, it will be even cheaper to buy. But what's interesting (and profitable) is that the rents in low-income areas are not much different from those in middle-income areas, where the price of the real estate is higher.

Think about this and tell me if it makes sense to you. If you can charge pretty much the same amount of rent, but pay significantly less for the building, will you have a greater positive cash flow? Of course you will. When you pay less for property, your mortgage payment will be lower and you'll have a better chance for a positive cash flow.

On the other hand, you're probably thinking that you don't want to have to collect your rents with a gun. But "low-income" doesn't necessarily mean "crime-ridden." As long as the human race has existed, in every economic system there have been low-income people, and there always will be. Someone has to provide housing for them—and that housing ought to be safe, sanitary, and decent.

Over the years I have owned plenty of lower-income properties, and I have no horror stories to tell. Low-income people may not have a lot of money, but they do have an immense amount of pride. If they are treated with respect and given a decent place to live, I have found they will care for their apartments as well as any middle- or upper-income person—sometimes even better. The landlords of low-income housing who have horror stories to tell are the ones who don't paint, fix the leaky faucets, or keep the lawns trimmed. You can't expect someone to take better care of your property than you do yourself. But if you take pride in your property, your tenants will, too.

In short, low-income properties can be serious cash-flow generators. They will appreciate over the years along with the rest of the market, and you can force their value up somewhat with improvements, but their primary advantage for the real estate investor is cash flow.

Middle-income properties have a higher unit price than low-income ones. Because you have to pay more for the property, your mortgage payments are more, but rents are not dramatically higher. The result is less positive cash flow, but the appreciation aspect will likely be better than with low-income properties. As the market goes up, middle-income properties will appreciate faster than low-income ones. Use middle-income properties to balance your portfolio *after* you've accumulated plenty of cash and a positive cash flow.

The final type of property, upper-income or prime, does not present any special opportunity for beginning investors, as a rule. Though the rents are higher, the per-unit cost is usually proportionately higher, too. The result with most upper-income properties is a break-even or negative cash flow—and that's not something I would advise as part of your wealth-building strategy. Upper-income properties are usually purchased by investors who are looking for shelters for their money but don't want to do any of the hands-on work. These are usually doctors, lawyers, and other highly paid professionals who often don't even know what's going on with their real estate.

Never buy a property solely as a tax shelter. You never have to lose money on real estate just to get a tax break, because with the right property you can have positive cash flow and tax benefits at the same time.

Ingredients for a Super Purchase

Though real estate is in general a great investment, you must be selective about what you buy. Any one or a combination of the following ingredients could mean you've found a money-making property or business.

Distressed Seller. A distressed seller is probably one of the most lucrative circumstances an investor will have the good fortune to come across. For our purposes, distress doesn't necessarily mean tragedy, but distressed sellers are under a tremendous amount of pressure to sell—much like I was when I put my New York properties on the market. This gives you as the buyer a great deal of leverage, and the ingredients are the same whether you are looking at a property or a business. Examples of distressed property sellers include someone who is facing foreclosure; a couple going through a divorce when neither partner can afford alone what they had together, or when they just want to get rid of a place that represents unhappy memories; an owner who is experiencing some sort of personal crisis, such as an illness, that has created a need for immediate cash; a property owner who has died, so that the heirs must sell and divide the proceeds; an owner who may be elderly and no longer able to handle the property or business.

Let me make it clear that I'm not recommending that you take advantage of or try to cheat anyone. But if someone is facing foreclosure, and your below-market offer is the only one they've gotten and it will prevent the total loss of their investment and a bad credit rating, then you've both made a good deal. Remember, they may be distressed, but they are not obligated to accept your offer; they have the option to hold out for something better.

It always pays to find out why the owner is selling. You may have to dig a bit for this information, since some sellers may feel that admitting to distress lessens their bargaining power. Pay attention to subtle clues and innocent comments that may tell you more than they mean to say.

Distressed Property or Business. In most cases, a distressed property or business doesn't take a lot of probing to discover. It's usually blatantly obvious: The grass is overgrown and the landscaping is shabby; windows are broken; the building needs paint; if it's a business, inventory is low and the shelves are bare. When owners of a distressed property or business are willing to sell, they are usually realistic enough to know they can't expect to get full market value. You can buy at a good price, make improvements, and create positive cash flow for yourself or a good investment to sell at a profit to someone else.

Distressed properties and businesses are often owned by distressed sellers, and that's a good combination for you. If the seller wants out bad enough, he'll help you structure a good deal and may even be willing to hold a major portion of the financing.

Lack of Management. Falling somewhere in between a distressed seller and a distressed property, the effects of lack of management are not always readily visible, but they can be capitalized on. The building may or may not be in good shape, and the seller may or may not be motivated. But when there has been lack of good management, there is opportunity for the buyer.

In one case, I came across an owner of a four-unit building who had become very friendly with two tenants who had lived there for a number of years. The neighborhood commanded about $550 in rent for comparable apartments, but these tenants were paying only $310 because the owner felt uncomfortable about raising the rents. When I negotiated the purchase, I did so with the current numbers and justified a lower purchase price based on the existing cash flow. Once I'd bought the building, I raised those rents to fair market value (legally, according to the leases, and with reasonable notice to the tenants), and was able to create an additional $5,760 in annual cash flow. That was like finding an extra $500 a month, just because I knew the market would support the higher rents.

I have also found properties suffering from mismanagement because the owners either didn't know what they were doing or didn't want to take the time to do it efficiently and profitably. They may have failed to make simple repairs that would have reduced other operating costs, such as leaky faucets that drive up water bills, or air-conditioning and heating units that use excessive energy because they need to be cleaned and serviced. They may have spent top dollar on the services they did provide, instead of finding a way to accomplish the same thing for less money. And their inattentiveness may have resulted in a higher-than-necessary vacancy rate. You'll see similar situations with businesses that are for sale, where owners want to retire, move, or for any reason just don't want to run a business. All of this gives you leverage as a buyer and the opportunity to increase your cash flow as an owner.

Lack of Owner Interest. Lack of owner interest can be due to a variety of reasons on the part of the seller. He may have bought the building and then realized he doesn't like managing rental property, but rather than sell, he just let it go. He may have a full-time job or another business, and is just not willing or able to take the time and energy to do a good job. He may live in another city; distance is one of the biggest problems property owners face. Or he may have bought the building as a tax shelter without realizing that rental properties don't run themselves. Owners lacking interest are not usually looking for a big windfall profit; they just want to sell and get out.

A classic example of this was a property I recently put an offer on with one of my students, whose name is Scott. It was a 20-unit apartment building in Marietta, Georgia (a suburb of Atlanta). I only had to put $9,000 down, and the property generated $4,100 a month in positive cash flow. The seller was the chief executive officer of a bank, and he lived more than an hour away from the property. He just didn't want to bother managing it anymore and wanted out. He was willing to hold the financing, so I didn't have to shop or qualify for a loan. Scott was 22 and had a job making about $22,000 a year; on this property alone, he would net over $24,000 a year and have plenty of time to work on other ways to get wealthy. In other words, this property could mean financial independence for Scott, and he found it just by looking. And this sort of deal is not unique; they happen all the time. You just have to be on the lookout for them.

These are the circumstances that will make a super purchase for you. But take a moment to think about how these circumstances could be turned around. In other words, take care not to let yourself become a distressed seller or the owner of distressed property. If you do, you'll only be helping someone else become wealthy—at your expense.

How to Know Your Market

When you see one or more of the ingredients for a super purchase—a distressed seller, a distressed property, lack of management, or lack of owner interest—you've got the potential for a real estate or small business bargain. But to know for sure, you must *know your market*.

There are no shortcuts and no exceptions to this rule. You've got to get out in the field and look at all types of properties. Read the real estate section of your local newspaper. Get comfortable with the language of real estate and the jargon most investors use. Know what the current market values are in various parts of your community for both property prices and rents.

Establish relationships with several real estate agents. You'll find they have different areas of expertise and differing opinions of the market. Learn from all of them. Let them know what you're looking for—ideally you should be starting with distressed low- and moderate-income properties—and that you're willing to look at any property, regardless of its condition. Remember, looking doesn't commit you to buying, and each time you look at a piece of real estate, you'll learn a little more.

Once you know your market, you'll be able to recognize and take advantage of bargains when they come your way. Remember, all this can be done on a very part-time basis. You don't need to quit your job; just make your off hours more productive by accumulating information and knowledge to get comfortable with real estate investing. And, who knows, you just might find a great deal in the process—because great deals are out there in abundance, being snapped up every day by people who are smart enough to look for them.

The Gold Mine Ad

Shopping for real estate investments can be time-consuming, but it doesn't have to be. As your experience and confidence level increase, you'll find ways to streamline your efforts. In the meantime, I'll share with you some of the shortcuts I've learned to find great deals fast.

One of the most effective methods I've found is what I call my Gold Mine Ad. It is a small classified ad I place in either the "Income Property for Sale" or "Real Estate Wanted" sections of the Sunday newspaper. It reads like this:

> *Private investor wants to buy income*
> *property. Will look at all, any condition.*
> *555-1234*

Be prepared for calls from plenty of interested people. When John Belden, one of my students in Atlanta, ran this ad, the response was so overwhelming that he had to stop the ad because he didn't have time to follow up on all the leads he got.

Be prepared, too, to discuss prospective properties as a knowledge-able investor. You have the psychological advantage, because people are calling you rather than the other way around. But if you don't sound like you know what you're doing, you could scare off a good prospect and a potential steal on a bargain deal.

You'll get calls from people with single-family homes, duplexes, triplexes, multi-unit apartment buildings, businesses, commercial buildings—just about every form of real estate there is. Your conver-sations with these people will give you tremendous insight into the seller mind-set and its many variations, so pay attention. Take notes; in fact, I suggest completing an A.P.O.D. (Annual Property Operat-ing Data) Sheet for each call.

Here are the basic questions you need to ask:

Is the property listed with a realtor? Find this out immediately. The best deals are usually the ones not listed, but don't automatically rule out a property that is. Just keep in mind that the seller will have the added expense of paying a commission (if he has not reserved the right to sell the property himself) and that may have an impact on the offer he will accept.

Where is the property located? Get the full street address and if you don't recognize it, ask what part of town it's in.

What is the asking price?

What is the appraised value and the market value? You can ask the

ANNUAL PROPERTY OPERATING DATA

Property Name _____

Property Address _____

Type of Real Estate _____

Number of Units _____

APPRAISED	Land:	$_____	0%
VALUE	Improvements:	$_____	100%
	Personal Property:	$_____	0%
	TOTAL:	$_____	100%

State your source of the Appraised Value please and attach verification:

_____

FINANCING

Type	Balance	Payment	Pmts/Yr.	Int. Rate	Term	Annual Payment
___	_____	_____	_____	_____	___	_____
___	_____	_____	_____	_____	___	_____
___	_____	_____	_____	_____	___	_____

TOTAL _____ _____   _____

- -

Note: If any category does not apply to your subject property, please place an N/A in the spaces.

OPERATING EXPENSES	YR. 1	YR. 2	YR. 3	YR. 4
Accounting & Legal	_____	_____	_____	_____
Advertising & Promotional	_____	_____	_____	_____
Office Supplies	_____	_____	_____	_____
Phone Expenses	_____	_____	_____	_____
Property Insurance	_____	_____	_____	_____
Employee Insurance	_____	_____	_____	_____
Property Management @ ___ %	_____	_____	_____	_____
Payroll - Resident Manager	_____	_____	_____	_____
Payroll Taxes	_____	_____	_____	_____
Maintenance Supplies	_____	_____	_____	_____
Pest control	_____	_____	_____	_____
Cleaning Supplies	_____	_____	_____	_____
Swimming Pool Expenses	_____	_____	_____	_____
Painting Expenses	_____	_____	_____	_____
Trash Removal	_____	_____	_____	_____
Services, Lawn & Snow	_____	_____	_____	_____
Other	_____	_____	_____	_____
Utilities: Gas & Oil	_____	_____	_____	_____
Water & Sewer	_____	_____	_____	_____
Electric	_____	_____	_____	_____
Miscellaneous	_____	_____	_____	_____
TOTAL OPERATING EXPENSES	_____	_____	_____	_____

seller for this information, but it's also a good idea to confirm it by calling a real estate agent or checking the tax rolls.

How many units?

Are they currently rented?

What are the gross rents?

Who pays the utilities?

What are the expenses? Specifically, you want to know the costs of taxes, insurance, water and sewer, licenses or permits, heating and/or air-conditioning, garbage collection, other utilities, and any other expenses of managing the property.

What are the present mortgages on the property? You need to know the balance of any mortgages on the property, the interest rates, the payments, the years left to pay on the loans, and if they are assumable—that is, if you can take over the payments. Though it's rare, in some cases people may be hesitant to provide you with this information; if you encounter resistance, just be firm and let them know you can't make an intelligent evaluation of the investment without having all of the applicable data. Usually this bit of firmness will get you the answer to the question and the needed respect for future negotiations on the property. If it doesn't, you're going to have plenty of other callers, so just move on.

Is the seller willing to hold some of the mortgage? You'll get a variety of answers to this one, and you may have to explain that your policy is to look for the seller to hold at least some of the mortgage.

Why are you selling? Listen carefully to this answer to be sure you get the real reason. If necessary, probe further to find out how motivated the seller really is.

How can I reach you? Get a telephone number and determine what are the best hours to call. If the seller works during the day, you don't want to waste your time calling his home while he's away.

Wrap up the call by telling the seller you want to have your appraiser take a look at the property, and if you're interested, you'll call him back. Having an appraiser sounds professional and organized; the seller doesn't need to know you do your own initial appraising. Then analyze the numbers (calculating return on investment and cash flow are explained later in this chapter) and decide if the property has good investment potential. If it does, go take a look. If not, move on to the next call.

Other Ways to Locate Bargains

The Gold Mine Ad brings the opportunities to you, but you'll also find some great deals by looking for them yourself. Here's how:

Keep Your Eyes Open. You can find distressed properties just by keeping your eyes open. I carry a pad and pen or a small tape recorder wherever I go. When I see a distressed property, I jot down the address. After I've accumulated a few, I stop by the county courthouse and look up the owners' names in the tax rolls. My next step is to write the owners a letter asking if they are interested in selling, and I follow up with a phone call. The response varies. If they're not interested right now, I ask them to keep my name, and I put the information in a file and check back with them in six months or a year. If they are interested, I find out how much they want for the property and try to negotiate a mutually profitable deal.

Get to Know Your Building-Code Officials. Another way to uncover distressed properties is to visit your city or county building-code enforcement agency. Let the people there know you are in the business of rehabilitating older, distressed properties, and ask them about their files on buildings that are condemned or have multiple violations. You'll be amazed at how helpful they can be. With this information, you can contact owners to discuss potential deals.

Pass Out Business Cards and Fliers. If you're going to be a serious investor, print up business cards and fliers. The printing itself is a nominal expense; it's an affordable way to enhance your image and get your message out. One of my first cards read, "I buy houses, duplexes, multi-unit apartments, and commercial. I will look at all in any condition," and then it listed my name and phone number. Another early card listed a business name, R & I Enterprises, along with my name and phone number. "We buy" was printed in the upper left corner, and directly under that was "Houses, apartments, commercial, terms, any condition." I handed out these business cards to anyone who would take them, because I never knew where a good deal was going to come from.

I also had fliers printed up with similar information, and every so often I'd pay one of the neighborhood kids a few bucks to pass them out. You never know when someone will stick that flier in a drawer or their glove compartment, then pull it out six months or a year later and call you with a property. I also put a flier into every piece of mail I sent out, including my mortgage payments, utility bills, credit card bills, and so on. You never know who is opening that mail and what their circumstances are. And I have gotten calls and ultimately purchased property from people who received my fliers that way.

Read the Newspaper. Your newspaper is, of course, a great source of bargains. You'll find some great leads in the "For Sale by Owner" and "Investment (or Commercial) Property for Sale" sections, but don't overlook the foreclosure ads and bulletins in the legal section. There are plenty of books available that explain how to purchase foreclosed properties, but I have found it easier and more lucrative to find out who the parties involved are and approach them with an offer before the foreclosure process is completed. This is a win-win situation, because I can get a good deal without having to compete with other bidders, and the owner can avoid the final foreclosure process.

Ask for Referrals. Finally, never underestimate the value of referrals. In any business, referrals are the easiest and most productive way to grow. The only way I know of to build a strong referral base in real estate investing is to spend time in the business and do some serious networking. Let people know what you are doing and offer to pay $100 for any lead they bring you that you buy.

Become a Bird Dog

If you need a confidence boost to get you out and buying real estate, consider becoming a member of my Bird Dog Program network and find properties I might be interested in. I have partners all over the country—I call them Bird Dogs—who scout out deals and present them to me. If they show good potential, I put up the cash and we buy them together. My partners manage the properties, and we split the profits.

It's truly that simple. In my Bird Dog Program, I'm looking for long-term investments. I want them in various geographic locations so my portfolio is not seriously affected by regional economic cycles. And I want partners who have a vested interest in the property doing the management, because I know from experience that's the most profitable route to take.

The benefit for my partners is that they get to use my cash to become a player in the real estate game. They get the experience and the prestige of property ownership, and they all go on to bigger, better, and more profitable deals.

If you're interested in joining my Bird Dog Program, call (800) 741-7877, or contact me using the coupon on the back flap of this book.

Do You Need a License?

Something I learned very early is that there is a major difference between real estate brokers and real estate investors. Real estate brokers and sales agents earn a living (sometimes a very good living, sometimes a very poor one) by representing sellers and buyers in real estate transactions. Real estate investors become wealthy using real estate as their profit-making vehicle. I'm not recommending that you pursue a career in real estate sales, but there are a few reasons why you might consider getting a real estate license.

First, the knowledge you'll have to acquire—usually through any one of a number of real estate schools—to get your license will help you with the nuts and bolts of buying and selling.

Second, when you find a property that is listed with an agent, you will be entitled to share the commission if you, too, are a licensed agent—even though you are also the buyer. This bonus money can make a big difference in the amount of money you'll have to pay out of pocket to purchase the property.

Third, some states require property managers to have real estate licenses. If you are considering a management and maintenance business, a license may be helpful.

A real estate license is easy to get; most states require the equivalent of a weeklong course that focuses primarily on real estate law, followed by a licensing exam. If you can read at the eighth- or ninth-grade level, this is not difficult.

If you have an active real estate license, you must divulge that fact on your purchase offers and sales contracts. It's usually a nonissue, and most people don't care one way or the other, but you do have to tell them. The primary drawback to having a license is that you may find it difficult to get other real estate agents to look for deals for you since they might view you as a competitor rather than a client. With your own license, you could make more money on each transaction; but by using other agents, you could do more transactions and make more money overall.

My advice is to get your license and try it both ways. You can always place your license on inactive status if that works better for you.

The Business of Being a Real Estate Investor

Successful real estate investing is more than just buying and selling. While you own the properties, you must manage them effectively if they are to continue to generate positive cash flow for you.

You could hire a property management company to handle this aspect for you, but I don't recommend it in the beginning. No one manages property as well as the owner, because no one else has the vested interest in it that the owner has. When I left New York and moved to Florida, I sold all my properties because I didn't believe I could have maintained the quality my tenants had become accustomed to if I became an absentee owner. Today, thanks to my Bird Dog Program, I am a partner in investments all over the country; I put up the money to buy good properties and split the profits with whomever finds and manages the property—but they must be willing to be a partner and owner with me, and do the management, or I won't finance the deal. For the maximum return on your investment, manage your own real estate at least until you accumulate a number of prime properties and have a substantial cash flow.

There are a number of good books on the market that deal with residential property management, and I would suggest adding two or three of them to your personal library. You should also join a property managers' association. It will give you an opportunity to network with and learn from others. Such associations have publications and programs that address common problems and serve as a resource for members' needs. You may also find this a good source for leads on properties you might be interested in purchasing.

The most important part of property management is to keep an eye on the property. I'm not talking about military-style inspections here, but you should visit every property on a regular basis to make sure the tenants are keeping things up and no special maintenance is needed. Multi-unit buildings have to be seen more frequently than single-family homes because of the number of tenants. The idea is to catch small problems and correct them before they turn into major, costly repairs. This also helps you maintain a positive relationship with your tenants and keeps your units rented.

Keep your vacancy rate low by maintaining the exterior of your buildings in an attractive manner, adding improvements based on tenant input whenever feasible, and setting rents at fair market value. I rarely have apartments vacant longer than it takes to clean them between tenants because people know I am a conscientious owner and I provide quality housing. Encourage your existing tenants to provide you with referrals when vacancies do occur; you may want to consider a small, one-time rent discount for bringing in new tenants. Otherwise, when you have a vacancy, post a "for rent" sign and consider placing an ad in the classified section of your local newspaper.

In multi-unit buildings, you may consider arranging for a resident manager to collect rents, show vacancies, and handle janitorial and landscape maintenance. Unless you have a very large complex, this does not have to be a full-time job and can be compensated with a rent allowance. And you will continue to be primarily responsible for your property because you'll be handling any major issues that arise.

Every one of your tenants should have a lease or rental agreement—no exceptions! If you buy a building that has units rented without leases, draw them up immediately. You can find standard lease forms in most office-supply stores, or you can contact my office for details on a complete book and software package of real estate forms. Also, remember that most tenants expect rent increases when a building is sold, so don't be reluctant to do this. The key is to do it right away, within the bounds of existing leases.

Always keep in mind that your relationship with your tenants is strictly business. You have agreed to provide them with safe, sanitary, well-maintained housing. They, in turn, have agreed to pay rent on a specified date and to exercise reasonable care with your property. In other words, "no ticket, no laundry." If they don't pay their rent, or if they violate other terms of their lease, you must take appropriate action up to and including eviction. Treat your property business as if it were a Wal-Mart or a grocery store. It's okay to be friendly with your tenants, but never let "friendship" get in the way of your initial business agreement.

Real estate is a business like any other business, but it's different because it has a significantly lower risk level. If you're thinking about going into business for yourself but you haven't quite made the decision, try a small rental property. You'll have to do everything you would have to do in any kind of a business, from management to marketing to record keeping, but on a small scale. That will give you the chance to get a feel for how you'll do in business for yourself. If you like it, you can either buy more property or another business of your choice. If you don't like it, you can sell the property, and you will have learned your lesson without having lost any money—in fact, you'll probably show a profit. Is there any other arena that will pay you to get an education without any future obligation? And, who knows, you just might create a small personal fortune along the way.

CHAPTER 7

Analyzing Your Deals

To be what we are, and to become what we are
capable of becoming, is the only end of life.

—ROBERT LOUIS STEVENSON

When I'm teaching people how to make money with real estate, the questions I hear the most often have to do with problems. What do you do if a tenant moves out, what do you do if the furnace breaks down, what do you do if something else happens? My best answer is to remind you that every business has its problems.

If you own a store, you'll probably lose some merchandise to shoplifting. Sam Walton built a $50 billion business out of Wal-Mart. Right now, somewhere in the country, someone is shoplifting something at a Wal-Mart. And there may even be a cashier stealing a few dollars from the cash register. But Sam Walton didn't say, "Gee, I think I'll give up this $50 billion in sales and close down all my stores because I might have a problem now and then." Instead, he set money aside in a reserve account to cover losses from theft; it's called the cost of doing business.

People have been renting property for hundreds of years. Owners have been making profits from renting property for hundreds of years. Just because you buy a rental property doesn't mean all the tenants are going to move out or the building will fall down.

Will you have an occasional problem? Sure. Everybody has problems. They're not special gifts reserved for an unfortunate few. But think about this for a moment. What are problems? Is it a problem when we can't buy a new car or pay our bills? Is it a problem that we can barely afford to take one vacation a year, not the four or five trips we'd really like to go on?

Those are problems. Also a problem is facing retirement with an income at or below the poverty level. A problem is not being able to give your kids the opportunities you'd like. A problem is driving an old car that breaks down once a week because you can't afford a new one. A problem is a boss nagging at you and having to punch a time clock. A problem is when lack of money causes so much stress in your marriage that you end up getting a divorce.

A tenant calling because of a drippy faucet is not a problem, it's progress. Having to put an ad in the paper to fill a vacant unit is not a problem, it's an opportunity. These are simply circumstances that go with the territory of being in business and building wealth.

The bottom line is that it doesn't matter what business you're in, you'll have problems occasionally. Set aside a little money so you can handle them, collect your profits, and live a happy, abundant life.

Evaluating the Property

Something that often scares newcomers to real estate investing is how to tell when a property needs too much fixing up to make it a good investment. I have bought and sold hundreds of properties, and I rarely come across any in such bad shape that they are beyond repair. The reason is simple: If the property is in really bad shape, the owner may be motivated to sell way below the market value of a similar property that is in good condition. If you are dealing with an extremely low sale price because the property needs repairs, you have more borrowing power for your repair or rehab loan. That means a greater opportunity for profits, and I'll explain that further in Chapter Nine.

However, you have to train your eye to know the difference between cosmetic distress and serious problems. A building might be so neglected that you're afraid it's going to fall down around you, but in reality a few trips to the dump, a fresh coat of paint, and some cleaner and disinfectant may revive the property to fair market value. Here are a few things to watch out for:

Structural Damage. Outside, look for a dramatic lean in any direction. Inside, look for floors slanted toward a corner of the house. These are indications of a possible foundation problem. Before you reject the property, call in several contractors and get free estimates on repairs, then use that information to negotiate a better price.

Termite Damage. Termite damage usually scares off investors, but termites can take up to 10 or 15 years before they do irreparable damage. I once bought a house that had severe termite damage in the supporting beams in the basement. The property had been on the market a long time and was bargain priced. Obviously the termite damage had scared off many other potential buyers. After I bought the property, I had a contractor replace the beams using mobile jacks as support; it wasn't particularly complicated or expensive. I pulled money out of the property up front with the rehab, and then made $15,000 a few years later when I sold it. You can make good deals on termite-infested properties. Just figure the cost of replacing the bad wood and exterminating the termites. If you can do that and still make money, buy it.

Roof Damage. Always examine the roof. You might also ask several roofers to do it for you. Pick their brains until you become proficient enough to do your own evaluations. Roofers make money by selling you a roof, so keep that in mind as you consider their recommendations. If it looks as if the roof will need replacing in the near future, calculate that into your offer. Set enough money aside from your home-improvement loan and let it accumulate interest until the roof starts leaking; then replace it.

Major Plumbing. When you are evaluating a property, turn on all the faucets, flush all the toilets, and make sure all the drains run freely. The most common way plumbing can become a problem is in older buildings with galvanized and/or cast-iron plumbing. After years of use, this type of pipe collects sediment, which builds up and causes a loss of water pressure and stopped-up drains. I have found a product called Drain Snake, available in plumbing-supply stores, which seems to remedy the problem. (When using this or any other chemical product, always use caution and follow the directions on the label to avoid personal injury or property damage.)

Furnaces. In larger multi-unit buildings, you may have one furnace that heats the entire building. Be sure it operates efficiently or that the cash flow will support the bill. Get a heating and air-conditioning contractor you trust to do the evaluation for you.

These are the areas in which you could have a major expense if there is a problem. In most cases, roofs and plumbing and heating units need major repairs or replacement only every 20 to 25 years, so problems with them are the exception, not the rule, but it's always good to check. When you do see a major problem, don't automatically rule out the property. If you can cover the repairs and still make money, the property is a good investment. If you can't, it isn't. The whole process is just that simple.

You might want to hire a professional inspector in the beginning to confirm your opinion, but eventually you'll get to the point where you can accurately evaluate a property on your own.

Calculating Return for a Super Bargain and Great Profits

There is only one hard, fast rule about when to buy and when not to buy: If you will lose money, don't buy. And you can figure out just how profitable a property might be with basic, elementary-school arithmetic.

To evaluate a property's profitability, you need to look at four areas:

Net Profit. The easiest to see and most simple to calculate, net profit is the amount of money you have left over after all your expenses are paid.

Appreciation. This is the amount your property increases in value. There are two types of appreciation: natural, which is the amount the market goes up; and forced, which is adding value with improvements or a higher and better use. During periods of moderate growth, natural appreciation usually ranges between 5 and 10 percent annually; in high-growth cycles, it could be well over 10 percent, and sometimes as much as 20 percent; in low- or no-growth cycles, the value may remain the same or increase only by 1 or 2 percent. To find out the current rate of natural market appreciation, call a couple of real estate agents. It's their job to know these things, but it's also always wise to check with more than one to be sure you're getting an accurate picture. Forced appreciation is the area through which the bigger and more short-term profits are usually made. Most real estate will appreciate naturally to a small degree if you do absolutely nothing; if you put a little money and effort into the right property, you can make significant gains.

Equity Buildup. A portion of each mortgage payment you make (which the tenants actually pay) is applied to reducing the principal balance of the mortgage. When rents are paying the mortgage, you can consider the equity buildup as part of your overall profit.

Tax Shelter. Real estate investing is a business, and you are therefore entitled to take a variety of business-related deductions on your income tax. Often these deductions will offset income earned from another source and reduce your overall tax liability. The deductions you can take by owning investment property include depreciation, interest (the interest portion of your mortgage payments), maintenance, and any other expenses related to managing your property, such as gas or car expenses for driving to and from the property, cleaning supplies, bookkeeping supplies, forms, and other administrative materials. Though we know that real estate typically goes up in value, the IRS will allow you to take a tax deduction for depreciation based on wear and tear on the building (not the land). The formula for calculating investment-property depreciation can change with changes in the tax laws, so check with your accountant.

Now let's look at how you use these areas of profitability to determine the return on your investment (ROI). Calculate your ROI by dividing your profit by the amount of cash it took you to achieve that profit. To illustrate ROI, I'll use the four-unit building I told you about in Chapter Five. I bought the building for $75,000. The owner was willing to hold the mortgage and take a 10 percent down payment, or $7,500. By arranging to close on the third day of the month (after collection of that month's rents, of which I would get a prorated share), I was able to purchase the building for $3,700 cash out of pocket. The building was fully occupied, and each unit rented for $500 a month. This is how the numbers worked:

NET PROFIT—Add up the gross rents. Add up all the expenses (taxes, insurance, maintenance, utilities, vacancy allowance, and so on) and debt service (mortgage). In our example, we're using 5 percent for the vacancy allowance, which is the amount of time each year we can expect the units not to have tenants. To determine the vacancy rate for your area, contact a realtor or property management company. You can ask the seller for documentation on the other expenses. Then subtract the expenses from the rents. That will be the net profit (or loss) for the first year.

Calculating Net Profit

Monthly gross rents (4 units at $500 each) = $2,000	
Annual gross rents (12 × $2,000)	24,000
Monthly expenses = $800	
Annual expenses	9,600
Gross annual operating profit	$14,400
Debt service (12 × $596.75, the monthly mortgage payment)	7,161
Net overall operating profit	$7,239

Your first-year ROI is the net profit divided by the cash out of pocket it took for you to buy the property, which is $7,239 divided by $3,700, or 196 percent return on investment.

APPRECIATION—If you know your market, you will be able to estimate how much specific improvements will increase the value of your property. Appreciation turns into a cash profit when you sell or refinance.

Original purchase price of property	$ 75,000
Cost of improvements	1,300
Revised appraised value of property	130,000
Forced appreciation	$ 55,000

Appreciation ROI on this property was 1,486 percent (the amount of appreciation divided by the investment, or $55,000 divided by $3,700). In this example, I used forced appreciation only—that is, I forced the value of the property up by improving it. When adding in natural market appreciation, contact a real estate agent for the figure that applies in your area.

EQUITY BUILDUP—As rents pay down the mortgage balance, the equity increase is considered profit. It is a paper profit until you sell or refinance, but it is there for you to use when you need it.

Initial loan amount	$68,000
Amount applied to principal	500
New principal balance	67,500
Equity buildup	$ 500

Equity buildup ROI is 14 percent (the amount of equity divided by the investment, or $500 divided by $3,700).

TAX SHELTER—With investment real estate, most of the time your expenses will offset most, if not all, of your income for tax purposes. You will make additional income gains by deducting depreciation and letting that offset the taxes on income from other sources. How much of a tax shelter you will receive depends on your tax bracket and sources of income. Generally, you can count on a 5 to 15 percent ROI from a tax shelter.

Now let's go back and total up the first-year ROI from the $3,700 I used to buy this building:

Return on cash invested	196%
Appreciation	1,486%
Equity buildup	14%
Tax shelter	10%*
Total ROI	1,706%

*average estimate

And this doesn't even consider the money I made later by refinancing the building on the increased appraised value. Is it any wonder so many great fortunes have been built through real estate?

On any investment, I look at the first-year anticipated net profit, and if that doesn't give me at least a 20 to 30 percent return on my investment, I usually don't go any further. The exception would be if there is a tremendous upside to the building—something I know will give me a greater return in the future. It might be that the building has a lot of vacancies I know I can fill, or that nearby property-use trends are changing and I can benefit from that. Don't put anything in concrete; be flexible and use logic and reason to make a good deal.

Increasing Your Cash Flow

It's critical that you look at all the expenses of the property. The owner should be able to provide you with documentation for taxes, utilities, water, sewer, trash collection, licensing, and any other permits you may be required to have. You may also require the seller to give you records detailing maintenance costs and actual vacancy rates.

After you purchase an investment property, you must always be on the lookout for ways to increase your cash flow. Here are some techniques I use:

Contract with individuals rather than businesses for any work you don't do yourself. In other words, don't call a painting contractor to paint your building; find two or three people who can handle a paintbrush and put them to work. If you use a painting contractor, you will also be paying his overhead and profit, and that will eat into yours.

Find a good handyman to do the bulk of your maintenance. It's a lot less expensive to have a $7- or $8-an-hour handyman replace washers in faucets than to call in a licensed plumber to do it. Once you own enough properties to keep a handyman busy full-time, consider putting him on your payroll.

Look for hidden costs. Worn-out washers can cause drippy faucets that run up your water bill. Windows that don't close tightly can increase your heating and cooling costs. (Check with your city or utility company on the availability of grants to pay for energy-conservation improvements; see Chapter Fifteen for more details on how various government agencies can help make real estate investing more profitable for you.) If you use a dumpster for trash collection, be sure it is just large enough to accommodate your tenants' needs; don't pay for more service than you require. This is just plain good management, and it puts money in your pocket.

Buy used appliances. When it's time to replace items such as stoves and refrigerators, shop for and buy used appliances. Your best deals will come from individuals, but shopping for and making them is more time-consuming than working with used-appliance dealers. If you're purchasing from a dealer, let them know that you're a property owner and that they can expect repeat business from you; that will give you some leverage for a better price and/or a better warranty.

Analyze all expenses. Never accept an expense at face value without researching the amount to be sure you're getting the best price possible. Shop around and negotiate for good deals.

Raise the rents. Keep your rents in line with the market; don't charge lower rents just because a tenant has been with you a long time. When your leases come up for renewal and you are aware from your knowledge of the market that rental rates are increasing, adjust your rents accordingly.

Verify the accuracy of your tax bills. Take the time every year to check your tax bill. Get copies of the tax bills for comparable properties in the area (this is public information and easy to look up at the county court house). If your taxes are higher, file a protest with your tax collector; this is every taxpayer's right, and it can result in a lower tax bill. You can get instructions for the specific procedure for doing this by calling your local tax collector's office.

Choosing the Right Wealth Vehicle

A question I'm frequently asked is what's the best type of real estate to start with. Should you invest in single-family homes or multi-unit buildings? Both can be very profitable, and I would recommend a balance of different types of properties. Remember, when you have a vacancy in a single-family home, that property is 100 percent vacant. When you have a vacancy in a four-unit building, that property is only 25 percent vacant and is still producing cash flow. The trade-off is that single-family homes generally require less management attention and often appreciate faster, so put both types of properties in your portfolio.

My advice is to start with small multi-unit buildings, build a healthy cash flow, then diversify and add single-family homes to your holdings.

Independent Thinking

Once you begin accumulating real estate investments, you'll have to consider the question of how long to own each property. There are two traditional schools of thought on this: the "keeper" theory and the "nonkeeper" theory.

The author of one of the first real estate books I read subscribed to the "keeper" theory. Essentially, his theory was buy, buy, buy, and never sell. His strategy was never to sell anything, but instead to wait until you have enough equity in the properties to either refinance them completely or take another mortgage out and let the rents cover the mortgage payments. The money you get from a loan is not taxable because it's not income. The income you get from rents is taxable, but if you follow this strategy, it will be offset by the deductible interest you're paying on your mortgage. In other words, you keep pulling your money out of the property in the form of mortgages.

That is a good strategy, but not for your entire portfolio. You need income, and you need capital to go into bigger deals that require more money.

When I first began investing, I didn't realize there were many investment theories, and that different circumstances required different approaches. Because I was successful from the very start, I was loyal to most of the literature that gave me the specialized knowledge to do what I had done. I treated the advice in some of those books as gospel and followed it to the letter—especially the "keeper" theory.

In retrospect, if I had sold a few properties and cashed in on the equity, I could have grown twice as fast because I would have had more working capital. And though money from loan proceeds is not taxable because it's not income, which is great from a tax-strategy angle, there's a negative aspect to making all your money this way. When you approach lenders, you'll find that they frown on making loans to people who show no income on their tax returns, and that makes getting financing difficult. Don't choke your growth by following the "keeper" theory exclusively.

Following the "nonkeeper" theory exclusively has some drawbacks, too. When you turn over properties quickly, you don't derive all the benefits of ownership, such as positive cash flow and tax deductions for depreciation. Also, the profit, or capital gains, you make when you sell is taxable as ordinary income.

Most important is the reality that the "nonkeeper" theory is based on buying very low and selling a little higher. It sounds great, but I don't believe that, on a consistent, full-time basis, anyone could find enough properties at low enough prices to buy and then sell and turn a profit. And if you're depending on the sale to make your money, what happens if you can't find a buyer?

There are times when turning a property quickly will be very profitable. I've done it many times, and, as I've already told you, I've made as much as $5,000 on property by owning it for just an hour or so. But there are also times when your wisest move is to hang on to property for years. So don't subscribe exclusively to either the "keeper" or the "nonkeeper" theory. Instead, do what I learned the hard way: Be an independent thinker.

Set up your investment goals to include a diversified game plan. Start with one or two of the techniques you've learned, master them, and move on to another one. Shelter as much of your income from taxes as possible, but show enough income to be considered a good credit risk. Hire competent attorneys and accountants and listen to their advice, but make your own decisions. Consider partnerships and joint ventures as sources for seed capital. Remember, too, that it's easy to get emotionally attached to the first few deals you make. Don't do this! Be willing to sell properties when the time is right to increase your wealth.

Everyone will have an opinion about how you should run your investment business. That's fine. They're entitled to their opinions, and they might even have some positive input you'll benefit from. But the final decision is yours. You decide when to buy, when to keep, when to sell—and, ultimately, when to become wealthy.

CHAPTER 8

Higher and Better Use

Do not follow where the path may lead. Go instead where there is no path and leave a trail.

—UNKNOWN

In Chapter Three, I told you how I turned a single-family house into a rooming house, which created what I call a higher and better use of the property. This concept can be applied to a variety of situations, and it's an excellent way to increase value and cash flow.

You could change an old warehouse into an office building, a house into apartments, or an abandoned factory into retail shops. You see this over and over in cities all across America. Older buildings often have a special charm and character, and people are often delighted to have the opportunity to move themselves or their businesses into these facilities.

Here are a few specific suggestions for higher and better use: Always look for ways to turn unused space into a revenue source, and to maximize the revenue you do get. If you find a duplex with a large attic, create new value by turning it into a third income-producing unit. One of my students bought a triplex and turned it into a remarkable rooming house. He converted each apartment into three rooms, creating a nine-unit rooming house with a common kitchen and bath for each three units. It was positively luxurious for a rooming house, and exceptionally easy to rent and maintain.

107

Another of my students lived in an area where two-bedroom, two-bath homes averaged $60,000, and three-bedroom, two-bath homes averaged $75,000 to $80,000. He looked for two-bedroom homes with large enclosed porches on the back. With an inexpensive partition and a little cosmetic work, he would add a third bedroom and create an additional $15,000 to $20,000 worth of value. That's what you can get by thinking in terms of higher and better use.

Pay attention to neighborhood trends and use your imagination. Learn to look at buildings from a different perspective. With a little foresight and determination, you can use the higher and better use concept to rake in the money.

How to Create a Rooming House

One of the easiest ways to apply the higher and better use concept is by converting a single-family home into a rooming house. This is most commonly done with older homes located in neighborhoods that are in what is called a transitional stage. Such neighborhoods usually have a mix of single-family, multi-family, and commercial properties. Often these neighborhoods are close to downtown or industrial areas.

If the neighborhood has a mix of single-family and multi-family homes, it's a fairly safe bet that zoning won't be a problem. If the property is not already zoned for multi-unit, call your local zoning board to find out how to make the change. You can also make your offer to purchase contingent on getting the necessary zoning to accomplish your goal of higher and better use.

In many cities, officials welcome the addition of rooming houses, which are often referred to as SROs (single room occupancy). People with limited incomes (the elderly, students, young people in the early stages of their careers, etc.) have trouble finding a place to live because they can't afford to rent an apartment or buy a house. But they can afford to pay $50 or $60 a week for a room. By creating a rooming house, you can provide a tremendous community service while you make money for yourself.

How do you do it? It's not complicated. In most older homes, the bedrooms are all upstairs, which means you'll have little, if any, remodeling to do there. What you do downstairs will depend on the floor plan you're working with, but you want to convert as much as possible to revenue-producing space. Leave the kitchen as is, because tenants appreciate kitchen privileges, and it will give your facility more value. Also, create a small common room as a sitting area or gathering space for tenants. They'll appreciate a comfortable, safe place they can use outside their own rooms. For the remainder of the downstairs, erect partitions and hang doors to turn the rooms into bedrooms. Be sure to plan your partitions so every room has a window, if possible. (Some areas require a bedroom to have at least one window; check with your local building code to be sure. Remember, too, that windows are easy to install—just cut a hole in the wall.) Your tenant/bathroom ratio will depend on how many baths the house has. Rooming house tenants expect to share bathrooms.

Once your partitioning is completed, you'll want to clean, paint, make any necessary repairs, and install new door locks. I always use Weiser locks and have a master key made. Each tenant gets a key to his or her room and the front door, but my key opens any door in the house. If anyone moves without turning in their key, I can just switch the locks with another unit—something that's easily done by a handyman and doesn't require a locksmith but still provides security for your tenants. You'll also want good locks on the bathrooms to protect tenants' privacy. You may also need to install an extra-capacity water heater and add some cosmetic touches to the exterior.

Your last major expense involves furnishings. When you're buying eight or ten rooms of furniture, you can usually negotiate a good price. Shop at secondhand stores, check out the used-furniture sales departments of furniture-rental companies, and watch for hotels that have recently remodeled and are selling their old furnishings. (These are the same techniques hotelier Conrad Hilton used when he was running rooming houses.) When choosing rooming house furniture, go for function and sturdiness over style. Each room should contain:

- A full-size bed (frame, box springs, and mattress). Single beds are not as well-received, so unless the room is extremely small, go with the full-size.
- Curtains. Windows must be covered for privacy and insulation.
- Nightstand.

- Dresser with mirror. Or you may choose a chest of drawers and hang a mirror on the wall.
- Lamp. If there is no ceiling light fixture, you must provide a lamp.
- Sitting chair. If space allows, provide a comfortable chair.

Furnish your common room with some easy chairs, a few small tables, and maybe a used television. You might also check into the feasibility of installing a public telephone here.

Managing Your Rooming House

A rooming house is more management-intensive than an apartment building, but many of the same basic principles apply. Here are the essential details you'll need to know.

Advertising for Tenants. Once you're open for business, place an ad in your local paper under "Rooms for Rent." Note the key amenities, and include the general location, price, and contact information. If your newspaper organizes ads in alphabetical order, try to start your copy with an "A" word to get it at the top of the listings. These are two examples I have used:

AA—Downtown, private rooms,
kitchen privileges, cable TV, all included,
$55 per week—555-1234.

A private room, central location, all
included, $55 per week—555-1234.

Screening Tenants. In rooming houses, you can't expect to screen for an upper-income clientele or you'll run a higher-than-necessary and quite unprofitable vacancy rate. My advice is to make sure that applicants are working and that their personal hygiene is decent. Other than that, the only qualification is cash. With experience you'll develop a sense for the type of tenant that will meet his or her obligations.

Rental Agreement. The rental agreement stipulates the amount of rent and the rules of the rooming house. You will find rental agreement forms in office-supply stores, or you can create your own; as with any legal document, have it reviewed by an attorney to be sure it conforms with your state laws.

Deposit. A deposit will help you compensate for incorrect judgment decisions in the screening process. If you feel a prospective tenant might not be of the best quality but you want the rental, ask for a $100 deposit on top of the first week's rent. On the other hand, if your instinct tells you you've got a decent prospective tenant but he is short of cash, you might allow him to move in by posting just one week's rent as a deposit. Never let someone move in without paying a deposit.

Rental Proration. It's more efficient to have all your rents due on the same day. Because Friday is payday for most people, I have found that's the best day to collect rents. When people move in during the middle of the week, prorate their rents by the day for the partial week. Remember that rents are always paid in advance, not in arrears.

Master Key. Master key all of your units, not just the rooms. It's much easier to carry one key that will get you into any of your units, rather than several jangling key rings.

Manager. Each rooming house should have a resident manager to enforce the rules and make sure the common areas are kept clean. It's best to train the manager to *manage,* not to be a maid for the other tenants. (Tenants are expected to clean up after themselves in the kitchen, bathrooms, and sitting room; this stipulation should be part of your rental agreement.) The manager should have a strong attitude and some leadership qualities. Offer this person a $20- to $25-a-week rent allowance for assuming these responsibilities.

Collecting Rents. Rents may be due on Friday, but that doesn't mean you'll collect them all on that day. Take steps to instill a pay-on-time attitude. One way to accomplish this is with a $1 per day late charge. Another way is to charge $70 rent for your $55 room, with a $15 discount if the rent is paid on time.

Despite the best screening and the most creative incentives to pay on time, you're going to have the occasional tenant who doesn't pay. This is something that happens in every business, and it shouldn't deter you from using a property to pursue your dreams. Just be prepared to handle it, and my advice is to not let a late payer slide. When the rent is due on Friday and not paid by Saturday, issue a written late-rent notice that day. This can be a simple form that reads:

Premises #_____

Rent for month/week of _____, 19_____

A rental payment of $_____ was due on _____

According to our records, a payment has not been received.

Kindly arrange to make payment at your earliest convenience. If you have already mailed your check, please disregard this notice.

THE MANAGEMENT

The best time to go after late payers is early Saturday morning. Knock on their door at 8:00 A.M. because they probably would prefer to sleep until 10:00. They'll get tired of you waking them up and start to pay on time.

If you haven't received the rent by Monday, post a "24-Hour Notice to Vacate or Pay Rent" on the door and put one in the mail. Here's what that document should look like:

This notice made this _____ day of _____, 19___.

To:_____ (name of tenant)

_____(address of premises)

_____(city and state)

You are hereby notified that you are indebted to the Landlord of the premises above mentioned in the amount of _____ dollars (\$ _____) for unpaid rent of said premises from the _____ day of _____, 19___, to the _____ day of _____, 19___, which you are required to pay within 24 hours of receiving this notice or vacate said premises. If payment is not made or premises are not vacated, the Landlord will take appropriate legal action to recover possession of the premises.

_____(SIGNATURE)

If by Tuesday you haven't received payment or a suitable explanation from the tenant, open the unit to see if he has vacated. If he has, you know where you stand. By leaving without notice, he has forfeited his deposit, so you are covered for the week's rent. Sometimes a tenant may give you a sob story, but you're in business. Stand your ground, be firm, and remember that in order to run a profitable business of any kind, you have to get paid. If the tenant still doesn't pay, refer to and enforce the terms of your rental agreement.

Remember, rent collection problems are the exception, not the norm. Rooming houses can be a very profitable real estate investment; just one or two of them can give you the financial independence you need to quit your job and start building your wealth. So don't let the fear that you might have to deal with an occasional late payer stop you from becoming wealthy.

Net $2,500 a Month Without Managing Anything after Working for 60 Days

Creating and operating a rooming house can be a source of significant and profitable cash flow, but there are other ways to benefit financially from this investment. Once you've got the rooming house up and running, you can earn a large cash profit and establish long-term income by selling it to another investor.

Let's say you bought a property for $100,000 and turned it into a rooming house generating $1,000 a month in positive cash flow. (That is, $1,000 a month more coming in than you have to pay out.) You could realistically put the rooming house on the market for $150,000. If you check your amortization book (the table that shows the repayment schedule for loans at different interest rates for various lengths of times, which is available in office-supply and book stores), you'll see that the monthly payments on a loan of $50,000 at 10 percent for 20 years are $483. That means the person who buys the property will have to pay $483 a month more than you're paying now, but he'll still be netting more than $500 a month from the income the rooming house generates.

You can sell the property for a minimal down payment, as low as $5,000, on a wraparound mortgage. That means you hold the financing and are still responsible for paying off the original mortgage. But the buyer will be making his mortgage payments to you and you'll have almost $500 a month left over after you make payments on the original mortgage. That money will come in every month for the next 20 years, and all you have to do is a few minutes of bookkeeping.

The buyer will net more than $6,000 the first year, which is better than a 100 percent return on investment for him. When you show a buyer that kind of profit, it's hard for him to justify trying to drive you down on either your price or your down payment because his return is so great to start with.

A word of caution about wraparound mortgages: Many conventional lenders insert clauses into their mortgage contracts prohibiting this technique, so if you have a conventional mortgage on your rooming house, you'll need to check this out. When you buy with seller financing, however, you won't have this obstacle. Also, remember that the primary concern of all lenders is getting their payments on time every month, and even conventional lenders may be willing to negotiate with you if you want to sell the property with a wraparound mortgage.

The only thing that can possibly go wrong is if the buyer defaults on his payments and you have to take the property back and foreclose. In a good, well-written wraparound contract, you don't have to go through a formal foreclosure; the process is more like an eviction, and it can happen very quickly if it's done right. Get a good real estate attorney to help you with the paperwork. If the buyer defaults several years into the deal, you're taking back property that has gone up in value and is probably producing higher rents and more cash flow than it did when you sold it. And you can either go back to managing it yourself, or resell it for a higher price.

This technique is great for any property you buy with the higher and better use concept, and it's something that doesn't take any special skill or a lot of capital to do. You just have to focus on the project and get it done. If you did just one of these deals a year for the next five years, you could set yourself up to get $2,500 a month for the next 20 or 30 years without having to manage anything. Do more than one a year, and you'll quickly build a mind-boggling amount of passive income.

CHAPTER 9

How to Borrow Money and Build Your Own Personal Fortune with It

It is one of the most beautiful compensations of life that no person can sincerely try to help another without helping themselves.

—RALPH WALDO EMERSON

You've learned how to borrow varying amounts of money, but before you run out and begin applying for loans, know the amount you're going to need and how much that money will earn for you.

Let me illustrate. Supposing I offered to give you a temporary job to help you acquire seed capital for your business, whether it's real estate or something else. We agree on your duties, and the fact that you will work for me for 35 days. But then I offer you your choice of compensation plans: I will pay you either a straight $1,000 a day or a penny a day, compounded daily at 100 percent. That means your pay rate will double every day.

Which would you choose?

The arithmetic on the first plan is simple: 35 days times $1,000 a day equals $35,000. Not a bad sum for five weeks' work, and it could well be just what you need to get you on your way to financial independence.

The arithmetic on the second plan is a little more complicated, and is based on the principle of compounding. That means the money you

116

earn immediately starts to earn more money for you. Let's see how the numbers work out:

Day	Daily Amount
1	$ .01
2	.02
3	.04
4	.08
5	.16
6	.32
7	.64
8	1.28
9	2.56
10	5.12
11	10.24
12	20.48
13	40.96
14	81.92
15	163.84
16	327.68
17	655.36
18	1,310.72
19	2,621.44
20	5,242.88
21	10,485.76
22	20,971.52
23	41,943.04
24	83,886.08
25	167,772.16
26	335,544.32
27	671,088.64
28	1,342,177.28
29	2,684,354.56
30	5,368,709.12
31	10,737,418.24
32	21,474,836.48
33	42,949,672.96
34	85,899,345.92
35	171,798,691.84
Total earned:	$343,597,383.68
	(*over $300 million!*)

When I present this proposition in seminars, most people choose the penny-a-day option, but only because they suspect a trick. When I ask them to tell me how much money the penny will turn into in 35 days, they never even get close. They guess $100,000, or even $1 million, or occasionally as high as $10 million, but no one has ever guessed $343 million.

My point is this: If you don't have money, or even if you do, you may want to borrow the funds to get your business started. But first take the time to understand the principles of compounding, and make sure you apply them to your investment. Look for ways to double that borrowed money quickly, then double it again, and again. That's a great way to build your own wealth with someone else's money.

You may be thinking that investing your money so it will double—and double quickly!—sounds good, but that it's not really possible. On the contrary, it happens every day. In Chapter Seven, I used a real property I purchased to show you how to calculate return on investment—and my ROI on that property was 1,706 percent! That was a good deal, but it wasn't an unusual deal. Those kinds of properties are out there all over the place, in every city and town in the country, just waiting for you to pick them up and make money.

As a simple example, let's say you put a $5,000 down payment on a $100,000 piece of property. A year later, it appreciates 5 percent (which is very realistic in most markets), and you sell it for $105,000. Your initial $5,000 investment has earned you a profit of $5,000, which is a 100 percent return on your money in just one year.

Most people think that getting a 100 percent return on investment in real estate means you buy a property for $100,000 and sell it for $200,000, but you don't have to see the property double in value to double your money. Real estate is bought using mortgages, so you measure your return on investment based on the amount of cash you have invested, not the total amount of the purchase.

Real estate brokers generally won't tell you this because in many cases even they don't understand it. I even tried to explain it to a member of Mensa (the high-IQ society), and she didn't get it at first. The problem is not that it's complicated, but that it's so simple it tends to escape most people.

This works in plenty of businesses other than real estate. For example, retail markups are tremendous. Most consumer goods—clothing, jewelry, furniture, electronics, etc.—are marked up anywhere from 100 to 300 percent. The process generally works like this: Items are manufactured and then sold in truckload or train-car-load quantities to a broker, who adds 10 to 15 percent to the manufacturer's price. The broker sells to a wholesaler, who tacks on a 30 to 50 percent markup before selling to the retailer. The retailer adds another 100 to 150 percent, so by the time the item gets to the consumer, it has been marked up 200 to 300 percent. When a retailer buys a pair of shoes for $20 and sells them for $40, he's making a 100 percent gross profit.

Doubling Your Money

When I make an investment, whether it's in a business or property or anything else, all I want to know is how much I have to put up and how much I'm going to get back, period. Everything else is incidental.

Do you see now that it *is* possible to double your money in a short period of time? Getting a good return on an investment is compounding in action, and compounding is one of the main keys to wealth! But remember, if you take the money out of the process too soon, you'll kill the compounding formula and put yourself back at square one. That's what happens to most people when they start building wealth. They make a little money and are so pleased that they "reward" themselves with jewelry, clothes, cars, and trips—and destroy the compounding formula. It's the same principle as when someone who is dieting loses five pounds and eats a hot fudge sundae as a reward. Don't reward your success by undoing what you've accomplished; reward your success by staying on track and achieving even more.

During my first year in real estate, I made $117,000, but I kept my job at the slaughterhouse for another full year. With that kind of money, why was I willing to spend eight hours a day doing hard physical labor in a disgusting environment? For two reasons.

First, I hadn't yet shaken off my middle-income, blue-collar mentality that required a job for security. Second, and most important, I was determined to reinvest that $117,000 in appreciating assets that would compound at 100 percent annually. Ingrid and I lived on the money I earned at the slaughterhouse, and I put every nickel of that $117,000 back into real estate. By the end of the second year, I had made $234,000, and a year later I had turned that into $500,000. My penny-pinching days were over. At that point, I could have easily pulled out $100,000 for a new Rolls-Royce and still continued to increase my net worth. If you, too, exercise the discipline to keep your money working for you until you have amassed your first significant amount of wealth, you will be able to afford all the toys and luxuries you want while your bank account continues to grow.

Take another look at the penny-a-day compounding example. If you spend $100 on day 15, you've spent a major portion of your income. But by day 30, you can spend thousands of dollars and not be seriously affected by it. So make your seed money work for you until it grows into a money tree.

Remember, financial independence is within your grasp—today. You just have to borrow smart, invest in appreciating assets, compound your money at a rate as close to 100 percent as possible, and don't touch your seed capital until you've turned it into a money tree that will be your own personal fortune.

OPM in Action

Shortly after my wife and I were married, we found an old house that was in such terrible shape that it was unlivable. There was no back door, the bathroom was on the back porch, and the only useful item in the kitchen was an old tub sink. We bought this palace in 1977 for $18,000. We used our hard-earned savings to make a $4,000 down payment, and the owner agreed to hold a $14,000 15-year mortgage at 8.5 percent.

I knew absolutely nothing about home repairs and remodeling, but I learned as I went along. With my brother-in-law's help and a lot of sweat, we made the house livable. The initial purchase price was well under market value because of the poor condition of the house, but we quickly built up "sweat equity" with the repairs we made. Then I went to a bank and asked for a loan to install aluminum siding at an estimated cost of $4,000. With the improvements I had already made, I felt certain the house was now worth $25,000 to $30,000, and I owed only $14,000.

The bank appraised it and offered to lend me $18,000—which was

72 percent of its assessed value—as a first mortgage. That meant I would have to pay off the existing $14,000 mortgage the seller was holding. Now, this was not an especially good loan for me; it was great for the bank, because it was well secured. You can easily borrow 75 to 80 percent on investment property these days, and 90 to 95 percent on your own home. But at that time, I only knew to ask for the actual cost of the aluminum siding I planned to install. That was one mistake I'll show you how to avoid.

When I decided to accept the loan, I was operating under the strong influence of two important factors: First, I wanted more cash out of the deal, and second, I had been doing my homework. So I called the man I'd bought the house from, told him that I'd done a great job making improvements on it and that I was planning to add aluminum siding. Then I asked him to come out and take a look at the house.

Keep in mind that as the mortgage holder, he had a vested interest in the condition of the property. When he came out, I showed him what I had done. I explained that I had to borrow the money for further improvements, but that the bank wanted a first mortgage position. I offered to give him $7,000 in cash if he would hold the other $7,000 I owed him in a second mortgage for 20 years at 8.5 percent. I'd already been paying him on time and the house was in better shape than it had been in years, so the offer was clearly a good, safe deal for him.

At the closing, the banker showed up with two checks: One payable to me for $4,000, and one payable to the seller for $14,000. We closed, the banker left, and the seller and I went into the next room to complete the deal. He gave me back $7,000, and I signed a second mortgage over to him. (All the paperwork was prepared by attorneys, so it was safe and legal for both of us.) I walked away from the closings with $11,000 in tax-free cash. The whole deal took about three weeks.

Think about that. In less than a month, I had as much cash as it normally took me a year to earn.

The name of this technique is "seller subordination," which means that if you have a property on which the seller is holding the first mortgage, you ask him to subordinate his mortgage position to second place so you can obtain other financing on the property.

At the same time I did this, I decided to try buying a distressed income property to fix up and rent out. I used part of the $11,000 as a down payment on a shabby duplex that was structurally sound but looked awful. Ingrid and I painted the outside, paneled the hallways, did some landscaping, and were able to raise the rents high enough to cover not only the mortgage payment on the duplex but the one on our home as well. Essentially, we were living free thanks to money that we had borrowed from the bank and that our tenants were repaying.

This is just one small example of how to build wealth using other people's money—a phrase popularly abbreviated to OPM. And the more money you make, the easier making money will become.

Though I first used this technique (buying run-down property, fixing it up, and then letting the rents pay the mortgage) on a very inexpensive house in a low-income neighborhood, it works just as well on higher-priced property. There are plenty of upper-income neighborhoods that have one or two run-down houses. Even in my neighborhood, where the houses go for $500,000 and up, there's a shabby, neglected house that's a real eyesore. I've tried to buy it, but the owner doesn't want to sell. But you'll find enough owners who *will* sell in all types of neighborhoods to use this technique successfully over and over, as I have.

The Secret Cash Machine of the 90s

Home-improvement loans are basically designed to finance home improvements, but for the creative thinker they can be consistent and profitable sources for sizeable lump sums of cash.

During the 1970s and 80s, people bought homes, saw them rapidly appreciate, and often sold them to use the profits for larger, more expensive homes. Though real estate continues to increase in value, the actual rate of natural appreciation has slowed. (Don't confuse this with forced appreciation, which you can control by improving distressed properties.) People are staying in their homes longer and upgrading by remodeling rather than moving. This has created an awesome opportunity for anyone to cash in big on home-improvement loans.

As I write this, the Federal National Mortgage Association (Fannie Mae) is introducing new and attractive remodeling financing options.

It is responding to predictions that more money will be spent on home remodeling and renovation than on new construction within the next decade. How will this help you build wealth? I'll explain.

Lenders are usually more lenient with the qualifications for home-improvement loans for property you own than with mortgages for property you want to buy. You can take out a home-improvement loan on the house you live in, improve your property, and still be able to generate capital for another project. But you do not necessarily *have* to live in the home you are improving, and it can be a multi-unit building. In other words, home-improvement loans are readily available for investment properties, too. I have used them on a very large percent of the properties I have bought, and they have provided me with millions of dollars in working capital over the years.

The first time I profited from a home-improvement loan was with a run-down property in New York. I knew my bank would lend up to $17,500 for home improvements. I found the proposal and contract forms, and had business cards made up in the name of R & I Contracting Co. The property needed work that was going to cost me $3,000 to $4,000. I submitted a detailed estimate for $15,000 with my loan application. The bank reviewed my plans, approved the price, and made the loan. I wound up spending $4,000 to get the work done, which meant R & I Contracting (me) finished with an $11,000 profit. The rents on the property paid back the loan, and I was able to use the $11,000 as a down payment on another property. This was my first realization that getting rich wasn't going to be nearly as hard as some make it out to be.

During my first year in real estate, I made $117,000, tax free, using home-improvement loans without really understanding what I was doing. Had I realized the tremendous opportunity and power of this type of borrowing, I could have increased my personal fortune much more rapidly.

To obtain a home-improvement loan, you must submit an application that includes a description of what you plan to do, with cost estimates from a contractor. Home-improvement loans may be secured by the property in the form of a second mortgage, or they may be unsecured, depending on the specific policies of the lender. Shop around for the best deal.

There are two ways to generate quick cash with a home-improvement loan. The first is the method I just described: Use the loan to make improvements that drive up the value of the property and take out a new first mortgage for a higher amount. The second is to act as your own contractor and take the contractor's profit from the improvements, a process I described in Chapter Five.

A Little-Known Loan That Can Get You $15,000 to $25,000 Quickly

One of the most attractive home-improvement loans is the Federal Housing Administration (FHA) Title I loan, which is insured by the federal government. The bank lends its own money at the prevailing rate; if you default on the loan the government will reimburse the bank for 90 percent of the loss, making it a very safe loan for the bank. These loans were designed to combat the discriminatory lending policies of some banks. These policies are called red-lining, because bankers would draw red lines on maps around the areas where they would not make loans. If a property was in one of the red-lined areas, they would find a reason to turn down a loan application. But the red-lined neighborhoods were often the ones most in need of rehabilitation, so the government came up with Title I loans to remove the risk for the lender and help people who were willing to improve housing in run-down neighborhoods.

I found out about Title I loans by accident. Back when I was first getting started in real estate investing, I had a property that needed some repairs, but I didn't have the money to do it. The bank would not approve me for a standard home-improvement loan, and I was afraid I would be forced to work on this property in bits and pieces over several months as I could afford it. Then I happened to be talking to a contractor friend and mentioned my problem. He told me about Title I loans. I was skeptical, but I headed back to my bank and asked. The people there said sure, just bring in the estimate, and they'd cut the check. I was surprised and delighted, and happy to be moving forward again.

To qualify for a Title I loan, you must have a reasonably good credit rating and show you have the ability to repay. The lender will consider the property's cash flow for this. There are no other major FHA qualifications, although the bank's internal policies may include some additional restrictions, or even be more lenient. Again, it's important to shop around for the best deal.

Currently, with a Title I loan, you can borrow up to $25,000 on a single-family home, and $12,000 per unit (with the total not to exceed $60,000) on multi-family residences. Loans up to $5,000 can be completely unsecured; loans over that amount are secured by a mortgage or deed of trust on the property being improved. Investment properties qualify for this loan, and the FHA does not require them to be owner-occupied, though individual bank policies may differ.

There is one important difference between Title I and other types of home-improvement loans. According to current FHA guidelines, you cannot take a contractor's profit with a Title I loan when you do the work yourself. But this is still a great loan; use it to improve your property, which increases its value and therefore your equity, and allows you to charge higher rents, which means more positive cash flow.

When people ask me if the best opportunities for making money in real estate have passed, I point out that when I first got started, you could borrow only up to $17,500 with a Title I loan. Just 17 years later, the maximum amount has increased to $60,000. Sounds to me like the opportunities have only gotten better.

You can get a full fact sheet and a list of Title I lenders in your area by contacting the Department of Housing and Urban Development. Lenders who offer Title I loans can change, so if you contact one that doesn't offer them anymore, keep searching. They are out there, and you can find them if you don't quit.

Profit from a Rehab/Construction Loan

You may be looking for a Title I or other type of home-improvement loan and find a lender who tells you that the only loan he has available is a rehab/construction loan. Don't let the term scare you; you don't have to be a builder to take advantage of this type of money.

A rehab/construction loan is a short-term, interest-only loan often referred to as a new-construction loan. If you were a builder, it would work like this: You determine the actual cost to build the house or do the renovation, add in your profit, and submit an estimate to the lender. After the loan is approved, the lender advances monies for construction as each phase of building is completed. Generally, the last draw of the loan includes your profit.

What's important to realize is that you don't have to build a house to take advantage of this type of loan. Some banks will offer rehab/ construction loans for remodeling or rehabilitation projects—which is a fancy way to say home improvement. You'll go through the same basic process: Submit the estimates and receive the loan proceeds in increments as the work progresses, rather than in one lump sum up front.

If the property being rehabilitated has a mortgage on it, you may have to get the mortgage holder to subordinate his mortgage to a second position to allow the lender the first mortgage position. As you recall, this was the technique I used to make $11,000 on my first house. All it means is asking the first mortgage holder to let his loan be designated as a second mortgage so you can get first mortgage money somewhere else.

The reason you'll have to do this is that you'll rarely find any conventional lender willing to lend with anything other than a first mortgage position on a rehab/construction loan. But there are plenty of other lenders, such as sellers who hold their own financing and second mortgage companies, both of which will assume a second or even third mortgage position. Shop for them in the Yellow Pages of your telephone directory (look under "Mortgage Companies," "Mortgage Brokers," and "Finance Companies") and the classified advertising section of your newspaper (check under "Money to Lend").

If you are buying property with the idea of obtaining a rehab/ construction loan, you'll have to apply the subordination technique we discussed earlier. This is usually done with seller financing and negotiated at the time of purchase. Simply include a statement similar to the following in your purchase contract:

"This offer is contingent upon the seller taking back a *second* mortgage at X percent interest for Y years. The second mortgage is not to be recorded until the first mortgage is in place and recorded."

Be sure to consult with an attorney and use the correct legal language according to your state's laws.

When the construction or rehab is complete and you have been advanced your final draw, the lender will often turn your construction loan into a longer-term mortgage. Of course, depending on the market and economic conditions, you may have to shop elsewhere for your mortgage; be sure you know going into the deal what your options are. Used correctly, a rehab/construction loan can finance your down payment and all of your rehabilitation costs, and put some tax-free working capital in your pocket for your next investment.

Rehab/construction loans also drive home a very important lesson. When you approach people at a bank and ask for a specific type of loan and are told they aren't making that loan right now, but they have other types of loans, listen carefully to the terms of the loan and think about how you can apply it to what you're doing.

One-Year Float Loans: Risky, but Worth Considering

A few years ago, I found a multi-unit building appraised at $225,000 that was in foreclosure. The owner just wanted out, and the two mortgage holders were willing to work with me to avoid the lengthy, expensive foreclosure process. My offer and eventual purchase price was $175,000. The first mortgage holder was willing to make some substantial concessions on the terms and the principal balance of his mortgage, and was also willing to subordinate his mortgage to get some cash out of the deal.

To complete the deal, I needed an $85,000 new first mortgage. The building was older and somewhat cosmetically distressed, but it had no serious structural problems and most of the units were occupied. Getting an $85,000 first mortgage on such a property should have been easy, so I was stunned when it wasn't. The first five lenders I approached turned me down.

I was about ready to give up when I noticed a small community bank just a few blocks away from the property. On the spur of the moment, and not really expecting anything to come of it, I went in and explained the situation to the senior vice president in charge of commercial loans. Our conversation was quite enlightening. First, he told me, at that time many banks were not lending long-term mortgage money for commercial properties. They were basing their lending decisions on economic cycles. Second, it would be easier to borrow commercial mortgage money if I was seeking $250,000 or more; commercial mortgage lenders just don't get real excited about an $85,000 loan—it's peanuts to them. It sounds crazy, but sometimes it's easier to borrow big money than small. (See Chapter Twelve for more details on the way banks operate.)

It was sounding as if I was going to lose this great deal when the banker said he could loan me the $85,000. He would amortize my payments over 25 years, but the loan would be callable in one year. What that meant was I would make monthly payments as though I had a 25-year mortgage, but at the end of a year, I had to pay the loan in full. The interest would float monthly at 2 percent above the prime rate. (The prime rate used to be the interest rate banks offered their best commercial customers, but that's not true anymore. Today, it's a figure set by the leading commercial banks, such as Citibank and Chase Manhattan, and is based on the cost of funds. The prime changes, and since there is no federal agency regulating it, it can change quickly. If you want to know what the prime rate is currently, it's published in the business section of most daily newspapers.)

This was a so-called balloon loan, and the terms made it extremely risky. But the potential reward was $75,000 in equity that I would eventually be able to put to work elsewhere. I had one year to arrange permanent financing.

The very first month I had the loan, the prime rate shot up two full points. Fortunately, I had enough positive cash flow to cover the higher payments. But, as the year went by, I was unable to find permanent financing.

This is an aspect of balloon loans that scares many people, and it used to scare me. However, after I had a few balloon loans that I couldn't pay—like this one—I realized there's nothing to fear. All you have to do is remember this: The banks don't want the property, they want their money. And if you've been making the payments on time, they're usually happy to renegotiate your loan. They may try to bluff you at first, and insist that the loan is due. Just be firm, businesslike, and honest. Offer them their choices: They can extend the loan, or they can have the property back. You'll find that you usually won't have a problem getting the loan extended. On this particular building, I was able to extend the loan on the same terms, which I maintained until I found a buyer and sold the property at a handsome profit.

If you use a one-year float, do it carefully. It is a last-resort loan and should be taken only when the potential profit is significant and no other monies are available. Remember, if the prime rate goes up sharply, so will your payments, and you must be prepared to meet them. Also, one year isn't a particularly long time in the world of banking, so don't wait until the loan comes due to begin your search for permanent financing on better terms.

Take Advantage of Seller Financing

Very often sellers of distressed property are forced to hold the mortgage because traditional lenders will not lend money on real estate in such poor condition. (The same can apply to a distressed business; many businesses are sold with seller financing.) Sellers are also motivated to do their own financing when conventional mortgage money is tight; it's often the only way they can sell their property. No matter what its condition, whenever you buy a piece of real estate, always ask about seller financing. And always try to get the seller to hold as much of the mortgage as possible before you look for other money.

Once you have seller financing, there are a number of ways you can pull money out of the property. One is seller subordination, which is what I did with my first house. As I described at the beginning of this chapter, we bought the property, improved it, and refinanced it. Part of the refinancing included asking the seller to subordinate his mortgage position and take back a *second* mortgage. If you've been making your payments on time and you combine this proposal with some cash, most reasonable sellers will go along with you. Other ways to pull money out of property are the home-improvement loan, rehab/construction loan, and, when the money supply loosens up, discount mortgages.

Perhaps the most exciting part of making money with other people's money is that you help them make money, too. Building wealth with the right kind of debt is a win-win situation.

CHAPTER 10

A Million in Debt Is a Million in Net

The first person gets the oyster, the second gets the shell.

—ANDREW CARNEGIE

There are only two times a banker will call you sir or ma'am, and that's when you have $1 million on deposit, or when *you owe* the bank $1 million.

As long as you make the payments, banks are happy to have you indebted to them. And you must understand that the only way to get wealthy is with debt—but it has to be *good* debt. If you owe $1 million or more on appreciating income-producing assets, your wealth will increase in direct proportion to your debt. Ideally the income should cover the debt service, and the assets will gain in value as the amount you owe decreases. When the loan is paid off, you will have an asset that has paid for itself; it can continue to generate revenue for you, or you can sell it.

This principle works on any scale, from a small house to a multi-million-dollar development. If you buy a house for $100,000 and rent it for enough money to cover the mortgage and other expenses, when your mortgage is paid off you'll have an asset worth $100,000 plus whatever appreciation in value it's gained over the life of the loan. If the house's value rose by 2.5 percent a year over the period of a

20-year loan (which is a very conservative figure), you'd have an asset worth $150,000 and your tenants would have paid it off for you.

The same thing applies to larger, multi-unit properties. It also works on businesses other than real estate. When you buy an appreciating asset, you start out with a big debt, but you use the income from the asset to pay the debt and ultimately turn it into a sizeable net worth. If you purchase an income-producing appreciating asset for $100,000 and it increases in value just 10 percent, you've made $10,000 over and above whatever profits the asset produces. If you purchase an appreciating asset for $1 million and it appreciates at that same 10 percent, you've made $100,000.

When you purchase a business, always try to buy the real estate as well, instead of just leasing. A woman I know bought a commercial building for her own business. She got a good deal on the building, and her business did well. When she decided to retire, she made more selling the building (she netted $1 million) than she did selling her business. I've seen this happen over and over: The business generates the cash flow, but real estate creates the true wealth.

Have you ever thought about how nice it would be if you could charge something and have someone else make the payments? That's how buying income-producing assets works, because the cash they generate makes the payments. And when those assets go up in value, your net worth has increased that much more.

Just remember that debt for appreciating and income-producing assets is a great way to build your personal fortune. By contrast, consumer debt *never* turns into net worth. It always turns into net loss—always!

I've had students proudly tell me that their only debt is their mortgage and they pay cash for everything else. While it's good that they have no consumer or credit card liabilities, these people are not going to get wealthy until they change their attitude about debt. Used properly, debt can be one of your greatest wealth-building tactics.

How Wealthy People Get Wealthier

Wealthy people consistently use other people's money to make more for themselves. More fortunes have been built on borrowed money than any other way. After more than 15 years as a real estate investor and business owner with a net worth in the millions, I still never use any more of my own money than I absolutely have to when I'm executing business deals. And neither should you.

In fact, I see using other people's money to make money as a game. It's fun, it's challenging, and it's a very profitable way to play. And the wealthiest people do it all the time. The big players who have the biggest money all use borrowed funds. They take on huge debt, because the larger the debt, the bigger the asset—and the more awesome their net worth becomes. Of course, the asset must be an income-producing, appreciating asset to accomplish this.

The other aspect of this policy is that I rarely, if ever, use anything but totally disposable income to purchase *depreciating* assets. I don't buy clothes or household furnishings with borrowed money. I don't finance my vacations. If I can't pay cash, then I do without the consumer item and focus on making enough money so I *can* pay cash. I owe money only on assets that will make me more money than I borrowed to buy them in the first place. And so should you, especially in your beginning stages of wealth building. Once you begin to accumulate money, you can blow some of it on frivolous things, but don't do that until you have it.

A technique that has worked well for me over the years is to designate the positive cash flow from a particular asset for a specific purpose. I would, for example, look at the cash flow from a given rental property as money for solving a financial problem—like paying for a vacation, buying a new car, or providing luxuries for my family.

How to Get Your Next Automobile Free

After I'd bought my first few properties, I realized I needed a new vehicle. The car I had wasn't in the greatest shape, and a pickup truck would have been more convenient, anyway. I had just purchased a building with positive cash flow, and I found a great deal on a new Toyota pickup truck. I used a $5,000 line of credit a bank had sent me (totally unsolicited) to buy the truck and used the cash flow from the property to pay it off. To me, that was like getting the truck for free, because the apartment building made the payments on it.

When to Turn the Bank Down

The advent of credit cards and the lack of education about how to use them has increased consumer debt to record levels. The result is that many of us have a very negative perception of credit and debt, even as we run up the balances on our accounts. There are many who will never get out from under their credit card debt, but *you* can. You just have to understand that credit is both good and important, that debt can be positive, and that even credit card debt is okay if it's used for appreciating assets instead of consumer goods.

Here's the rule about borrowing money: *Borrow money only when you can use those funds to make more money.* Use borrowed money to invest in appreciating assets, that is, only assets that will increase in value. Use borrowed money to invest in income-producing assets—preferably ones that show a positive cash flow, meaning that you have money left over after meeting your loan payments and expenses each month. For example, if you borrow money to purchase a rental property, your rents must be higher than the total of your mortgage payment and expenses. You learned how to analyze a property's profitability in Chapter Seven; what's important now is that you understand and accept the policy of borrowing money *only* to purchase appreciating and income-producing assets.

Never use borrowed money to purchase consumer goods. Never buy clothing, jewelry, or new cars with borrowed money. And if banks or other credit companies try to lend you money and you don't need it, don't take it. Ask them if they will establish a line of credit so you will have quick access to the funds when necessary, but never borrow money you're not going to immediately use to make more money with.

Big merchandisers like Sears, K mart, and Wal-Mart, along with the credit card companies, continue to spend millions of dollars on advertising campaigns to entice you to charge up your cards with consumer items. They want you to take vacations, go out to eat, and buy frivolous items with money you borrow from them at exorbitant interest rates. And they know you'll never pay the money back. You'll pay the interest, month after month, and you'll never be able to reduce the balance, so you'll be paying them forever. Who's getting wealthy with that deal?

Consumers are getting an incredibly mixed and confusing message. On the one hand, merchants and credit card companies are saying, "Buy, buy, buy." On the other hand, economists are saying how bad things are because we owe so much money. But nobody is pointing out that owing money on the right kinds of things is positive and productive.

Have you ever seen any of the major credit card companies air a commercial that suggests you use your credit card to invest in a good piece of real estate? No, and you probably never will. The reason is simple: If you make a few good investments and start building your personal wealth, you'll have enough money to pay cash for the things you want and you won't need to use their credit cards. It's much more profitable for them to encourage you to charge consumer goods, so you'll stay in debt and they'll keep on raking in the bucks.

You're being bombarded with the "buy now, pay later" message hundreds of times every day, but it's for consumer items. If you listen to it, it will keep you broke. I'm going to bombard you with the "buy now, pay later" message, too, but I'll teach you to focus on items that will generate positive cash flow now and will go up in value while you own them, and on terms that are set up so someone else pays the debt for you. If you listen to me instead, I'll help you build your personal fortune.

Which would you prefer?

Interest Rates Don't Really Matter

Credit card companies justify their high interest rates because they are essentially offering unsecured loans at a higher level of risk than other types of loans. That in itself is understandable, and my problem with credit cards is not the interest rate but the type of purchases that are generally made with plastic.

I'd like to tell you a story that clearly expresses my feelings and policy about interest rates. Not too long after I'd reached financial independence and quit my job, I applied for a loan at the bank I'd been doing business with since I first got started at the age of 20. I was surprised when the people there turned me down, and totally shocked at their reason. They said I was growing too fast, and they thought I should slow down.

I argued with them. I pointed out that my property business was in beautiful condition, every unit was rented, every building was profitable, and I was making all my payments on schedule. If anything, I thought I should speed up so I could make more money, both for me and for the bank. I was so insistent that they finally agreed to make the loan I wanted, but at a higher interest rate because they claimed I was risky. Interest rates at the time were fluctuating between 7 and 8 percent; they charged me 16 percent. I was too naive to know I could negotiate this; I needed the loan for a good property, so I analyzed the deal and took the money on the terms they offered.

But here's the point about interest: If you have money left over after you pay your mortgage and expenses, don't worry about the interest rate. When that banker offered me the money I needed at 16 percent, I calculated my rents and expenses, factored in my down payment, and figured out that I would still have a 100 percent return on my investment in the first year—even paying twice the going interest rate!

This was another advantage being a high school dropout gave me. If I had been too educated, I might have realized the bank was taking advantage of me, and I probably wouldn't have accepted the loan on those terms—and I would have missed out on a very profitable investment. What's more, the entire situation taught me a very valuable lesson about conventional thinking. Insisting on the lowest interest rate can stop you from making money. Though I do try to get the lowest rate I can, I'm willing to pay more if I'm going to get a good return on my money. It's just something that wealthy people do.

This is the principle that made many people wealthy with investment bonds in the 1980s. Basically, bonds are loans. The people issuing the bonds want to borrow *your* money, and they'll usually pay a higher rate of return than a conventional savings institution because you're taking a risk with their idea, project, or business. The reason they're able to pay higher interest is that if whatever deal they're attempting to finance works out, they'll make even more than the 12 or 15 or 18 percent they're paying on the bonds.

I was young and naive, and it hadn't been long since I had been dirt poor, but I had the common sense to realize it was worth paying a higher interest rate on that loan because I would still get a good return on my investment. The very wealthy people know this. It's the people stuck in the middle who either don't understand or aren't willing to take advantage of this exciting money-making concept.

CHAPTER 11

Walk Away from the Settlement Table with Cash Every Time You Buy

Every problem has within it the seeds of its own solution. If you don't have any problems, you don't get any seeds.

—NORMAN VINCENT PEALE

For many people, one of the most memorable and gut-wrenching parts of a real estate or business purchase is the four- or five-digit cashier's check they are required to bring to the closing. But these purchases don't always mean you have to shell out big bucks. You can buy a property at a fair price, make a reasonable or low down payment, and still *make money* when you close.

I had to try this technique of financing several times over a span of years before it began working for me. No one ever showed me how to do it; I had to figure it out myself. But I'm going to show you. It may seem a little complicated, so study it carefully before you use it. It needs the right combination of circumstances to work, but you can create those circumstances with many income-producing assets. Your goal with this strategy is to get the seller to sell you his property, take his down payment out of the mortgage money, and allow *you to make money* at the closing. You'll get your best results with a highly motivated seller, a cosmetically distressed property, and any other cir-

136

cumstances that will encourage the owner to participate in creative financing. Show the seller the improvements you plan to make and convince him to allow you to finance those improvements out of the closing proceeds.

The mechanics of this technique usually involve the use of a promissory note from the buyer to the seller that represents your down payment. A promissory note is a negotiable instrument that can be bought and sold like cash. It is the instrument you sign along with a mortgage that is essentially an IOU. The note is your promise to pay; the mortgage is evidence of the collateral.

PROMISSORY NOTE
General Form

$_____ City of _____, State of _____ Date _____

FOR VALUE RECEIVED, I (or we, jointly, jointly and severally) promise to pay to the order of _____ the principal sum

of _____

dollars ($_____) in lawful money of the United States, with

interest thereon from _____ at the rate of _____ %

annum until paid, payable on _____ and _____ thereafter, and if not paid as it becomes due, to be added to the principal

and become a part thereof and to bear interest at the same rate.

_____ (SEAL)

_____ (SEAL)

Begin by locating the property and deciding how much you want to offer and the amount of the down payment. The terms of your offer are that the seller will hold a second mortgage on the property contingent upon your obtaining a suitable first mortgage. On the offer the lender receives as part of the mortgage application, you show your down payment. But rather than cash, the seller has your promissory note for the agreed-upon down payment.

At the closing the bank will give the seller the first mortgage check. The two of you (seller and buyer) go to your title company's office, where the seller writes you a check for whatever the agreed cash-back balance to you is. Then you give the seller a second mortgage totaling the down payment amount plus any cash you received. Once this is completed, the seller returns your promissory note because you have now satisfied it with the second mortgage and a new note for same. Essentially what happens is that instead of giving the seller a cash down payment, you've agreed that the down payment can be made over time instead of at the sale, and you've secured that agreement with a second mortgage.

This type of financing, which was commonly called overfinancing during the 1980s, is usually used with large, multi-million-dollar deals, although it can work very effectively on smaller properties and even businesses under the right circumstances. The reason you don't see it more often on smaller deals is that people either don't know about it or don't think they can do it. But it's a very practical and useful technique that can be used to complete a deal that might not otherwise happen.

It's true that overfinancing was part of the problem with the bad real estate loans many S&Ls made. But it wasn't the technique that was bad; it was a lack of ethics that caused the problem. People got their money up front, then hung the banks for the loans. If you decide to overfinance, be prepared to meet your obligation and make the commitment to yourself to follow through.

Before you try this technique, be aware that some banks insert clauses into their mortgages that restrict you from obtaining secondary financing on the property without their approval. I don't understand the reason or need for this clause, because any junior mortgages you might add to the property will not affect their position as a first mortgage holder or the security of their loan. But since some banks do this anyway, you can make it a point of negotiation. If you see the clause, tell the banker that you may want to eventually seek secondary financing and ask that it be removed. At the very least, demand additional language to the effect that permission to obtain secondary financing will not be unreasonably withheld by the bank.

How Creative Financing Works in Real Life

The first time I successfully used this technique was to purchase a wood-frame, two-story, single-family house. The property had minimal cosmetic distress and was ideal for an inexpensive conversion to a rooming house. The seller wanted to leave the state and be near her family, so she was motivated.

She was asking only $32,000 for the property and was willing to hold a second mortgage. I needed $5,000 to pay for the improvements. I agreed to pay her full asking price and give her a $15,000 down payment, which would come out of the $20,000 first mortgage money that I would seek and secure. She would hold a second mortgage for $17,000. At the closing, the banker gave her a check for $20,000; she gave me $5,000 of that money, and we drew up the note for the second mortgage. Here are the terms of the offer:

Purchase price	$32,000
Down payment (promissory note until closing)	15,000
First mortgage	20,000

Here's the end result:

Purchase price	$32,000
Down payment	15,000
First mortgage	20,000
Cash to buyer (me) at closing	5,000
Second mortgage at closing held by seller	17,000

The property was now financed for $37,000. Though that was $5,000 over the selling price, I walked away from the deal with $5,000 in cash, and the improvements I made with that money quickly forced the value up to exceed the loan amount. It was a great deal for everyone: The woman was able to sell the house; the bank made a good loan that was eventually paid off; and I was able to finance the property with enough money to make the necessary improvements to generate a substantial cash flow as a rooming house.

This financing method works best with a motivated seller and a property that can be improved to enhance its value. We gave an example with a modest purchase price, but the creative financing formula can work equally as well with million-dollar properties. Just use caution and common sense; be sure your cash flow will cover all of the debt that's created with this technique; and consider having your documents reviewed by an attorney to verify that the deal conforms to your state laws.

This technique is also more likely to work when you are dealing with a repeat seller. This is when you have bought a property and the seller is impressed enough with the transaction to contact you when he has something else to sell. Not only do you go into the deal with confidence and respect already established, but you are operating from a position of strength because the seller has come to you.

Cash Back to You

Another way to get money at a closing is with a repair and redecorating allowance. This is money the seller gives you out of the sale price to cover the cost of repairing or redecorating the property. To actually take cash away at the closing, you need a seller who is willing to accept a purchase price that is less than the appraised value and who will work with you to put together the deal. You can also use a repair and redecorating allowance to reduce your down payment.

Once you've agreed on the amount the seller wants, the repair and redecorating allowance is added to the price and presented to the lender for financing. At closing, the seller turns the amount of the allowance over to you from the loan proceeds.

Let's say you find a house appraised at $100,000, but the market is slow and the seller is very motivated, so he agrees to accept $88,500. You write the offer to show a sale price of $99,000 with a $10,500 repair and redecorating allowance. Then you apply for a mortgage loan based on 90 percent of the sale price, or $89,100, which just about any bank will be happy to provide on a property appraised at $100,000 if it's going to be owner-occupied.

At the closing, the bank gives the seller $89,100 and you give the seller $9,900 as your down payment for a total sale of $99,000. Then the seller gives you $10,500 back for the repair and redecorating allowance. You don't have to physically exchange thousands of dollars, you can just have the seller bring $600, which is the difference between the amount of the mortgage and the sale price, and you walk away with that cash. (Had this been a purchase of investment property with financing of only 80 percent available, you could have used the repair and redecorating allowance to significantly reduce the amount of cash you need to make the down payment.) If the seller is worried about paying taxes on the repair and redecorating allowance, you can ease his mind by explaining that it can be written off as an expense related to the sale.

This is often done with both residential single-family and multi-unit buildings, as well as commercial properties. A friend of mine who is a real estate agent has used this technique to make some great deals for himself and his clients. No one dictates just how much work really needs to be done on the property, or how much it will actually cost, as long as the numbers work for everyone involved. It's a simple and easy way to reduce the down payment, and it sometimes even allows you to get cash at closing, especially when you are buying the property with the intention of living there.

When you come to the negotiating table with a sound knowledge of techniques like these, you have a distinct advantage over most buyers and sellers. With the clout and power this knowledge gives you, you can make great deals happen.

Let the Seller Make Your Down Payment

When you are buying occupied rental property, always arrange to close (take ownership) on the third or fourth day of the month. The logic is simple: Most rents are due on the first, which means that whoever owns the building on the first is obligated to collect them. But rents are paid in advance, so if ownership transfers a few days after those monies are collected, the new owner is entitled to receive a prorated share of them.

Earlier I mentioned two construction workers, Jim Avisa and Mike Bartlett, who became millionaires by investing in real estate. They purchased their first multi-unit building using this technique, and *walked out of the closing* with a check for $6,000—and a building that generated $800 a month in positive cash flow.

Here's an example of how this worked for me. Earlier I told you about a run-down four-unit building I bought for $75,000 with a 10 percent down payment. But I didn't have $7,500 in cash. I did, however, have $5,000 credit available in the form of passbook/signature loans. Obviously that wasn't enough and I also needed additional cash to handle the needed repairs. So in my offer I stipulated that the closing take place on the third of the month.

The building was fully occupied, and the rents totaled $2,000 per month. To determine the daily rents, divide the monthly total by the number of days in that particular month. In a 30-day month, that meant daily income of $66.67. By closing on the third, that meant the seller would owe me 27 days of rental income, or $1,800.

Here's another consideration when purchasing rental property: The owner collects and holds security deposits on each unit. The amount of the deposit will vary depending on the location and lease, but it's usually one month's rent.

Let me be very clear here: That money belongs to the tenants. But it is held by the owner, and when you become the owner, the funds are transferred to you. That meant another $2,000 the seller had to give me at closing. You get to use the deposit money until you sell the building or a tenant moves out and you refund his deposit. Check with your state laws to see if there are any special requirements about the handling of security deposits. But remember, even if a tenant moves out, you'll soon have another moving in with a new deposit.

I was able to make a $7,500 down payment with only $3,700 cash out of pocket after deducting the monies the seller had to transfer to me at closing. I still had enough money to pay for the improvements necessary to increase the value of the property and qualify it for new financing, so I could pull $33,000 out of the deal just one month later. At that point, I could have sold the property for no money down, held the mortgage, and walked away with all the cash and no debt.

Even today, I make a practice of closing on the third, fourth, or fifth day of the month when I purchase multi-unit buildings, because it's always worthwhile to get the benefit of the prorated rents. One thing you need to check on is that the rents are due on the first, and not a different day. It's rare, but sometimes rents are due on the fifteenth, or sometimes the owners use an odd lease by which the rents are staggered throughout the month. Rents due on any day other than the first will affect the amount of prorated dollars you can take off your down payment, so check it out.

Also, if you're buying a business of any sort, do some research on the payables and receivables to see if you can take advantage of prorations.

Most sellers will never question the closing date. If they do and want to close on the first of the month, or at the very end of the month when there would be little benefit from prorations, just tell them you won't be available. Say you have a prior commitment or you're going to be out of town, and that the closing must take place on the third, fourth, or fifth. Remember, your choice of dates will rarely be challenged, but if it is, all you have to do is be firm. There's no reason to be afraid of losing the deal over this issue. When you're confident of your own knowledge and ability, you can accomplish just about anything at the negotiating table.

CHAPTER 12

Insider Banking Secrets

Can't never could.

—JIM PAYNE'S MOM

Banks are money stores. Just as a restaurant is in business to sell food and department stores are in business to sell clothes and furniture, banks are in business to sell money. Banks are for-profit enterprises with stockholders who want to see a profit on their investment. They make money in two primary ways: first, through interest on loans, charging points and origination fees for loans, closing costs, and other service fees; and second, by making loans that are sold to other lenders who are looking for investments.

So loans are very important to banks, and bankers are under a tremendous amount of pressure to make them. But here's the catch: They are under a tremendous amount of pressure to make *good* loans— that is, loans that will be paid back on schedule. When a loan goes into default, all eyes turn to the guy who made it. Bankers have been known to lose their jobs when big loans or too many loans go bad. In fact, the whole S&L crisis was caused primarily by banks making bad loans and becoming insolvent as a result.

What you always have to keep in mind is that banks are not some benevolent entity that lends you money when you need it just because you need it. They are *businesses*—just like the business you either have or will have—and they are in business to make a profit.

Why Are We So Insecure about Bankers?

Even though you may intellectually understand that by borrowing money from a bank, you are a customer and the bank is making money on your loan, you may still be intimidated by bankers. Let's take care of that right now, once and for all.

Bankers work hard at projecting a very respectable, conservative image. They dress in respectable, conservative gray, brown, or blue suits. They drive respectable, conservative automobiles. They belong to respectable, conservative professional organizations. And they do all this because they work in what is supposed to be a conservative, respectable industry.

What's important for you to remember is that just as there is good and bad in any industry, there are good and bad banks, and good and bad bankers. Most bankers fall under the 95 Percent Rule: They go to work every day and do their job as best they can, but they will never stand out or achieve anything remarkable.

I'm not trying to make fun or be nasty or critical of the profession, but you need to know how the system works. Even the most important banker in town doesn't necessarily earn a lot of money. Many bankers don't even have a lot of business experience; they come out of college and into bank training programs, and their knowledge of business and investing is more from textbooks than from practical experience. If you follow my methods, you'll probably make more on your first real estate deal than a junior loan officer makes in six months.

So why are so many people intimidated by bankers? There are several reasons. First, we don't understand banking, and it's common to be intimidated by something you don't understand. But let's get that into perspective. If you put a basic algebra exam in front of me, something that most high school seniors would knock out easily, I would be lost—and probably intimated by all the x's and y's and other unfamiliar symbols. That's because I don't understand algebra; I never learned it. But I can look at the most complicated closing statement and figure it out fairly quickly, because I've taken the time to learn and understand closing statements.

Learning banking is just like learning anything else. For the most part, bankers are ordinary people who have learned their profession through college and on-the-job training programs. If they can learn it and be trusted to make loans, why can't you learn whatever it is the banker knows?

Getting to know your bankers on a personal basis can also take a lot of the mystique out of what they do. You can meet bankers by asking friends and business associates for introductions, and by getting involved in your community. Banks encourage their senior staff people to be involved in chambers of commerce and other civic organizations. Join those same groups and begin building your banking relationships. Introductions made now will pay off in the future; you might meet a junior loan officer today who will become president of the bank in ten years, so keep in touch with him or her.

Another reason we're intimidated by bankers is that age-old fear of rejection. I'd like to tell you that bankers don't reject people, that they only reject bad loans, but that's not true. Certainly they do reject bad loans, but sometimes they also reject people. What I can tell you is that rejection isn't fatal, and if you get rejected by one banker, move on to the next and try again.

Bankers are human, and they will discriminate based on their own personal experiences and biases. A male banker in his sixties may decide that a 30-year-old single mother who is applying for a small business loan is too risky. A 32-year-old female banker who is divorced and has children may applaud her ambition and approve the exact same loan package. In my early days of investing, I had bankers tell me I was growing too fast and should slow down—the very same bankers who were reaping the benefits of my on-time mortgage payments. It doesn't always make sense, and it certainly isn't always fair. But life isn't fair. Business isn't fair. Banking isn't fair. Sometimes you get turned down for a loan for no good reason, and when that happens, you'll just have to deal with it and not take it personally.

The reality is that rejection is an unavoidable part of the process of becoming wealthy, and that's why it's important to develop banking relationships with several bankers. Find bankers who can relate to who you are and what you're trying to accomplish. Search out bankers who have the authority to lend money and want to work with you. This is an ongoing part of being in business.

A third reason many people are intimidated by bankers is related to privacy. We don't know much about them, but through our loan application and credit report, they learn a great deal about us—sometimes things that even our closest friends don't know. But don't worry if your credit report is flawed by past financial problems. We'll examine the subject of credit in depth in Chapter Sixteen, for now let me reassure you that your credit report can be a very small part of any commercial loan application. Most people have had credit problems at one point or another, and bankers know that. Your primary concern should be to focus on the deal and put together a loan application package they can't resist.

The Type of Loan You Want Is More Important than Your Credit

Banks are heavily regulated, and part of that regulation says they must have balanced portfolios. That means they can lend only so much money on particular types of loans. If the bank has reached its limit on the specific kind of loan you want, you won't get yours approved no matter how good it looks.

For example, let's say a bank makes loans for automobiles, boats, home improvements, and vacant land. The marketing department creates an advertising program that pushes land loans, and people flock in and the bank makes plenty of loans. But then a government auditor comes in and says the bank's portfolio is lopsided. Too much money is lent on land. If there's a dip in real estate, the bank could be in trouble. The auditor can actually tell a bank not to lend any more money on land and to focus on other types of loans.

What's more, when auditors think a bank's portfolio is not balanced, they can force the bank to do what is called a downgrading of the loans in the areas where it was lending too much money. By downgrading, the auditors are saying that the loans are not as safe as they could be. So the bank has to take money out of profits and post it to reserves to cover any bad loans. When this happens, investors tend to get nervous, the bank's stock may drop, and stockholders get upset.

What does all this mean to you? It means that you can go into a bank, and even if you have great credit, a good loan proposal, and a track record with that institution, it still has to turn you down if it's not lending that kind of money right then. And usually the loan officers won't tell you the real reason; they'll make it look as if there's something wrong with you. But you could take that same application to the bank next door and very likely it could make you the exact same loan without any problem at all.

It may give you some comfort to know that even with all of my excellent banking relationships, I can't always get the money I want the first time out. Here's a classic example that happened to me not long ago.

I use a television show to promote the investment seminars I hold across the country, and every week we have to change the commercials on the show for the city we're in. The production costs to do that were running $5,000 to $8,000 a month. I realized I could buy the necessary equipment for about $150,000, make a 25 percent down payment, and have payments of $1,900 a month. That meant I'd net a minimum of $3,000 a month in money that I wouldn't have to spend once I had the equipment in-house. Having the equipment would also allow me to bring a lot of our other video production in-house for a significant savings.

From my point of view, buying the television equipment was a profit item. But the bankers saw it as a depreciating asset, and no less than 30 banks (I counted them, and I'm not exaggerating) turned me down for the loan—and several of those banks were institutions I had done business with before. But I kept trying, and I finally found a bank willing to make the loan. The reason? It had just gone through an audit, and had been told it had too many real estate loans. So it was scrambling to make other types of loans, and my television equipment was perfect.

Banking Games You Can Play

For the first 10 years I was investing, I was like 95 percent of Americans in that I didn't understand how this banking game was played. It wasn't until after I was well established financially and had reached an age where the bank presidents and other senior officials were my peers that I finally learned the inside story. Because now these bankers are my friends and we socialize together, they'll tell me the truth. And because I know how the system operates, when I get turned down for a loan, I can find out the real reason—even when it's one the bank doesn't want the general public to know. I see no reason not to share my inside knowledge with you.

If you present a great loan package and get turned down, try giving the banker a knowing smile and saying, "Portfolio's a little heavy on investment loans, is it?" The answer you'll get will probably be the truth.

Share some of the stories I'm telling you and let the bankers you deal with know that you know how the game is played. If they realize you know what you're doing, they'll be more comfortable sharing the real story with you. And it's refreshing for them to be able to do that, because there are very few of their customers they can totally relax with. Though they may try to convince you otherwise, bankers are human, and they like to talk and gossip just like anyone else.

Think Commercial, Not Consumer

Remember when I said there are only two times a banker will call you sir or ma'am, and that's when you have $1 million on deposit, or when you owe the bank $1 million? Well, 95 percent of Americans will probably never get to that point because they think like consumers. They see banks as a place to borrow money for cars, boats, and vacations. These loans are relatively small (definitely small in the bank's view), fully amortized, and usually paid back over a span of two to five years. Keep in mind that a $10,000 car loan may be a lot of money to you when you're making only $20,000 a year, but it's not much money to even a small bank with $50 or $100 million in assets. When banks lump all their consumer loans together, they're very profitable; but taken one at a time, they're no big deal.

So when you go into a bank thinking like a consumer and ask to borrow $5,000 at whatever the going interest rate is, assuring the banker that you'll pay it back in monthly installments of $159 over the next three years, he's going to discreetly cover his yawn, guide you to a clerk, and focus his attention on people who are talking about *real* money.

Commercial thinking is different. When you think commercial loans, you think of much larger dollar amounts. You generally think short term, often just six months or a year. You negotiate the payment schedule, which may be monthly payments, but it may also be no payments or interest-only payments until the note is due. You approach the banker with confidence; he's a peer, not a superior. He's not doing you a favor by lending you the money; you're doing *him* a favor by borrowing from his bank.

Banks Prefer Customers Who Have Jobs

This is one of those silly contradictions that might not make any sense to you, but trust me on it. Bankers may prefer to make commercial loans rather than consumer loans, but they want to make those commercial loans to people who have jobs. One phrase bankers hate is, "I'm self-employed."

We all know there's no such thing as job security anymore. In my opinion, self-employed people are better risks because they have control over their income and working status. Just because you have a job today doesn't mean you'll have one next month. But bankers want their loan packages to show steady income. It's one way they measure "good" loans. If the loan goes bad, they can point to your employment as justification for having made the loan in the first place.

I found this out the hard way. It was easier for me to get loans as a slaughterhouse worker grossing $11,000 a year than it was as a self-employed investor making $250,000 a year. Why? As a slaughterhouse worker, I had predictable income. As an investor, I didn't—at least in the banker's view. But remember that bankers are only human, and it's human nature to like and feel comfortable with people who are like you. Bankers are also by nature conservative, and they see entrepreneurs—no matter how successful—as risk takers. I'm not a risk taker at all; when I make a deal, I have very carefully calculated the investment, the profit, and what I have to do to make it all work. But to a conservative banker, that still looks risky. To be successful, I have to understand that and work with it. Bankers are people who have jobs, and they like other people who also have jobs.

Yet, here I am, encouraging you to achieve financial independence so you can quit your job. But if you do, you'll have a harder time getting your projects financed. Is this a catch-22? Not at all. There's a simple solution: Give yourself a job.

Create a company, give yourself a title, and pay yourself a salary. If you have a rental property, your company could be Ace Property Management, your title could be general manager, and your salary could be $500 a week. Write checks to yourself every week so you have the check stubs to prove it. It doesn't matter if you take that salary and put it back into your business account so you can pay yourself next week; you've shown the banker steady income, and that's what he needs to see.

It's not necessary to form a corporation or go through any major hassle to create your company; it's a simple sole proprietorship of which you are an employee.

Even today, Russ Whitney, self-made millionaire, could have a hard time getting a loan. But Russ Whitney, president of WIN Computer Systems, who draws a salary as an employee of the corporation, gets loans on a regular basis. And yet I make my money the same way I always have: with real estate and other investments, and through the ownership of small and medium-sized businesses. The first time I did this was when I created R & I Enterprises, which was the company name my wife and I used when we first began investing in real estate.

A word of caution: Don't confuse creating a company for loan purposes with creating a company for tax purposes. For loan purposes, you are simply documenting steady income. For taxes, work with a qualified and competent tax adviser.

Understanding the Different Kinds of Financial Institutions

So far we've been using the term ''bank'' in a generic way, but there are several different types of financial institutions. I didn't really understand this in my early days of investing. I got around and got things accomplished, but I could have done much better if I had had a clearer picture of the differences between the various institutions. Understanding what they do and how they operate will make dealing with them easier and more efficient and give you a significant edge.

Commercial Banks. This type of institution generally handles checking accounts (they call them demand deposit accounts), savings accounts, and certificates of deposit, as well as consumer, automobile, home mortgage, and commercial loans. They are usually well capitalized and more diversified in their services than savings and loan associations. Some banks provide brokerage services, annuities, mutual funds, and other investment services. The Federal Deposit Insurance Corporation (FDIC) protects depositors at commercial banks to a maximum of $100,000 at any one bank. Federally chartered banks are required to be members of the FDIC; state-chartered banks need not belong, but most of them do.

Savings and Loan Associations. Often referred to as S&Ls or thrifts, these institutions were initially created to house savings and offer home-mortgage loans. During the 1980s, S&Ls attempted to diversify, which ultimately led to the infamous S&L crisis, which we'll discuss in more detail in Chapter Thirteen. Many surviving S&Ls are returning to the operating guidelines they followed prior to the 1980s. Deposits are insured by the FDIC.

Credit Unions. Credit unions are nonprofit financial cooperatives that offer members many of the services provided by banks. They vary in strength, size, and assets. Membership requirements vary according to the institution, and may be based on occupation, geography, employer, or some other requirement. Credit unions generally have lower overhead expenses than commercial banks, and can usually offer more attractive savings interest rates and loan rates than commercial banks do. Deposits are protected by the National Credit Union Share Insurance Fund (NCUSIF), a federal agency that insures credit unions the same way the FDIC insures banks. Generally the level of financial expertise and credentials is lower at a credit union than at a commercial bank.

Mortgage Companies. These institutions are in the sole business of leading mortgage money. Many mortgage companies are satellites of savings institutions based in another part of the country; others are individually owned and operated, with their own funding sources.

Second Mortgage Companies/Consumer Finance Companies. These institutions offer personal loans, home-equity loans, and second mortgages at consistently higher interest rates than those charged by banks and S&Ls. Some, but not all, of these institutions may be more lenient with their lending requirements than a conventional bank, and some financial experts believe that providing riskier loans than banks is one reason for their higher interest rates. They also do not have access to low-cost depositors' funds and must obtain their monies from commercial sources at money market rates. Often this type of lender is more willing than others to participate in creative financing packages.

Mortgage Brokers. Though mortgage brokers are not lending institutions, this is the best place to explain their role in the banking industry. Mortgage brokers are essentially middlemen who represent many lenders. They know who is lending what kind of money, and they can help you prepare a good loan package. Mortgage brokers are especially helpful to the beginning investor who may be insecure about dealing with bankers. I found them especially valuable when I was just getting started, since the broker dealt with the banker on my behalf, and the banker never had the chance to make a potentially negative judgment based on my age. Also, since mortgage brokers put together your documentation, if you're unsure of anything (though if you follow my advice, you shouldn't be) they'll be able to help you.

Mortgage brokers are paid a commission out of the closing proceeds of the loan; never use a mortgage broker who asks for an up-front fee. I learned this the hard way when I paid a broker a large fee (which the small print said was nonrefundable) but didn't get the loan. Good brokers won't waste their time with you if they don't think they can get you the loan, so they're happy to take their fee out of the loan proceeds.

Once you have a specific property in mind, interview several mortgage brokers before selecting one to handle your business. Tell them you're looking for loans for investment properties and ask about their parameters, their lenders, what types of loans they have, what the interest rates, points, and origination fees are, and in general how the process works.

Hard Money Lender. Sometimes called an equity lender, this type of institution will finance an average of 65 percent of the equity in a property, often without any credit or other background check, relying solely on the property to guarantee the loan. Often their interest rates are higher than other lenders'. You'll find these lenders advertising in the "Money to Lend" category of the newspaper's real estate section, or you may be referred to one through a mortgage broker. Michael Keiter, one of my students in Colorado, used a hard money lender to buy a house that was in foreclosure. To avoid the foreclosure, the owner was willing to sell at less than market value. The property was appraised at $65,000, and Mike found a hard money lender who was willing to lend him $42,000 on the property alone—no qualifying, no credit check, no down payment. Since the seller was only asking $39,000, Mike walked away from the closing table with cash in his pocket and equity in the property.

The Clout of Compensating Balances

Compensating balance is a fancy phrase for cash flow. It's not the amount of money you have, but the amount of cash you control. And if you control significant amounts of cash, you can have significant clout with a bank.

Let's say you started a property management company and picked up five contracts. The buildings have 50 units each with average rents of $400 a month. That means every month you collect $20,000 from each building, or $100,000, to deposit in the bank. In a year, that's over a million dollars, and that makes you a million-dollar player. Even though it's not your money, you get credit as the person who places those funds in the institution. If you control where it goes, it doesn't matter if it's your money or not.

Of course, you're going to be paying out $85,000 to $90,000 every month to the property owners, but there will be a certain amount of lag time between the deposits, when you write your check, and when that check is cleared. That lag time is called float, and it's a time when banks can use that money to make more money for the bank. Anytime money is in a bank more than 24 hours, the bank is earning money on it. So while those deposits may be little more than a bookkeeping chore to you, they are very valuable to the banker.

Remember, deposits are the lifeblood of a bank. Deposits make the banker look good. Some bankers even get paid a commission or bonus based on new deposits and new good loans they generate. And a million-dollar account makes a banker look very good, indeed. Bankers will do a lot of nice things to attract and maintain accounts of that size. They'll take you to dinner, they'll give you rebates on loan closing costs, they'll pay for having your taxes done—I've even seen banks pay for the lease on a car for a good customer. And if you happen to control a lot of money but have poor personal credit, you'll even find bankers willing to help you get loans. In short, when you have a large compensating balance, you have clout.

Property management is not the only business with the potential for significant compensating balances. The typical McDonald's, for example, may net only $100,000 a year, but it may gross *$1.5 million,* and that money has to be cycled through a bank. One of the companies that I have an interest in, EquityCorp. (a mortgage servicing company; more about this in Chapter Fourteen) has millions of dollars in compensating balances in several trust banks, and, believe me, those bankers appreciate that business.

You don't necessarily have to have money of your own if you have compensating balances. You just have to realize how much clout you have and use it to your advantage. Keep your eyes open to opportunities to control where other people put their money, and let the banker know when you do have that control.

How to Document Yourself for a Loan

The specific contents of a loan package will, of course, vary depending on the type of loan you are seeking. What should be consistent is that you present yourself in a polished, professional manner each time you approach a lender. Your loan package is essentially a marketing piece for yourself and your project; it is a tool you can use to sell yourself to the banker. And since so few people ever take the time to put together a sharp loan package, yours will stand out.

Put your documents in a folder with clips on each side. I put my tax returns on one side and the rest of the information on the other. You can choose any arrangement you prefer, as long as there is a logical sequence to your documents. Be sure everything is typed and on good-quality paper. If you are including copies of a form you have filled out by hand, be sure your writing is neat and legible. Make sure photocopies are clear and easy to read. Remember, complete documentation will increase your chances of approval and speed up the loan process.

Documents Necessary for Any Type of Loan

COVER LETTER ABOUT YOURSELF—This is basically a résumé in paragraph form. Don't address this letter to anyone specifically. Put your name and address at the top and describe yourself: what kind of work you do, what your general background is, why you are a stable and reliable person who can be trusted to repay this loan. If you are involved in any community activities, list them; you may find you have something in common with the banker, and remember, bankers like to loan money to people who are like themselves. Keep it brief and to the point, but make it a strong sales piece.

YOUR FINANCIAL STATEMENT—A listing of your assets and liabilities, that is, what you own and what you owe. The difference between the two figures is your net worth.

COPIES OF YOUR CREDIT REPORT—If you have copies of your credit report, include it. If there are any derogatory entries, explain them in a brief statement.

COPIES OF YOUR FEDERAL INCOME TAX RETURNS FOR THE PAST TWO YEARS—Copy the entire return, not just the front page.

Documents Necessary for a Real Estate Purchase

A STATEMENT ABOUT THE PROJECT—Describe the details of the project, including the history of the property and what you plan to do with it. Make it clear you have given thought to all the aspects that may affect the property's profitability.

RENT ROLL STATEMENT—This should include current and projected figures for the property's gross monthly and yearly rents and expenses. Break out your projected net cash flow so the banker can clearly see the profit potential.

YOUR ACCEPTED OFFER—A copy of the offer the seller has accepted.

CONTRACTOR'S ESTIMATES—If you are applying for a home-improvement or rehab/construction loan, include detailed contractors' estimates for the work you plan to do.

LEGAL DESCRIPTION AND ANY OTHER GENERAL INFORMATION ABOUT THE PROPERTY—Any additional information you can provide about the property will demonstrate that you have researched it thoroughly.

PHOTOS OF THE PROPERTY—Snapshots taken with a good 35mm camera are best.

DETAILS ON OTHER PROPERTIES YOU OWN—If you have bought and fixed up other properties, include before and after photos along with details such as the figures on positive cash flow or, if the properties have been sold, your profits.

Documents Necessary for a Business Loan

Because the types of business loans vary greatly, it's impossible to state exactly what you need for a business loan. If you are looking for funding to purchase an existing business, you'll need all the documents related to that business. If you want to start a new business, you'll need your business plan with short- and long-term (at least five years) projections. If you need a loan for a specific purpose or expansion, provide the appropriate details. The key is to anticipate any questions you think the lender may have, and answer them in your loan package.

Buzzwords That Open Doors

One of the most important elements of success in any business is establishing a comfort level for yourself. That also applies to borrowing money. The fastest way to become comfortable with borrowing money is to learn the language of bankers and other lenders. It will help you understand them, and your knowledge will make them feel more confident about making loans to you.

Here are some basic loan terms you need to know:

Adjustable-rate mortgage (ARM). A mortgage loan that allows the interest rate to be changed over the life of the loan. Since their introduction about 15 years ago, ARMs have generally saved borrowers significant sums over fixed-rate loans. *Caution:* Be sure any ARM you accept has both annual and lifetime interest rate caps; the most common is 2/6, which means the interest rate cannot increase more than 2 percent each year, with a maximum increase of 6 percent over the lifetime of the loan. Also check how long the current interest rate applies; most are for one year, but some are guaranteed for as short a period as three months, others for up to five years. Never accept payment caps instead of interest caps; a payment cap means your payment won't go up but your interest rate might, and the result could be negative amortization. For example, if you had a 20-year mortgage at 7.5 percent, your payments would be $403. At 8.5 percent, the payments would be $434. If you took an 7.5 percent ARM with a payment cap of $425 but no interest cap and the interest rate went up just 1 percent, you would be adding $9 to your principal amount each month.

Amortize. Amortization is the process of reducing a debt through installment payments of both principal and interest. An amortization table or schedule (also referred to as a loan and mortgage payment table) is a chart that shows the monthly payments for loans at varied interest rates and time periods. Use an amortization table to calculate your monthly repayment amount before you apply for a loan. These tables are often included in real estate handbooks and are available in bookstores and most office-supply stores.

Assumable mortgage loan. A mortgage loan that can be taken over by another person. Some assumable loans require no qualifying (many VA and FHA loans fall into this category); others require qualifications just as they would on a new loan. If interest rates have changed, the lender may elect to adjust the rate of the loan before allowing a new buyer to assume it.

Equity. The difference between the value of the property and the principal balance of the loan, or what you owe.

Fixed-rate mortgage (FRM). A mortgage loan for which the rate of interest stays the same throughout the life of the loan.

Home-equity loan. Similar to a second mortgage in that the loan amount is based on the amount of equity in a home, with widely varying terms.

Home-improvement loan. A loan for the specific purpose of financing home improvements. The lender may or may not require a mortgage or other collateral to secure the loan.

Junior mortgage. Any mortgage that provides a lien subsequent in priority to another mortgage. A second mortgage is a junior mortgage.

Lien. The term used when a lender has interest in rather than title to the property being used as collateral for a loan. Liens can also be attached to property to satisfy unpaid debts. Under those circumstances, the lien holder is paid before the owner receives any money.

Mortgage. A document providing written evidence of the right of a creditor to have property of a debtor sold upon default and foreclosure. Also used to describe the process of using real estate as collateral for a loan.

Mortgagee. The lender or mortgage holder; the one to whom the property is pledged.

Mortgagor. The borrower; the one pledging the property as security for a debt.

Negative amortization. The situation that occurs when a loan payment is less than the interest alone. Even though the payments are made in the correct amount and on time, the amount the borrower owes increases.

Second mortgage. A mortgage using the equity of a property as collateral for a loan. Mortgages are generally recorded in the order of date placed, but an existing first mortgage holder can elect to take a second position if circumstances warrant. In this case, the term "second" is not necessarily a chronological reference; it means the position the mortgagee holds when collecting in the case of default and foreclosure. It is possible for properties to have multiple mortgages.

Seller financing. When the seller of a property agrees to hold the note and accept payments rather than one lump sum.

A Few Final Banking Basics

A banking relationship is not a single event, it's an ongoing process. Banking has changed significantly in the last decade, and it's going to keep on changing. You have to stay in tune with those changes and keep working the system to your advantage.

It used to be that most banks were community banks and the bankers were longtime members of the community. They knew just about everybody, and everybody knew them; documenting loans was more of a formality than anything else and lending was pretty much an old boy network kind of thing. Today, with all the bank mergers, takeovers, and failures, it's all different. And, like a lot of other things in my life, I learned it the hard way.

When I first moved to Florida, I had all my money in one bank. I had a good relationship with the banker, I made large deposits, and I got all the loans I applied for. But then the bank was taken over by a bigger bank, and the rules changed. Suddenly, despite my excellent track record, I couldn't get a loan—and my banker couldn't do anything about it.

So I moved my accounts to another bank. I established a rapport with a loan officer and had received several loans when that bank was taken over—and, again, the rules changed. This happened to me two more times. Then I went to a new community bank that was now headed up by the banker I had originally worked with several years before. We had a good and mutually profitable relationship, and I learned a valuable lesson from the whole experience.

Here are some of the rules about dealing with bankers I've developed over the years:

Never deal with just one bank; establish relationships with several banks. When a bank can't provide what you need, whether it's because the timing is bad, it doesn't make the type of loan you want, or it has been taken over and the rules have changed, you need a backup lending source, and you'll usually need it quickly. So build several solid banking relationships by dividing up your deposits and your loans among different institutions.

Interview the banker—it's a privilege for him to loan you money.
You need a banker you are comfortable and compatible with. Remember, bankers are human and they will discriminate, even if it's unconscious. Find a banker who believes in you and what you're doing. That's the banker who will go to bat for you. Also, make sure the banker has real authority. Early in your relationship, ask him what his lending limits are. If he doesn't have the authority to make the kind of loans you'll need, find out who does. If you tell him what you want and he stalls, you're probably not dealing with the right person. Especially in large banks, it's common for people in the branches to have grand titles but little real authority. If the loan decisions are made downtown, you should be dealing with someone downtown, not with someone in the branch who can't help you.

Be professional. Though you may eventually become personal friends with your banker, your banking relationship is a business one. Your first meeting should always be done by appointment and, if possible, with a referral from a high-powered mutual acquaintance. Subsequent meetings also require appointments; it shows that you value both his time and your own. And use your selling skills (the ones you'll learn in Chapter Seventeen) in every contact. Yes, it's true you're the customer, but you want the banker strongly on your side, and you're going to have to sell him to get him there.

Give your banker all the ammunition he needs to work with you. Put together complete, attractive loan packages. I always bind my loan applications in an attractive cover, and I try to anticipate any question the banker may have and include appropriate documentation so he doesn't have to ask. Bankers tell me repeatedly such a presentation has a very positive impact, but fewer than one out of every 100 applications are prepared this way.

Let the banker buy lunch. The person who picks up the tab for lunch or dinner is usually the person who benefits from the relationship. Remember, the banker is benefiting from your business, so always let him buy lunch. If you feel comfortable with the banker paying the bill, you've learned what I'm trying to teach you. If you feel intimidated about putting the banker in a position to buy, read this chapter again and work on your industry knowledge and communication skills. Most of the time, if you've done your job right, the banker will reach for the check. Remember, too, that there are no absolutes in this world. There may be a time when your strategy involves giving yourself the psychological advantage of playing the big-money host. Just always remember how much the banker stands to gain by lending you the money you need to become wealthy.

Become Your Banker's Adviser

As you get to know your banker, you may find yourself assuming the role of investment adviser. This probably won't happen if the banker is nearing retirement, but if he's still got a number of years of working ahead of him, he'll appreciate your information. And whether he uses what you tell him or not, bankers are always intrigued with how financially independent people make money.

Not long ago, I met a banker who didn't own any property at all. We were both involved in Little League, and we got to know each other on a personal basis. I showed him a few of my properties and explained why he shouldn't be renting. He saw the wisdom in my advice, and less than a month later he'd bought a foreclosure deal he found out about through another banker. He has since bought a second property, and he'll probably make real estate investing a sideline business for the rest of his life.

He's also been a tremendous help to me. Besides going the extra mile for me when it comes to my loans, he teaches at our quarterly five-day Millionaire University training camp (an intensive wealth-building seminar), so our students learn the real story about banking from a banker. If you take the time to teach your banker what you know, it will come back to you many times over.

CHAPTER 13

Cashing In on the S&L Crisis

═══════════════════════════════

Progress always involves risk. You can't steal second base and keep your foot on first.

—FREDERICK WILCOX

The headlines have been blazing about America's savings and loan crisis for some time. The government has taken over hundreds of banks and S&Ls across the country, and thousands of depositors lost their savings investing in bad deals. Some wealthy investors made fortunes—and some have gone to jail for illegal activities related to failed institutions. The Resolution Trust Corporation (RTC) has great deals. The RTC has bad deals. The American taxpayers will be paying for this debacle for generations to come.

How much of all this is true, and how much isn't? And what does it mean to you?

Well, everything I just said is true. The government has taken over hundreds of banks and S&Ls. A lot of people lost money investing in bad deals. A lot of people made money, and some of them have gone to jail for stepping over the line. (Interesting note: Some of those jailed were bankers.) The RTC does have great deals, but it also has lousy deals. And yes, the American taxpayer will ultimately pay for the bad deals.

But the good news is that average Americans can get wealthy by learning how to find great deals through the RTC. You can make a lot of money, and you can help a lot of people in the process. Or you can just pick up a good deal for yourself. I personally have seen four-bedroom, two-bath houses in good neighborhoods sell for as low as $2,000. Janet Claussen, one of my students in Florida, bought a duplex in good shape with both sides rented for a total price of $500. Another one of my students in Kansas City, Missouri, bought a two-bedroom, one-bath house with a full basement for $128—and the RTC paid $1,000 in closing costs. He also bought a three-bedroom house for $500. He has the smaller house rented; the larger one needs about $500 worth of work before he can put a tenant in it, but it will take him only a couple of months to get his full investment back when he's finished.

In 1992, the RTC allowed more than 12,000 families to get into properties with low down payments and mortgage payments that were less than their rent had been. It's not difficult; you just need to know how to do it, and that's what we're going to discuss in this chapter.

S&L Bailout Myths and Realities

Just about everybody has something to say regarding the S&L disaster, but most people don't really understand what they're talking about. Let's take a look at some of the myths you may have heard, then clarify them with a look at the way things really are.

Myth: The good properties have already been taken.

Reality: In a recent period, the RTC closed four times the number of banks as were shut down in the first three months of its operation. Good properties are available and will continue to be available for some time.

Myth: All the opportunities are in the Sun Belt (Florida, Texas, and California).

Reality: S&Ls have failed and are failing across the country. In addition, banks are not limited to investment properties in or near the area where they are located. There are plenty of opportunities all over the United States.

Myth: The early investors got the best bargains.

Reality: The RTC continues to adjust its practices; those buying at auction now will pay a fraction of what the first bidders paid.

Myth: With tougher banking restrictions, the average investor can't get financing.

Reality: There is more financing available than ever before, including direct RTC loans.

Myth: The Affordable Housing Disposition Program (see below) precludes participation by investors.

Reality: It gives every starting investor an opportunity to participate with minimal risk or capital.

How We Got to This Point

A wide variety of factors, circumstances, and just plain bad timing contributed to the S&L disaster. But the real cause was a change in the way Americans do business.

Sam Walton changed the way rural America shops by building giant Wal-Mart stores in small communities across the country. The huge corporation with its purchasing and marketing abilities has been the catalyst that put many small retailers out of business. The small stores couldn't match Wal-Mart's prices and variety, and were eventually abandoned by their customers. Some see Wal-Mart as a villain, using tactics that are technically legal but morally unfair to capture large market shares and force independent businesses to close their doors. Others see Wal-Mart as a savior, bringing a previously unavailable resource to rural America while it creates jobs and promotes American-made goods. Whatever view you take, the reality is that Wal-Mart altered the way many Americans shop.

Along the same lines, large commercial banks changed the way Americans conduct their personal financial business. Prior to the 1980s, savings and loan associations were just what their name implied: a place where you could save and borrow money. The savings accounts were primarily passbook; the loans were predominantly home mortgages; and the institutions themselves were carefully and stringently regulated.

Because of the limited scope of their services, most S&Ls were like relatively small specialty stores. The supermarkets of the industry were the large commercial banks with their lengthy menu of services. Just as Wal-Mart captured customers who had belonged to local merchants, the large commercial banks launched expansion programs supported by clever marketing campaigns and began to pull customers away from the S&Ls. And just as the small shops that had the misfortune to be in Wal-Mart's path went out of business, the S&Ls began to fail at an ever-increasing rate as they lost customers to the commercial banks.

The S&Ls began campaigning for changes in the banking laws that would allow them to be more competitive with commercial banks. After some legislative dancing, Congress chose a solution referred to as deregulation. You may find the term confusing, because it did not mean that banking regulations were eliminated. What did happen was that certain policy restrictions on what thrifts (as S&Ls are sometimes called) could do with their customers' deposits were abolished and federal regulations governing S&L capital requirements and the percentage of assets that must be liquid were relaxed. This meant that S&Ls had the freedom to make a variety of loans on tremendously risky ventures and that they reduced the level of their cash reserves. We saw a boom in commercial building, junk bond sales skyrocketed, and everything looked rosy—for a while.

But at the same time Congress deregulated the S&Ls, the price of oil dropped. It was an unfortunate and untimely coincidence. America's marginal oil fields began cutting back, and the economies of numerous states plummeted. The overall economy took a general downturn (as part of a normal economic cycle), and the real estate industry slowed to a standstill. Compounding the problem was the Tax Reform Act of 1986, which eliminated many of the loopholes—including several relating to real estate—that investors had used to shelter income. The consequences were devastating to an already sluggish market.

That there was definite mismanagement within the S&Ls themselves is clear, and many S&L officials have been held accountable for both poor judgment and criminal activities. But the real problem went much deeper. An entire industry bet its future on an upswing in the economy that failed to materialize. Federal regulators started to sound the alarm. The S&Ls and their supporters fended off the regulators who, by then, were overwhelmed by the enormity of the situation. The President and Congress held their breath, almost as if they, too, shared the secret dream that a sudden upsurge in the economy would make the problem disappear.

Finally, it became apparent that a major catastrophe was at hand, and we weren't going to be able to simply wish it away. On August 9, 1989, the Financial Institution Reform, Recovery and Enforcement Act of 1989 (FIRREA) became law. This act created the Resolution Trust Corporation.

What Is the RTC and What Does It Do?

Despite its somewhat misleading name, the Resolution Trust Corporation is not a private corporation but rather a federal agency. It was established to take the place of the Federal Savings and Loan Insurance Corporation (FSLIC) and the Federal Home Loan Bank Board (FHLBB), the federal entities that previously supervised and insured deposits in S&Ls. Those agencies were abolished with the same legislation that created the RTC.

What the RTC does is step in to manage the assets of S&Ls when they fail. The sequence of events goes like this. All S&Ls are monitored by the Office of Thrift Supervision (OTS), which is part of the Department of Treasury. When an institution is not operating up to standard, the OTS decides if it should be closed. Once the OTS makes that decision, it sends in a team to take control of the entire facility, including accounts, physical assets, and all outstanding loans. These are immediately placed under control of the RTC, which begins the process of selling the assets.

Now, if you had a savings account in an S&L that failed, you'd be pretty anxious about your money—and justifiably so. If the S&L had adequate cash reserves and safe investments, it wouldn't have failed. Your one comfort is that your savings are insured by the federal government up to $100,000.

The goal of the RTC is to liquidate the assets in a way that keeps the amount of money the government has to pay to depositors as low as possible. While the agency is in the process of attempting to sell those assets, it must also manage them—a fact that complicates the RTC's task but will work to your advantage.

It's interesting to note that the RTC has received a tremendous amount of publicity involving the sale of real estate, yet the agency itself states that real estate comprises only about 10 percent of all the assets they manage and have sold. Other assets include cash and securities, mortgages, delinquent loans, investments in subsidiaries, and a considerable amount in the catchall category of "other."

What this means to prospective investors (that's you) is that since real estate is a small portion of the RTC's responsibility, its response time will probably not be as fast as you'd like. (Keep in mind that what is "small" to the RTC is an astronomical number and a tremendous opportunity to us. As I write, the RTC has an estimated 68,000 pieces of property in its inventory, and that number is expected to increase over the next decade.)

RTC officials are very mindful of the mismanagement and fraud that contributed to this disaster. To protect themselves, most decisions are made by committees. However, if you know the system and understand how the RTC bureaucracy works, you can help control the pace of the process and take advantage of this incredible real estate bonanza.

How the RTC Sells Property

The goal of the RTC is to get the best possible price for any given property, and to get the properties sold as quickly as can reasonably be expected. RTC properties are sold in two primary ways: on the open market or through a competitive bid process. The open market process is very similar to any real estate purchase; you see a property, come up with the price you're willing to pay, and make an offer. If your offer falls within the RTC's guidelines on what it will accept on the property, you'll have a deal.

Properties not sold on the open market go through a competitive bid process, either a sealed bid or a live auction. Both are forms of auctions, where you essentially compete with other bidders to buy the property. The scheduling of auctions is set up to give you as a bidder the opportunity to find out where the properties are and to inspect them so you can make an intelligent bid. In a live auction, you know how much other people are bidding and have the opportunity to top their bids. In a sealed-bid process, your offer is submitted in a sealed envelope by a specified deadline. After the deadline has passed, the bids are opened, and the one the RTC determines is best is accepted. You'll find notices of RTC sealed-bid and live auctions listed every Friday in the *Wall Street Journal* and often in your local paper.

I recommend that you attend an RTC auction before you're ready to buy just to see what it's like and to get a feel for how it works. You'll see all kinds of people from all economic backgrounds buying property. It's an exciting, entertaining process, and seeing the action will make you more comfortable when you get ready to bid on properties yourself.

How You Can Benefit from the S&L Crisis—and Why It's Okay

A couple of years ago, one of the newsmagazine shows did a feature on investors who bought properties from the RTC at extraordinarily low prices. The properties were in various stages of distress, from needing slight cosmetic improvements to major repairs. The new owners were fixing them up and either renting them out or selling them, and they were making a lot of money doing so. The slant of the feature was that these investors were ripping off the government and the taxpayers by paying way below market value for single-family homes and small apartment buildings. More than one bystander was interviewed, saying the investors should have paid more money for the properties.

That's ridiculous. Those bystanders probably just didn't take the time to research and figure out how to take advantage of the situation themselves.

The investors who are now purchasing property from the RTC didn't have anything to do with causing the S&L crisis, but they are contributing to the *resolution* by buying the assets of the failed S&Ls. They are helping to reduce the government's and the taxpayers' liability for the entire disaster. They are buying and rehabilitating properties, returning them to the tax rolls, and ultimately providing housing for people who need it. That they are building wealth for themselves is a bonus they have earned.

We must remember, too, that the RTC is a government agency—and government agencies are usually mediocre at best at managing real estate. Just take a look at the public housing projects in any major city to see what I mean. It is in the best interest of everyone for the assets currently under the RTC's control to return to the private sector as quickly as possible.

This is one of the major reasons the S&L crisis offers a unique chance for beginning real estate investors to get into the game without a lot of up-front cash. It's an opportunity our parents didn't have and our children won't—and it's an opportunity that 95 percent of Americans may not even bother to take advantage of. But if you want to be among the 5 percent of the 95 Percent Rule and become wealthy, let this timing and the RTC help you.

Finding RTC Bargains

How do you go about taking advantage of what the RTC has to offer? It can be as simple as looking at a newspaper once a week, going to the library, or, if you own a computer, accessing the RTC listings directly. RTC listings are also usually included in the "Real Estate Corner" of the *Wall Street Journal* on Fridays.

As part of its public information services, the federal government has designated libraries throughout the country as official depository libraries. This means all federal public information—including listings of RTC properties—is automatically sent to them. You can make photocopies or take notes from the pages that interest you. Check with your local library to see if it is a designated official depository, or call the RTC Asset Inventory at (800) 431-0600 for the location nearest you. Another excellent source is the RTC sales office that supervises the location you are interested in. You can visit the office or write for a copy of its latest property listing.

If you have a computer and modem and are a serious investor, you can access listings of RTC properties through WiNet. This is an up-to-date listing of the RTC inventory, and it also includes thousands of other government properties and individual foreclosures. For details on how to access this data base, contact WiNet at (800) 741-7877.

When you do get information from the RTC, you'll notice it carries a very strong disclaimer in language that will either scare you to death or put you to sleep. What it means is that the RTC doesn't guarantee any of the information it provides, so you have to check out and confirm the details of the properties that interest you. Of course, you should always do a property inspection on any RTC property—or any other property, for that matter.

Investors should view the RTC process as similar to prospecting in the Gold Rushes of the past: You must filter through a lot of pebbles to find the golden nuggets.

Are there good deals available? Plenty. Are there great opportunities available? You bet! RTC properties are just like any other investment property you may consider: If they produce positive cash flow and are in reasonably good shape structurally, they're a good deal. If they don't pencil out, move on to the next one. Invest the time and energy to do the necessary cleaning up and fixing up, and be prepared to manage the property properly.

Here's what I recommend you look for in an RTC property:

- The property must have a positive cash flow.
- It must be priced at least 20 percent below market value.
- You must be assured of a 30 percent return on your investment the first year after calculating rent prorations.
- The property must have an up side—that is, it must have the potential for dramatic appreciation through improvements, or a higher and better use with minimal investment on your part.

When you find these four elements, you have found your gold. Go for it.

The Affordable Housing Disposition Program

The purpose of the Affordable Housing Disposition Program (AHDP) is to create home ownership and rental housing opportunities for low- and moderate-income households through the sale of residential properties held by the RTC. There are still a tremendous number—literally thousands—of them available. Some of these may not be especially glamorous, but they are the ones you should be looking for. If the RTC is a gold mine, the AHDP is where you'll find plenty of gold nuggets.

The program works like this: When the RTC takes over a bank, all properties that fall into the residential category are screened, and those under a predetermined price level are assigned to the AHDP. For the next 90 days, only qualified buyers may make offers. After 90 days, the property is either placed in the general inventory or given to the auction program.

Qualified buyers are nonprofit organizations, public agencies, and individual investors whose total family income does not exceed 115 percent of the area median income. That means if you're a family of four in Los Angeles, you can earn up to $50,050 and still qualify to purchase affordable housing from the RTC. In Boston, it's $54,650 or less. In Chicago, it's $53,900 or less.

Under the single-family unit program, nonprofit organizations and public agencies must either resell to a low-income family or rent the property. If they choose the rental option, they may not charge more than 30 percent of the renter's income, as adjusted by a HUD formula. Individuals must commit to make the property their home and live there for a minimum of one year. The federal government considers a single-family dwelling anything under five units, which means you can buy a four-plex and live free in one of the units while you rent out the other three.

With multi-family units, the guidelines are similar. A qualified investor, a public agency, or a nonprofit organization may bid for these properties, providing that, as part of their offer, they commit to reserving 35 percent of the units for lower-income residents and not less than 20 percent for very low income residents.

The fun begins when the RTC puts out a notice of "Ready to Market" for a multi-family unit. If you think the property has potential, you write a short letter saying you're interested and include a financial statement, evidence of a funding source, and a statement that you'll adhere to lower-income occupancy requirements. This is called a serious intent notice, and is not as complicated as the government language makes it sound. The property contact—the person listed on the property information who has been designated by the RTC to act as the agent (seller)—will assist you in putting together the appropriate documentation. The contact's job is to help prospective buyers and to get the properties sold.

At the end of the marketing period, the RTC will provide the minimum terms and conditions to all those who expressed an interest. Your next step is to submit, within 45 days, a package containing the following:

- A formal offer.
- A sales contract and earnest money deposit.
- A conditional commitment for financing from a lender.
- A written commitment to meet the lower-income occupancy requirements, and an explanation of how you plan to do it.
- A reaffirmation or revision of the original serious intent notice.

Preference is given to the offer with the highest percentage of lower-income tenants and the longest time commitment. If you want to purchase more than one multi-family property, you may package offers of intent and your package will get priority treatment at the RTC.

If the idea of low-income tenants scares you, it shouldn't. The government defines "lower income" as 80 percent of the median income or below, and "very low income" as 50 percent of the area median income. Under these terms, the tenants you will rent to are going to be working-class, blue-collar families. In New York City, a lower-income family of four can earn up to $32,400, a very low income family up to $20,250. In Miami, the low-income cap is $34,000; very low income is $19,000. Phoenix, it's $28,400 and $17,750, respectively. These are definitely tenants who can afford to pay rent, and you'll be able to screen them as you would any other tenants. The RTC's Affordable Housing Disposition Program is an opportunity both beginners and serious investors should definitely pursue.

Your Step-by-Step Guide for Buying an RTC Property

Once you find a property that interests you, here's what to do:

1. Find out if the property is still available. Check with the property contact, whose name and telephone number is included in the listing, to make sure the property has not been, or is not being, sold. With such a large organization, it could be weeks before a sale is recorded on the asset register, and you don't want to waste your time on properties someone else has already purchased. However, if you find a property you think you might be able to do something remarkable with

but it's under contract, let the property contact know of your interest. If the first deal falls through, you could still get it.

2. Find out how long the property has been marketed. Note that there is a difference between how long the RTC has had the property and how long it's been marketed.

3. Do a property analysis as you would on any potential investment to see if the project will produce a positive cash flow. Use the guidelines in Chapter Seven.

4. Calculate what it will cost the RTC to carry the property, if it doesn't sell, for the same amount of time it has already had it. Consider factors like management and maintenance costs, insurance, lost tax revenues, and marketing expenses. Deduct this amount from your offer.

5. Make sure the title is clean. Ask a title company to do a quick preliminary check to make sure there are no potential liens or problems; the title company will usually do this for free if you let it do the formal title search later.

6. Physically inspect the property. Do a simple, top-to-bottom check, again using the guidelines in Chapter Seven.

7. If you're not confident in your own abilities to evaluate a property's condition, arrange for a property inspector to take a look. A certified inspection will cost $200 to $300.

8. Consider the property's up side, or what it will be worth in two or three years. What will the demand for such a property be, based on your knowledge of the market?

9. If everything looks good, put in a bid. In most cases, your bid will be very similar to an offer you might make to a private seller. Remember, the property contact will help you in preparing your paperwork.

Timing Is Everything

With the RTC, as with any business, timing is important. The longer it has been marketing a property, the less it is willing to take for it.

By law, the RTC must try to get the highest price it can on its properties to keep the taxpayer burden as low as possible. The agency bases the minimum price it will accept on a percentage of market value—95 percent in distressed states and 90 percent elsewhere. But it has it own interesting definition of market value that can mean bargains for investors.

The RTC essentially defines market value as the highest price a buyer is willing to pay, and it arrives at that figure based on the opinion of "qualified professionals" (usually real estate agents). Then the RTC takes pricing one step further. It calculates the net realizable market value (NRMV) and is usually willing to accept an offer comparable to that figure. NRMV is simply a government term for a price that has been lowered further.

To determine the NRMV, the RTC considers how much money it will save by selling a property quickly: the real estate taxes that won't be paid until a private owner takes over; the cost of property maintenance, insurance, and security; and how much the property may go down in value if it's not being managed properly while the RTC owns it. All of these factors will help justify a lower price for the property.

Before putting any property on the market, the RTC has already estimated what the NRMV is. And the longer the property stays on the market, the lower the NRMV goes. As an example, let's say you are in an area where the RTC has to obtain purchase prices of 90 percent of market value. You're looking at a property with a market value of $100,000, so you would think the minimum offer the RTC will accept is $90,000. But you may be able to do even better. Simply factoring in the NRMV may reduce the value from $100,000 to $80,000, and an offer of $72,000 might be accepted. And because you know the RTC loves clean deals, you offer cash (which means no government financing) and get a 15 percent cash discount; now a property that had a minimum price of $90,000 can be purchased for $61,200.

The NRMV isn't set in stone. It's an abstract number, so part of your strategy is to estimate a comparable figure yourself. If you come up with a reasonable, documented NRMV that is lower that the RTC's, it will seriously consider your offer. Here are some guidelines for determining market value:

- 80 percent of appraised value if the property has been adequately marketed for a period of up to 6 months.
- 60 percent of appraised value if the property has been adequately marketed for a period of 6 to 18 months.

- 50 percent of appraised value if the property has been adequately marketed for a period of 18 to 24 months.

If the property needs repairs, prepare a contractor's estimate just as you would for a home improvement loan, outlining what repairs are necessary and what they will cost.

The NRMV can be used in AHDP housing, too. If the property has been marketed for 90 days, the upset price (the lowest price the RTC will accept for the property) starts at 80 percent of the market value. From there the price for AHDP single-family (five units or less) properties can go down. For example:

- Properties in the AHDP for 30 days or less may be sold at 70 percent or greater of appraised value.
- Properties in the AHDP for 31 days or more may be sold at 40 percent or greater of appraised value.
- A property in the AHDP that has not sold after 60 days may be marketed through a widely advertised sealed-bid sale or auction, and those properties may be sold without a minimum sale price.

Auctions Are Great, but . . .

Though you can pick up some fabulous deals at an auction, be sure to avoid what's called auction fever.

The rules for successful bidding at auctions are simple:

- Never bid on a property at auction unless you have completely inspected and analyzed it for profitability.
- Determine your highest bid price before you go to the auction, and never go higher—no matter how tempted you are by the excitement.

When one of my students, Randy Curry, found some great Bird-Dog RTC deals, I decided to go to the auction with him. He had located seven properties we thought were all worth at least $100,000 each. (It turned out that they eventually appraised at $163,000 each.) I set the limit at $45,000 each.

The bidding began, and we got the first one for $35,000 and the second one for $40,000. By the time the third one went on the block, other people had figured out we were on to a good deal. That property went for $51,000 and, boy, was I tempted to top that bid. I had the cash and it still would have been a steal, but I didn't do it.

Thanks to auction fever, the other four properties were bought by other investors for well over $100,000, which was closer to their actual value—not a bad deal, but when you do your homework, take action, and stick to your guns, you get the best deals and make the most money without any fear of losing.

What the Future Holds for the RTC

The S&L crisis is far from over. Some economists are even predicting that by century's end 50 percent of all our financial institutions will disappear, some by merger and, yes, a lot more by failure. Over the next three years, the number of properties the RTC will take control of and sell is expected to triple. This means a giant window of opportunity for you and me—average people who want to invest in real estate.

Not since the 1860s, when the government opened up the West, has the average investor had such a golden opportunity. More fortunes will be made in real estate over the next several years than in any single period in U.S. history.

Will many old real estate tycoons build a second fortune? Of course.

Will large corporations race in and grab a major portion of the pie? They have already started to do so.

Will you have the patience, foresight, and perseverance to make your mark, achieve your dreams, and let the RTC be one of your tools as you build your personal fortune?

I hope so.

CHAPTER 14

How to Find Continuous Prosperity

Chance favors only those minds which are prepared.

—Louis Pasteur

I've made millions of dollars in a number of businesses, though my initial fortune was made in real estate. If you look at the portfolios of most other wealthy people, you'll see the same or even a higher degree of diversity. They find businesses that generate profits, then park that money in real estate and watch it grow. That's how the top 2 percent of income earners become wealthy. That's how wealthy people become wealthier. And it's also how plain, old, average folks like you and me can build our personal fortunes.

Use real estate to build a little capital and credibility, then think about the business you've always dreamed of, or the thing that you've always said you would do if you had the time and money. You may already know what kind of business you ultimately want to be in, or you may still be searching. If you haven't yet chosen a business, there are plenty of books and magazines on the market that discuss various opportunities and that will give you at least some of the information you'll need to make a decision.

My advice to you on this topic is simple: Be sure you choose something you will love doing; be sure it has the potential to generate the income you need to meet your financial goals; and be sure you're building a business, not just making a job for yourself.

By something you will love doing, I mean that life is too short to spend the majority of your waking hours doing something you hate. Choose a business that will be fun, one that you can approach with the enthusiasm you give your favorite hobby.

By the potential to generate the income you need, I mean you must seriously examine the profit potential of a business. Find out what kind of revenue similar businesses generate. Compare that with your financial goals, and be sure you have a match before you make a commitment.

By building a business, I mean something that will generate cash flow whether you're working in it or not. This is an area of special caution for home-based businesses. There are plenty of so-called experts out there who will tell you how to start a résumé-writing service, or a child-care service, or a disk-jockey service, or any one of hundreds of other operations they call businesses, but in fact they are teaching you how to create a job for yourself.

A job is something that, when you stop doing it, it stops making money.

A business is something you can design, establish, pay other people to work in, and make money from whether you participate in the day-to-day operation or not.

It's hard to get wealthy if all you have is a job; it's much easier and much more fun when you have a business that is making you money whether you work or not.

The Gold Watch Syndrome

It's certainly true that owning a business requires a significantly higher degree of commitment than having a job, but it doesn't mean you have to keep it, and own it, and run it for the rest of your life. I have created or bought into a variety of different businesses; some I built up and sold, others I continue to own. And I'm always on the lookout for new opportunities.

Let's compare this philosophy with having a job. Just a generation or so ago, people were expected to get a job and stay with that company until they retired and collected the traditional gold watch. Today, the average employee will hold ten or more jobs in two or three different career fields over his lifetime. In fact, for people interested in climbing the corporate ladder, changing companies is an effective way to move up quickly. Having several different employers on your résumé is no longer a sign of instability; it's a sign of ambition and perseverance.

We've pretty much shed the gold watch mentality when it comes to jobs; now it's also time to take a new look at business ownership. There's absolutely no reason why you can't own several different businesses at the same time, and just because you buy or start a business doesn't mean you'll have to own it forever.

Let's say you enjoy real estate, but you also like working with animals. You could own some income-producing rental property, a property-management company, a pet-grooming salon, and a boarding kennel. At any given point, you could sell off one of those businesses and invest the proceeds in something else. Even better, you could consider setting up the grooming salon or boarding kennel as a franchise and earn royalties from other entrepreneurs who want to copy your methods.

My point is that business ownership gives you the opportunity to pursue not just one dream, but all of your dreams. The only restrictions you'll have to deal with are the ones you place on yourself.

Open Your Eyes to Opportunity

Getting started with your first business, no matter how small it is, will give you the confidence you need to keep going and growing. You've heard the saying "No man is an island"; the same thing applies to businesses. They have suppliers, they have customers who need other products and services, they have competitors with ideas and needs of their own. These are all situations that can offer potential for you if you're paying attention. Always be on the lookout for opportunities because they're around us all the time.

Developing businesses can be a lot like free-association word games, where one person says a word and the other says the first thing that comes to mind. My first business, real estate, led me into publishing, public speaking, mail order, computers, and more. I became a millionaire by reading and following the advice in business self-help books and literature on developing a better attitude. But even though I was successful, I knew from experience that there was plenty the books didn't say, and a few things that I had learned how to do better through trial and error. So I decided to write my own book, *Overcoming the Hurdles & Pitfalls of Real Estate Investing*. It was rejected by several major publishing houses before a seminar company agreed to publish it if I would go on the lecture circuit to promote it.

That's how I got into the public-speaking business. Public speaking is a $38 billion a year industry, and 90 percent of the people who make money on the speaking circuit are industry experts, not show business or political celebrities. I traveled around the country giving talks on real estate investing, promoting my book, and making lots of money— sometimes as much as $40,000 for a two-hour speech. The more I learned about seminars, the more I realized this was something I wanted to do myself. So I created my own seminar company and my own publishing house to produce my books and tapes. I found bright people with good information to share, helped them put together books and tapes, and set up seminar programs around the country.

Public speaking is a great business, because even though we all work hard, we are helping people change their lives for the better and we make good money doing it. It's also a tremendous opportunity for anyone who has expertise in a specific area. More than 16,000 seminars are held every day in the United States alone, which makes motivational and educational public speaking a virtual gold mine. If you can teach and entertain at the same time, this is a business you should give serious thought to pursuing.

Once my seminar company was up and running, a natural progression was into mail-order sales of my books and tapes. Though I often poke fun at "mail-order millions" when I talk about my initial search for a way to get wealthy, the reality is that you *can* make millions in the mail-order business. I know, because I've done it.

Just about anything you might imagine can be bought through mail order, including clothing, furniture, gadgets, food, and even livestock. Since today's busy consumers never seem to have enough time for shopping, they welcome the opportunity to make purchases comfortably from home without the hassle of fighting the crowds at malls.

The potential to make money in mail order has never been greater—but neither has the competition. The key is to find a unique product and develop an effective marketing strategy. If you currently have a business with products that are suitable for selling by mail, consider establishing a mail-order division to broaden your customer base and increase your profit. If you don't have a business you can expand through mail order, study the industry carefully before jumping in with a new idea or product. Before I established my mail-order business, I looked at how other information companies sold their products; I improved on their methods, and was able to make millions of dollars in mail order. (Mail-order millions, how ironic.)

Do you see what happened? I took my personal desire to teach people how to become wealthy and turned it into four very successful, very profitable businesses.

I didn't stop there. Because I do practice what I preach, even though I had made millions in real estate, I continued to study the industry. I traveled to Canada, where I was introduced to the basic concept of biweekly mortgage payments. After some careful analysis, I designed the Mortgage Reduction System™ (MRS) and created EquityCorp. to market and administer the program. I'll explain that program, and how you can participate, later in this chapter.

In the process of doing this, I developed computer software that would analyze an individual's mortgage and calculate the benefits of MRS, and in the process created a software development company. That package is provided to our consultants when they get into the business. But not everyone who saw the opportunity and wanted to become a consultant for EquityCorp. owned a computer to run the software on. That's when I got into computer sales.

Do you see how business opportunities are very much interrelated? For me, it all started with refinancing my own home and using that money to invest in a duplex. Where will it start for you? You must get into the game somewhere to start opening up the doors to success and prosperity.

It Doesn't Have to Be Related

Don't limit yourself to related businesses; let your imagination and personal preferences lead you to other opportunities. For example,

I've had a variety of real estate businesses, a television production company, a publishing company, a computer company, and so on—and right now, I'm investigating coin-operated car washes. Do you see any relation? Neither do I, but I see an opportunity. I live in a growing area, where the need for services is increasing. It occurred to me that a coin-operated car wash might be a profitable business that provides significant passive income without being management-intensive.

But I didn't know anything about car washes, so I had to find out. I started with a publication available through *Entrepreneur* magazine that is essentially a manual on the car-wash business and includes a list of car-wash equipment manufacturers and sales agents. I've contacted about 20 of those companies, and now I know what I'm looking at in terms of cash investment, financing, operating procedures and costs, and potential income—and it looks great. So now I'm getting ready to open up a string of car washes, and I expect to be adding at least $1 to $2 million a year in net profits to my income with this venture alone within the next 18 months, while someone else manages the operation.

I can't stress this enough: Whenever you see a need not being adequately met or a changing consumer trend, you are seeing a business opportunity. Do some research, figure out how to take advantage of it, and let your powers of observation make you wealthy.

Cut Your Mortgage by One-Third

I have made a few references to Mortgage Reduction System™ and EquityCorp., an ancillary business I started several years ago. Before I show you how you can become a part of this business and make money helping people reduce their mortgages, let me show you how you can save money doing the same thing yourself.

If you have a typical 30-year mortgage, you'll pay as much as three times the purchase price of the house over the life of the loan. Here are a few examples:

Amount borrowed	Rate	Finance charge	Total repayment
$ 90,000	8%	$147,740.40	$237,740.40
120,000	9%	227,598.00	347,598.00

I used a fixed rate for illustration, but this is also true if you have an adjustable rate; the actual numbers will change a little as the interest rates fluctuate, but the impact is still the same.

What's more, the way American banks calculate interest on mortgage loans, you have to pay on the loan for 8 or 10 years before you begin making any significant reduction in the amount you owe. In the first year of repaying a $100,000 loan at $1,000 a month, you'll reduce your principal by only about $400—just slightly more than 3 percent of the total amount you paid. Why? Because lenders force us to use the most ridiculous loan-repayment method in the world. We pay interest in arrears, we pay interest on the unpaid balance, we pay compounded interest, and to top it off, most of us believe the bankers who tell us that 30 years is the way we should pay back mortgage loans.

It's an absurd amount of interest to pay, especially when you consider that our house payment is the largest payment most of us make each month. However, there are ways to beat the system and save yourself substantial amounts of money.

One solution is a 15-year mortgage. You'll pay off your loan in half the time and reduce your finance charges by 50 or 60 percent. But the bad news is your monthly payments will be approximately 20 percent higher than they would be on a 30-year mortgage.

A better solution is a biweekly mortgage. This provides for payments every two weeks, or 26 times a year, rather than 12 monthly payments. Because most people are paid on this schedule, it makes sense to set up your single largest expense on the same schedule. The bonus of a biweekly mortgage is that you are actually paying the equivalent of 13 monthly payments every year, so you'll reduce your principal faster and pay less interest. As you can see from the comparison, the savings are tremendous.

Read this section carefully, because even if you have an existing mortgage, this is a way you can still save money without refinancing. Does this mean you can give your bank a call and tell them you're going to go on a biweekly payment program? No. Very few, if any, banks offer biweekly mortgages. Even if they do, they will not likely change your repayment terms if you already have a mortgage unless you refinance. That means taking out a whole new loan, and if you do that, you'll have to pay points (a point is 1 percent of the amount

Mortgage Reduction Comparison Date: 10/20/92

For: Samantha Jones
1516 Main Street
Fort Myers, FL 33907
Loan Account# BFD666
By: Miss Yu

Principal: $98,707.96
Rate: 9.500 %
Term of Loan: 30 Years, 0 Months
Payment: $829.99

Length of Term	30yr/0mo	21yr/0mo	- N/A -	22yr/3mo	25yr/0mo	24yr/3mo
Interest Paid	200,088.51	135,651.77	- N/A -	138,756.70	159,970.22	153,990.31
Effective Rate	9.500%	8.504%	- N/A -	8.58%	9.024%	8.921%
Interest Saved	0.00	64,436.74	- N/A -	61,331.81	40,118.29	46,098.20

Year Begin-End	Standard Payments	Biweekly (PI)	Additional Equity	Option 1 . . .	Option 2 . . .	Option 3 . . .
1993-1994	98099.29	97269.30	829.99	97347.09	97689.60	97599.29
1994-1995	97430.20	95687.85	1742.35	95851.17	96570.16	96380.58
1995-1996	96694.72	93949.45	2745.27	94206.77	95339.63	95040.92
1996-1997	95886.23	92038.51	3847.72	92399.17	93986.96	93568.30
1997-1998	94997.51	89937.92	5059.59	90412.17	92500.05	91949.53
1998-1999	94020.58	87628.85	6391.73	88227.97	90865.57	90170.10
1999-2000	92946.70	85090.61	7856.08	85826.99	89068.87	88214.06
2000-2001	91766.23	82300.46	9465.77	83187.72	87093.85	86063.89
2001-2002	90468.61	79233.39	11235.21	80286.51	84922.81	83700.32
2002-2003	89042.20	75861.93	13180.27	77097.36	82536.31	81102.18
2003-2004	87474.22	72155.85	15318.37	73591.69	79912.94	78246.17
2004-2005	85750.63	68081.95	17668.67	69738.10	77029.22	75106.72
2005-2006	83855.97	63603.73	20252.24	65502.04	73859.29	71655.68
2006-2007	81773.27	58681.06	23092.21	60845.57	70374.76	67862.13
2007-2008	79483.87	53269.82	26214.05	55726.95	66544.39	63692.08
2008-2009	76967.25	47321.53	29645.72	50100.32	62333.87	59108.17
2009-2010	74200.86	40782.89	33417.98	43915.27	57705.47	54069.31
2010-2011	71159.92	33595.30	37564.62	37116.36	52617.71	48530.36
2011-2012	67817.17	25694.36	42122.81	29642.68	47025.00	42441.68
2012-2013	64142.66	17009.27	47133.39	21427.25	40877.23	35748.71
2013-2014	60103.46	7462.21	52641.25	12396.46	34119.30	28391.49
2014-2015	55663.39	0.00		2469.38	26690.67	20304.07
2015-2016	50782.64			0.00	18524.76	11414.00
2016-2017	45417.50				9548.41	1641.61
2017-2018	39519.87				0.00	0.00
2018-2019	33036.93					
2019-2020	25910.56					
2020-2021	18076.92					
2021-2022	9465.81					
2022-2023	0.00					

financed; banks charge varying numbers of points to originate a loan) and other closing costs. It could cost you several thousand dollars out of pocket to change your payment program.

If you're wondering why more banks don't offer biweekly loans, the reason is simple. In most cases, when you take out a mortgage loan, the bank doesn't wait for the 30 years you'll be making payments to get its money back. A high percentage of first-mortgage loans are sold on what is known as the secondary-mortgage market, where the loans are traded as investments. Insurance companies, the Government National Mortgage Association (known as Ginnie Mae), quasi-federal agencies (such as the Federal Home Loan Mortgage Corporation, known as Freddie Mac), and private corporations (such as the Federal National Mortgage Association, known as Fannie Mae) purchase these loans and package them into investments known as mortgage-backed securities. When you invest in a government-insured, mortgage-backed security through your local investment broker, what you're buying are home loans just like your own.

Banks sell their loans because they don't have a bottomless well full of money to lend out, and this gives them a way to replenish deposits and lend more money. If your bank has sold your loan, it can't change your repayment schedule because it doesn't own your loan anymore. It may still be servicing your loan—that is, collecting your payments and forwarding them on to Freddie Mac or Fannie Mae or whatever organization owns the loan, and earning a fee for that service. This is why most people never realize their loans have been sold.

Another reason that banks won't switch you over to a biweekly payment schedule is that they are just not set up to handle the paperwork in that manner. So how can you take advantage of this intelligent and simple loan repayment method?

Your best option is to contract with a company that is set up to simulate a biweekly mortgage. There are a few very good ones that will do all of the work for you at a nominal charge. They will draft your checking account every two weeks for half of your regular mortgage payment and hold those funds in escrow. Each month, they will make the payment to your mortgage holder as you normally would, but at the end of a year you will have accumulated an extra payment, which is then applied to reducing your principal—ultimately shortening the life of your loan by as much as one-third. Be sure the biweekly mortgage service company you choose is insured and that the bank it uses is a trustee of the fund, so your money is safe.

Perhaps the biggest advantage of a biweekly payment plan over a standard 15-year mortgage is flexibility. With a 15-year mortgage, you are committed to the payment amount. With the biweekly plan, if you encounter financial difficulties or for any reason need to reduce your payment amount, you can go off the program and make the lower payment. When you're ready, you go back on the biweekly program.

There are a number of financial writers who are very vocal in their criticism of companies that provide biweekly mortgage services. Their argument is that you could do this yourself without having to pay any service fees. And though you could, you probably won't. I have been explaining this concept at seminars for years and have found that less than 1 percent of the people will actually act on the information by making that extra payment on their own. What's more, the average person does not know how to check to verify that the additional monies are being applied to the principal. Many banks will apply extra payments to prepaid interest, which means all you've done is pay more interest sooner. Some apply extra payments to the back end of the mortgage, which means you get no benefit until you're very close to paying off the loan. Without a professional helping you, you could waste a lot of time and money, and not gain the benefit of principal reduction. The small fee a biweekly mortgage company will charge is pennies compared to what you'll save with the program.

A biweekly mortgage is the safest, most efficient way for you to maximize the benefits from probably the biggest investment you'll make in your lifetime: your home. But students have asked me, if the biweekly mortgage is so good, why don't they hear about it from their attorney, their accountant, or their real estate broker? It's very simple. Your attorney, accountant, and real estate broker won't make any money by giving you this advice. They don't get paid to help you figure out the best way to repay your mortgage.

Another criticism that has been leveled at biweekly mortgages is that their very positive results—that is, reducing the term of your loan and the amount of interest you'll have to pay—cause you to lose a tax shelter. Yes, a home mortgage is a tremendous tax shelter for the average American. But it's foolish to spend $80,000 more than you have to over the life of your mortgage loan just so you can deduct it from your taxes. If you need write-offs, start a business. Give money to charity. But don't give up building equity in your home.

Help Others Cut Their Mortgages, Too

When I first discovered the concept of biweekly mortgage payments, I was so enthusiastic that I created a company to administer such a program—the first company of its kind in the United States. We developed a system to help people all over the country save money and make money by sharing this technique with others. It's called the Mortgage Reduction System™ (MRS), and is offered through and serviced by EquityCorp. Since it was introduced in 1986, thousands of homeowners across the United States have realized tremendous savings in mortgage interest and are paying off their mortgages earlier.

Some people who chose to get involved in this company have earned hundreds of thousands of dollars just by showing others how MRS works. Our mortgage consultants earn a substantial fee each time they put a home owner on the system. Some do this as a part-time way to generate extra income; others work it as a full-time business and hire other consultants to work for them. Some of the really creative and successful consultants also encourage their clients to use MRS with other loans, such as for automobiles, boats, and home improvement. MRS works with any loan that has compound interest and is amortized over several years. Funds deposited into the MRS account for disbursement to lenders are fully insured by the federal government and run through the Federal Reserve System, just as any typical electronic transfer is handled.

A number of companies offer biweekly mortgage payment programs and in doing so provide a tremendous money-making opportunity for consultants. The best in my opinion is, of course, EquityCorp. If you'd like more information about setting up your own mortgage on a biweekly program and/or becoming an MRS consultant to provide this valuable and much-needed service, contact EquityCorp. at 800-741-7877.

Financing Your Dreams

Many people who dream of owning lucrative businesses will use the techniques in this book to find seed money and use real estate to fund their companies. But wealth is not always measured in dollars. Plenty of people don't particularly care about having huge bank accounts; they're looking for something to pay the bills while they pursue dreams that have nothing to do with business, such as acting, singing, painting, any other creative field, or various types of community service.

Unless you are one of the few people who achieve superstar status, working in the arts can mean a very unpredictable income. Billy Hufsey ("Fame," "Days of Our Lives") says his real estate investments provide him with the financial freedom he needs to pursue his acting career. Billy uses my techniques to maintain his lifestyle when he's not performing.

Remember, if you can find something that will generate enough passive income to cover your basic expenses, you have financial independence, and you can do whatever you want to do. Start a business, do volunteer work, go back to school, join a theater company, run for public office, secure your future—the dream and the choice are yours. You can still live comfortably without millions of dollars once you've started to develop your personal fortune.

CHAPTER 15

The Government Will Help You Become Wealthy

You don't get to choose how you're going to die, or when. You can only decide how you're going to live. Now!

—JOAN BAEZ

Some of the best-kept secrets in our country are how government agencies help people in various businesses become wealthy. Even when those secrets get out, many Americans believe they can't take advantage of the programs that have been put in place to help them. Our view of the government is usually shaped by what we see and hear in the news: scandals, mistakes, and mismanagement by bureaucrats, and fraud by welfare and other entitlement recipients. And when we must have contact with government agencies ourselves, it's usually the Internal Revenue Service, which is never fun, or standing in line at a licensing agency.

But this is truly just the tip of the iceberg when it comes to what the government does and how it works. In fact, the government wants you to take advantage of its programs to establish your business, because businesses create jobs and economic prosperity—two things that are important to politicians who want to stay in office. When all was said and done after the presidential election of 1992, the reason George Bush lost was summed up in one political slogan: *It's the economy, stupid.* And your particular congressional representatives will be happy to see you take advantage of government programs, because then they can point out how much federal money they brought home to the district.

Setting politics aside, there's another aspect to letting the government help you build wealth. During the early days of westward expansion in the United States, land grants helped our country and its people grow and prosper. The modern-day version of those land grants is financial assistance in the form of loans and grants to entrepreneurs to help them build healthy businesses. These programs are generously funded, and they always will be—regardless of who is in the White House or which party is controlling Congress.

Donald Trump built a portion of his empire on government programs designed to encourage and reward the rehabilitation of rundown property. (No matter what people may think of Trump personally, and in spite of his many problems, most of his real estate ventures have very been successful.) When Lee Iacocca took over Chrysler, the first thing he did was get the government to guarantee $1.5 billion in loans to save the troubled automaker. EDS, the business that Ross Perot sold to General Motors for billions, made its profits largely from government contracts. Even success stories like Federal Express and Apple Computer were financed in part through venture-capital programs funded by government money.

But don't think only the already wealthy can get their hands on government money. There are hundreds of thousands of people just like you and me across the country who have received anywhere from a few thousand to hundreds of thousand of dollars in grants and loans from the government to start or expand business in just about every category. Recently I helped my area's Chamber of Commerce develop a marketing seminar to educate the local business community on the various government programs that are available to them. I have been using government loans and grants since my early days of investing, and even I was surprised at the tremendous scope of the programs that are available.

What the SBA Can Do for You

The Small Business Administration (SBA) is one of the most underused resources in the United States. The SBA has only a few grant programs, but they have a variety of short- and long-term loans that can be used for just about any legitimate business purpose. In 90 percent of the cases, the SBA does not actually lend the money; it guarantees repayment of loans made through private lenders.

SBA loans require the same documentation as any business loan. The lender and the SBA want to be sure you know what you're doing and that you'll be able to pay the money back. To help you through the application process, the SBA has set up agencies in all metropolitan areas; contact the SBA in Washington for a referral to the one closest to you. If you do the paperwork correctly, your loan will be processed quickly—sometimes in a matter of days, rarely longer than two or three weeks. Loans up to $750,000 are available for all types of business needs.

In addition to serving as a funding source, the SBA can help with various aspects of building your business. Call the SBA Answer Desk toll free at (800) U-ASK-SBA for complete details.

The Government Will Help You Buy Real Estate

Government loans and grants for real estate are amazingly simple and easy to get. The reason is that the government, in its curious wisdom, doesn't consider real estate a business. If you apply for a business loan or grant, you have to provide documentation on your business idea, the marketing you plan, your own experience, how much capital you have from other sources, and more. Real estate loans and grants are very different. Most are administered locally, so they are easier to process. In many cases, you don't even have to qualify for the funds; it's the property or your planned use for it that qualifies, and you may not even have to submit a financial statement. After Randy Curry and I bought two four-plexes in Pompano Beach, Florida, from the RTC, Randy went to the people at the local Department of Economic and Community Development and asked them about the availability of grant money for fixing up low-income properties. They had more money than they had applicants. Without requiring a financial statement or credit check, they allocated $36,000 per property in grant monies to rehabilitate the buildings. We didn't have to qualify for the money; the properties qualified because of their location. The only thing we had to do was commit to putting low-income tenants in the units. And now we have properties appraised at $193,000 each, for which we paid less than one-fourth of that amount.

You don't have to be rich, famous, or even particularly well connected to take advantage of government loans and grants. You don't have to be a business whiz, belong to a minority group, or have great credit. You just have to be willing to go after the money.

Dealing with Bureaucrats

The most important thing to remember about bureaucrats is they are people, and they respond the same way other people do. In other words, be friendly, professional, and courteous, and you'll probably get all the help you need. Be abrupt, impatient, or condescending, and you won't get anywhere.

Call the government agency responsible for the loan or grant you want to pursue and ask what the application procedure is. (See the self-help resources in the back of the book for a list of potential loan sources for entrepreneurs and real estate investors.) Be prepared to describe what you are planning to do and what you want. Also, don't become discouraged if you are shuffled around to a number of different people before you get to the person who can help you. Remember, the phone will be answered by a clerk, but you want to talk to the person in charge of the loans or grants, and you may have to be filtered through a few people before you get to the one you need. This can happen in any large organization, either public or private. So treat it like a game: If you can get to the right person, you win—and the prize is wealth and security for your future.

Tips on Applying for Money

If you do your homework, you'll usually find that you are eligible for several different loan and grant programs. *Apply for all of them!* Simply applying for government money does not mean automatic approval, but by seeking assistance from different agencies you'll increase your chances of getting all the money you need—and maybe even a little more.

You'll find that money is made available in the following forms:

Loans—money lent by a government agency for a specific period of time with an expectation of repayment. Loans may or may not require payment of interest; often the interest rate is below the general market rate.

Loan guarantees—programs in which a private lender makes the loan to the borrower, but the government agency agrees to pay back all or part of the loan if the borrower defaults.

Grants—money given by a government agency that does not have to be repaid. Some grants are paid in one lump sum; others are paid over a period of time.

Direct payments—funds given to individuals, private firms, and institutions by government agencies. The funds may be for a specific purpose or for unrestricted use.

Before you fill out the application, take the time to contact a program official to go over the form. It's best to do this in person; many agencies have field offices all over the country to assist you. If a face-to-face meeting isn't possible, then do it by phone. Whatever you do, don't skip this important step. This discussion will help you gain valuable insight into what the government's expectations are for the program and what the officials who will be evaluating your application want to see.

Then give the government the exact information asked for—no more, no less, and even if it seems silly. It's the government's game. Play by the rules and you can win. If your proposal is rejected, find out why and try again. Sometimes the reason will be minor and may even seem petty. Do what you can to correct it, and resubmit your application.

There may be times when, despite your best efforts and all your selling skills, you're not getting what you want. When you need help dealing with a federal agency, you can always call your congressional representative for assistance. Check the government section of your telephone directory for his or her local office listing. It's highly unlikely that you'll talk directly to the member of Congress; you'll probably deal with someone on the staff who's been designated to handle constituent problems. Tell that person whom you've called and what has happened, so that he is adequately prepared when he approaches the agency's officials. He can make a few phone calls on your behalf and help you cut through the clutter and red tape. Though this technique can be a very effective one, use it as a last resort; don't abuse the service.

There's More than One Government, and More than One Type of Assistance

Though I've used the term "government" in a generic way, remember that there are several layers of government—federal, state, and local—with programs you can apply for. Don't overlook any resource; do your homework thoroughly to identify every opportunity.

For example, in my own community of Cape Coral, Florida, the city and local banks have formed a partnership to give low- and moderate-income people the opportunity to buy a home. The city is identifying abandoned homes, many of which have been left vacant or partially completed by developers. The properties are condemned, refurbished, and then sold under a special loan program. The banks are offering these low-down-payment, low-interest, no-point loans in part to meet the standards of the federal 1977 Community Reinvestment Act, which requires banks to invest a certain percentage of their profits (referred to as CRA funds) back into the community. Keep this in mind when talking to bankers. Ask them if they have CRA funds and what kind of properties or vehicles they are looking to invest those monies in. These questions will establish you as a knowledgeable investor and help you get the information you want about how much money is available and for what purposes. Cities and towns across the country are developing programs similar to the one in Cape Coral. All you have to do is a little bit of research to find out what programs are available and how you can participate.

Government agencies usually apply a "use it or lose it" mentality to their grant money, which means that if they don't use all the money designated for a certain function this year, they won't get as much next year. What's more, the purpose behind the programs is to improve something—the economy, the labor market, housing availability, etc. In fact, federal, state, and local governments have always allocated monies for the renovation and rehabilitation of low- and moderate-income housing. Virtually every city and town in the United States has some sort of grant and loan programs available for housing. Housing improvement funds are the easiest and quickest money you'll ever find, with some of the best interest rates and most liberal borrowing terms. You can build your own wealth as you provide a decent place to live for people who need a hand. Clearly, it's in everyone's best interest to see that these monies are used.

Most local governments, at either the city or county level, have someone whose job it is to make sure that all the government money is used. This person is highly motivated to give away money; his job depends on it. Chances are the mayor, city council, or county commission is pressuring him to give away as much money as possible so they can apply for more the next year. I have seen situations where the person in charge of government grant and loan programs in a particular city didn't give away enough money and was fired because future allocations were cut back. Believe me, his replacement was hustling to find recipients for government loans and grants.

Think about what a great position this puts you in. How do you take advantage of it? Simple: Most communities have an organization that focuses on community development. It will be named the Economic Development Commission, the Department of Economic and Community Development, or something similar. Call and set up an appointment to meet with the director of this agency; tell him you're an investor, you've got some property, and you want to know what's available in the way of funds and support from the government. Especially if you're willing to provide safe, sanitary, and decent low-income housing, you'll find yourself welcomed with open arms.

Once you have determined your own wealth-building strategy, apply for government funds at the local, state, and federal levels. Use the resource list at the back of the book as a starting point for sources, and really put your tax dollars to work for you.

Guarantee Your Rent Payments

When you own rental property, one of the easiest ways to keep your units occupied and your rent payments coming in on time is through the federal government's Lower Income Housing Assistance Program Section 8, often referred to as Section 8 rental subsidies. The program is designed to assist low-income families in affording decent housing by paying a portion of their rent directly to the property owner. In addition, the costs to repair damages of assisted housing units are reimbursed up to the equivalent of two months' rent.

In order to be eligible for Section 8 direct rent payments, you must provide safe, sanitary, secure housing. You don't have to do anything more than keep your units clean, painted, and in good overall shape. A government representative will inspect your units to verify that all health, safety, and security standards are met, and to determine a fair market rent rate. You have the right to screen tenants as you normally would, and you'll receive tenant referrals from the program, which can keep your vacancy rate at virtually zero.

Many property owners are afraid of Section 8 tenants because they believe low income means low quality. This is not true! Section 8 tenants can be the best tenants you'll get. They receive counseling in the proper care of apartments and facilities. What's more, if the tenant damages the dwelling or does not live up to the lease, you have the right to terminate the tenancy. But Section 8 tenants know such action will jeopardize their ability to receive future rent subsidies, and they don't want that to happen.

Many cities have waiting lists for Section 8 rent subsidies because there is not enough eligible housing, not because there is not enough federal money. The vouchers are there; all you have to do is apply for the program. To get details on what's available in your area and to get the qualification process going, contact your local HUD office.

Getting Your Share Allows You to Do More than Your Share

Every year the government gives billions of dollars to cities and towns across America to pay for building and maintaining roads, bridges, sewers, and other infrastructure projects, to revitalize disadvantaged areas, to provide housing for low- and moderate-income people, and for a variety of other reasons. I have seen some of my students become specialists in government grant and loan programs, and provide a vital service to their communities with the renovation and rehabilitation of low- and moderate-income housing. Believe me, there is no more satisfying way to build your own wealth than by helping others—in this case by providing safe, decent housing to people who otherwise might not have a place to live. And doing this lets you do more for people who need help than you probably could do by just having a job and doing a little volunteer work for a charity in your spare time.

Let the government help you become wealthy while you use government programs to help your community. This is absolutely the best example of a win-win situation I have ever seen.

CHAPTER 16

Credit: Build It, Repair It, Use It to Become Wealthy

It had long since come to my attention that people of accomplishment rarely sat back and let things happen to them. They went out and happened to things.

—Elinor Smith

In the United States and in many parts of the world, conventional credit is not absolutely essential in order for you to start acquiring assets. However, it can definitely help. So let's take a look at how to establish credit, clean up bad credit, and play the credit game in general.

Though credit can be a component of wealth, it's also what keeps many people in poverty. The average middle-income American applies more than 75 percent of his income to various forms of debt repayment. You already know my view on borrowing: It's good when whatever you're borrowing for will appreciate in value and ultimately make you more money than the amount you borrowed; it's bad when used for consumable items or depreciating assets.

A financial reality is that the economy of the United States and many other countries is based on the extension of credit. If credit were eliminated, the result would probably be an immediate and prolonged recession. In most financial situations, whether a simple household or a giant corporation, having credit available can be very helpful. But it can also be disastrous if you don't use it properly. The key is to make credit work *for* you, rather than *against* you.

How Knowing the Rules of the Credit Game Can Help You Become Wealthy

Good credit means that over the years you have borrowed money for various things and always repaid it on time, and that makes you a good credit risk. You might believe that bad credit means just the opposite, but that's not necessarily so. Many people have late payments, judgments, and even bankruptcies on their credit histories, and they can still get credit because they know how to play the game. There are many degrees of so-called bad credit, and, as you learned in Chapter Twelve, plenty of factors other than your payment history will influence a lender who is considering your loan application.

You can begin applying your wealth-building strategies even though you may have limited or poor credit, but a decent credit rating will definitely be helpful if you are to achieve long-term success. Even if you currently have established credit, understanding how the credit system works will make it easier for you to maintain and improve positive relationships with current and future creditors.

Let's begin with a look at basic credit terms and what they mean.

Credit bureau. A credit bureau is a private, for-profit business that collects and distributes credit information on consumers. The largest national credit bureaus are TRW Information Services, CSC Credit Services, Inc., and Equifax, Inc. In addition, many smaller firms serve specific local markets. Lenders who subscribe to specific credit bureaus provide information about consumers that is then disseminated to other subscribers.

Not all lenders report credit data to a bureau, and not all subscribers are lenders. Typically, institutions or lenders that report to credit bureaus include:

- major banks
- travel and entertainment credit cards
- bank credit cards

- major savings and loan associations
- major department stores
- finance and consumer loan companies
- collection agencies

Institutions or lenders that are not likely to (but may) report to credit bureaus include:

- some small banks and S&Ls
- individuals who hold seller financing
- utility companies
- oil companies
- insurance companies
- small- and medium-sized credit unions
- medical care providers
- apartment building owners and other residential landlords
- mortgage companies

Credit bureaus also acquire information such as bankruptcies, judgments, liens, and wage garnishments from public records. Employers may subscribe to a credit bureau in order to use credit reports in evaluating prospective employees.

Credit report. This is the document issued by a credit bureau that contains a consumer's credit information; it is your basic financial history.

Credit rating. This is commonly considered your personal credit score, but in reality credit bureaus do not assign credit ratings to consumers. Lenders make their own determination about your creditworthiness based on their own standards, the amount and purpose of the credit requested, the information you provide as part of your application, and the credit report.

Credit correction agencies. These are organizations that help consumers with credit problems. The primary nonprofit agency is Consumer Credit Counselors (CCC), which operates under the National Foundation of Consumer Credit and is funded by businesses; the consumer clients do not pay for its services. Private, for-profit agencies charge consumers for assistance. Both CCC and for-profit agencies review and correct credit reports, work out budgets and debt repayment plans, hold credit cards, and make payments for clients; in general they serve as go-betweens for consumers and creditors. The for-profit agencies are sometimes referred to as credit-repair consultants.

Know the Six C's of Credit

Lenders, especially bankers, use a formula known as the six C's of credit when evaluating a credit application. Understanding them will help you make your applications as attractive as possible.

Character. This is essentially a summary of the individual. Creditors look for people who appear to be trustworthy and reliable, and who are willing and able to meet their financial obligations.

Capacity. This is the individual's ability to repay the loan; it is based on present and anticipated earnings balanced against existing debts.

Collateral. The item pledged by the borrower as security for the loan, which may be real estate, stocks, savings, a mortgage, etc.

Conditions. Both regulatory and economic conditions are considered. Regulatory conditions apply to the lender's individual circumstances; for example, when banks are not lending in specific areas. Economic conditions determine the lender's general policy toward loans. Both are affected by the current economic cycle.

Credit. This is the individual's credit history.

Capital. This is the net worth of an individual as indicated by a personal financial statement.

Take a moment to notice how far down on the list credit is. It's fifth—the next-to-last consideration. Notice where character is. It's first. Any banker will tell you that character—his personal judgment and assessment of you—is a key part of the loan decision. Remember, bankers are human, and their personal assessment of you is going to have a great influence on their decision about your loan.

Most people think that if they have a good credit report and a good job, they can get a loan. The reality is that if you do not have a positive rapport with the banker, he may go to the loan committee with your request and say, "I know this person has credit, I know he has a job, but I just don't feel good about him. There's something I don't like."

If that's the way the banker presents your loan, do you think the loan committee is going to approve it? Highly unlikely.

However, you could have marginal credit and some late payments, and that loan officer can go in to the loan committee and say, "I know this person has had some late pays, but she's solid in the community, I have a good feeling about her, and I think the bank would be doing her an injustice by not giving her a hand." If that happens, in many cases, you will get the loan.

The point to remember is that credit does not carry the weight most people think it does. Projecting an image of good character, trustworthiness, and professionalism is a much more important part of the loan application process.

A Few Facts about Credit Reports

Of course, credit can be important when you're looking for conventional loans. Let's take a look at your credit report and what it includes.

Identification. Consumers are identified by complete name, address, previous address if they've been at their present address less than two years, Social Security number, and date of birth. Some credit bureaus include employment information and salary history.

Credit inquiries. When a report is requested on a consumer, a note of the inquiry is made in the file and retained for approximately one year.

Public records. Credit-related information gathered from courthouse documents that are public record.

Collection accounts. Information reported by collection agencies.

Credit history. Entries from each reporting subscriber that generally contain the date the account was opened, original balance, credit limit, terms, monthly payment amount, payment history, the date of the last subscriber input, and any other important or unusual information about a consumer's account. The subscriber may indicate details such as an account being in dispute, having a co-signer, being secured by collateral, being written off as a loss, or that the consumer has co-signed other debts.

Consumer statement. A 100-word statement from consumers regarding any item on their reports that they wish to dispute or clarify.

The format and presentation of a credit report may vary with the reporting agency; when a copy of the report is sent to consumers or subscribers, most agencies will include instructions on how to read the report and an explanation of the abbreviations used.

No one may see your credit report unless you authorize it. If you notice credit inquiries being made by companies you don't recognize, you can and should challenge them. Call or write the reporting agency and request the full contact name and address of the company that made the inquiry. Then send a letter to that company, advising that you know it made an unauthorized check of your credit report and ask why it did so. You may want to remind the company that unauthorized inquiries are against the law; if you are not satisfied with its response, consider filing a complaint with the Federal Trade Commission.

Remember that a company checking your credit this month will know who checked your credit last month because it will appear on your report. Too many inquiries may cause a lender to wonder why you are seeking so much credit and thus to suspect a hidden risk. Too many inquiries without a corresponding opened line of credit or account may cause a lender to think others have turned you down, and that he should also deny your credit application.

After a specified period of time, negative credit items must be removed from your report. For most items, it's seven years; for bankruptcies, it's ten years from the date you filed. Most credit bureaus automatically do this, but if you are coming up on the anniversary date of a negative entry, follow up to be sure. Contact the credit bureaus your primary lenders use (you can find this out just by calling and asking) and request a copy of your credit report.

Keep in mind that some lenders have their own more lenient standards for considering negative items. For example, it may be an internal policy for a lender to consider a bankruptcy only if it occurred within the past four years, even though the entry remains on your credit report for ten. This is one reason why, if you have negative entries on your credit report, some lenders will approve your loan and others won't.

It is not uncommon for individuals to have more than one file with the same credit bureau. These alternate credit reports are usually caused by clerical errors, and the credit bureaus will usually make every effort to correct them. The most common way an accidental alternate file is discovered is when a consumer is denied credit and begins researching to find out why. If you determine this has happened to you, notify the credit bureau in writing and ask to be advised in writing when the situation is corrected.

It's possible to manipulate the system and use alternative credit reports to cover up bad credit or even create a new identity. This is fraudulent and may be prosecuted under different state laws. If a credit repair consultant suggests this, get out of his office as fast as you can. There are plenty of legal, ethical ways to build good credit and overcome bad credit, and I'll be sharing them with you. Don't be tempted to cheat. You can make your personal fortune legally and ethically. You can push and be aggressive, but there's never any reason to step over the line. Honesty, ethics, and good morals will always win in the end.

Correcting an Erroneous Credit Report

You can't correct an error you don't know about, so the first step in maintaining an accurate credit file is checking it on a regular basis. Recent negative publicity about errors in consumer files has led at least one major credit bureau, TRW, to provide consumers with a copy of their file at no charge once a year—but you must ask for it. (Write TRW's National Consumer Relations Center, 12606 Greenville Avenue, P.O. Box 749029, Dallas, TX 75374-9029, or call (214) 235-1200, ext. 251.) You are also entitled to receive your credit report free if you have been denied credit in the previous 30 days. Otherwise, credit bureaus charge from $5 to $20 for a copy of the report, which is still a wise investment for you in the early stages of wealth building.

The number of credit bureaus is a major frustration in maintaining a positive credit report. One bureau may be reporting your information accurately; another may have errors that are causing you to be turned down for credit. You can locate the credit bureaus serving your area by checking the telephone directory, or by asking a few lending institutions which credit bureaus they use. Contact each bureau by phone to determine the correct procedure and fee for gaining a copy of your report, then follow up with a letter making the formal request. Be prepared to provide your name, current address, addresses for the past five years, Social Security number, and birth date.

Once you receive the report, study it carefully for accuracy. Make note of any item with which you disagree. Then send the credit bureau a letter outlining the points you are disputing and why. Ask for the items to be investigated and for an updated copy of your report to be sent to you when the investigation is complete. Don't make threats or provide lengthy explanations, just ask the bureau to verify the information it has. Keep copies of all correspondence. In your file, note all telephone contacts, with the time and date of the call, the person you spoke with, and the result of your conversation.

If after four weeks you have not received a response to your letter, follow up with another letter and then a phone call. Maintain a professional, businesslike demeanor at all times—no foul language, no threats, and no shouting, and be sure your paperwork is presented in a neat, orderly fashion. Letters should be typed or word-processed; be sure the ribbon on your printer is fresh so the final copy is legible. If you do not have access to a typewriter or computer, print neatly on white paper, and be sure your name and address appear on each page.

Remember, credit bureaus report only what they are told by subscribers, and they can change information in your file only if advised to do so by the creditor involved. About half the time, your initial request will succeed in having a disputed item removed from your file. If that doesn't work, request a reinvestigation. Do this in writing, and also ask for the name, address, and telephone number of the creditor the bureau is contacting. If your requests to the credit bureau don't produce the results you want, you can go directly to the creditor.

If you must contact a creditor, it is best to do so in person. Make an appointment in advance, and be sure you'll be meeting with a manager or someone who has the authority to take the action you want. If a personal meeting is not possible, send a letter and follow up with a telephone call. Use the selling skills you'll learn in Chapter Seventeen to persuade the creditor to help you. Again, a calm, businesslike presentation is important; simply tell the creditor what the situation is and how you want it resolved. Allow a reasonable length of time for the action to be processed, and follow up with the credit bureau to make sure your file is changed.

What to Do When the Negative Reports Are True

Though mistakes account for a significant portion of the negative entries in credit files, all too often the reports are accurate. Your credit file may indicate a period of late payments and you know the reason is that you were unemployed, going through a divorce, facing a medical emergency, or any number of other legitimate reasons that can cause a financial bind. This happens to a lot of people and lenders know it, so you can overcome this situation fairly easily. If you've declared bankruptcy, it's going to be more difficult, but there are still ways you can gain credit.

Begin by making sure all of your bills are paid on time, so your current record is good. Then tackle the history. You *can* erase bad credit records from your file—even though they may be true. Remember that credit bureaus must be able to verify everything in your file, or they have to take it out—no matter what it is, even a bankruptcy. You don't need a reason to ask for a verification.

If the creditor verifies a negative report and refuses to change its position, it's time for a personal meeting. Assuming the item involves a poor payment history, explain the circumstances to the credit manager. If you are still a customer, point out that you are interested in maintaining a positive relationship for the future. If there is an unpaid amount involved, make arrangements to handle it. Sometimes creditors will accept a partial cash payment as payment in full, in much the same way that a mortgage holder will accept a discount. Be sure you negotiate the removal of the negative item in your credit file as part of your payment agreement, and get it in writing.

If you are unable to get the unfavorable reports removed, balance them with as many positive reports as possible. If you have good credit with a company that does not subscribe to the credit bureau, ask the bureau to include that record in your file; there may be an administrative fee involved, but it's worth the effort. Also, get statements concerning your payment habits from these companies so you can use them with credit applications to balance any negative information provided by the credit bureau. Cleaning up a bad credit report isn't difficult, if you are systematic and follow up carefully.

Respond if You Must

You are entitled to include a 100-word explanation of any unfavorable report in your credit file, and any inquiry must be provided with your statement. Include the details of what happened and how you attempted to correct it. If you feel the creditor was uncooperative, say so, but do it in a calm, unemotional manner. Finally, ask the bureau for an updated copy of your credit report once the statement has been included so you can verify its accuracy.

Having said that, let me add that I never bother with this, and I don't recommend it. You'll never find any monied businessperson whining to the credit bureau about his misfortunes or mistreatment by a lender. A better way to deal with negative credit reports is to provide your own professional explanation at the time you apply for your loan.

When I put together a loan package, I include a copy of my credit report and an explanation of anything that might raise a question. For example, I had a judgment against me that was listed in my credit file. However, the judgment was in litigation, and I believed it would ultimately be removed. (I was right.) I explained this in a brief letter and directed the lender's attention back to all the positive information I was providing. The result was that I was able to get the loans I needed. This is the best way to minimize any negative information in your credit file.

You may, however, want to flag the questionable entry on your credit report with a statement that reads, "There is a dispute on this entry. Please see application and personal financial statement for explanation." This will prevent a lender from making a snap judgment based on either a negative entry or a short written explanation that may not tell the whole story.

Establishing Credit for the First Time

The importance of establishing credit at an early age cannot be stressed too strongly. Consumers over 26 years old without a credit history are viewed with great suspicion by lenders. If you do not have credit with at least four different sources, begin building that credit immediately.

Your first step should be to use the passbook/signature loan process described in Chapter Four. You may also want to apply for a secured credit card, which means you secure the amount of your credit limit by placing that much on account with the card issuer. After making payments promptly for a while, ask that your security deposit be released. If it is not released, try another credit source, because now you've established a payment history other card issuers will respect.

If you are in college, you may be eligible for a credit card even though you have no credit history—and no job! Banks issuing Visa and MasterCard, as well as American Express and Discover, have special programs to encourage students to apply for their cards. It's a great deal for them, because initial credit lines are relatively low, which means a limited risk, and the earlier they gain a customer, the more money they will make over that person's lifetime. (Remember, credit card companies make money both from the interest cardholders pay and the fees the merchants pay.) If you're not in school and have limited or marginal credit, consider enrolling in an inexpensive night school class to take advantage of this easy credit source. The credit card applications are usually available on campus just about anywhere students gather, from the bookstore to the registrar's office.

If you apply for and receive one or more of these cards, exercise care and discipline to charge only what you can pay in full each month, and never let the lure of instant gratification and easy credit tempt you to build a debt you could spend years paying off.

Other ways to establish credit are to apply for charge accounts with a department store or an oil company. These are usually easier to get because they have lower credit limits and therefore less risk than bank cards. You must use these accounts for them to have a positive impact on your credit, but be sure to avoid accumulating debt you cannot afford to repay.

Several of the major automobile finance companies offer special first-time buyer loans, and independent companies are often willing to work with people who do not have a strong credit history. Once you receive a car loan, be sure your payment record is reported to the credit bureau.

Once you have established a payment history, consider closing accounts you don't use. Too many open accounts, even with zero balances, can be a red flag to prospective lenders. They think that if you have access to a lot of credit, you might be tempted to get in over your head. It's an insulting attitude, but it's there, and fighting it will get you nowhere. Ideally, you should have two bank credit cards, an American Express card, and lines of credit for times when plastic isn't appropriate.

Whenever you are turned down for credit, call the credit manager and find out why—even though you should receive a letter stating the reason. Let him know you want to do business with his company, and ask if there is anything you can do to change the negative decision. A tactic that works well is to ask what he would do if he were in your position, and then consider following his advice.

Get Rid of Consumer Debt

The best thing you can do for your credit rating is to clear up your consumer debt. I can hear what you're thinking—that paying off your debts is easier said than done! But if you follow the steps I'm sharing with you, getting out of debt is easier than you think. More important, getting out from under a mountain of useless consumer debt is an essential step toward becoming wealthy.

The approach you take will be determined by the level of your debt, so begin by doing a financial statement. List your assets, liabilities, income, and expenses. Don't rely on your memory, *write it down!* You'll probably be shocked when you total the numbers and realize how much you owe on depreciating assets. Once you know where you stand, set up a budget and begin paying off your bills. Here are a few budgeting tips to keep in mind:

Be realistic. Don't create a budget so tight you won't be able to stick to it. Remember to include small items that add up, such as tolls, parking, newspaper and magazine subscriptions, haircuts, and so on.

Allow for entertainment and recreation. It's okay to go to a movie or have dinner in a restaurant once in a while. Don't eliminate everything you enjoy doing or you will associate "getting out of debt" with "pain," when in fact it should be a pleasurable goal.

Don't go into additional debt for consumables. It's okay to continue using credit cards for convenience, but pay off the current charges in full every month.

Remember the rule of compounding. As you begin implementing your wealth-building strategies, reinvest your returns into additional appreciating assets.

Have a purpose for each investment. If you are deeply in debt, you will want to use some of your returns to pay off bills. One strategy is to designate a specific investment for a particular purpose, either to pay off a certain bill or to fund a particular expense. For example, years ago I bought a house for each of my kids. The mortgages are being paid off by rents, I have a little cash flow, and the houses are appreciating in value. By the time my kids are old enough for college, there will be enough equity in those houses to finance their education. Just be sure to reinvest enough of your earnings to maintain your financial growth.

Consider negotiating with lenders to reduce debt. Some creditors may be willing to take a smaller amount than your balance due in order to cancel your debt. Do this only if it will not cause a negative report in your credit file and if the lender will release you in writing from any future obligation. Generally you'll have more success with smaller, private lenders, though you may find a conventional lender who will negotiate with you if the account is in danger of being turned over to a collection agency. This also works with business debt to independent vendors. For example, we had a balance of $70,000 with one of our vendors and were paying it according to the original terms of our agreement. But when he got into a cash crunch and needed money, he asked me for $50,000 to cancel the debt. I offered $40,000 and he accepted; the debt was canceled at a discount of $30,000.

Let your creditors know what you're doing. Especially if you're finding it difficult to make payments, tell your creditors what is happening *before* your accounts get in arrears. Many will lower your monthly payment or interest rate to avoid a problem account on their books. (Remember, bankers in particular can suffer serious career consequences if they have made too many bad loans.) Even if they don't make any concessions, creditors will be less likely to take aggressive collection action if they know you are working to pay off their bill. Remember, creditors don't want to repossess whatever property you put up for collateral, and they don't want to take you to court—

they just want their money. They may try to bluff you at first, but if you communicate with them and work with them, they will usually work with you until you get over your tight spot. Creditors live in the same world you do, and they have a lot more flexibility than you might imagine.

Live like a Millionaire

Don't confuse lifestyle with wealth. People who live glamorous, big-spending lifestyles may have big incomes but may not necessarily have a significant net worth. There are plenty of people who earn $200,000 a year and owe $205,000. One lost paycheck could cripple them economically. One unexpected bill would bankrupt them. By contrast, many millionaires live below their means because they would rather invest their money in wealth-building vehicles than in depreciating assets. Most millionaires do not have significant credit card debt; in fact, they would rather do without than charge.

Just as aspiring actors study the methods of great performing artists and medical students learn the techniques of established physicians and surgeons, if you are going to become a millionaire you must copy the behavior of other millionaires. And as I have said before, millionaires may have thousands of dollars worth of debt. But they have gone into debt only to acquire assets that will eventually add to their millions.

CHAPTER 17

Communication Skills That Will Make You a Millionaire

Many receive advice, few profit by it.

—PUBLILIUS SYRUS
(First Century B.C.)

If you take a look at people who have made a lot of money—regardless of the circumstances or the vehicle they used—you'll find they have at least one trait in common: They have learned and developed top-notch selling skills. Lee Iacocca may be a talented automobile designer, but he was able to turn Chrysler around by selling people on the company's cars. Federal Express is the largest start-up ever funded by venture capital, but only because Fred Smith was able to sell investors on his idea of an overnight delivery service. The individual most identified with Apple Computer is Steven Jobs, who did the selling; Stephen Wozniak was responsible for the initial technology, but you rarely hear about him. When founder Dave Thomas went on television to sell Wendy's hamburgers, profits rebounded and more than doubled in two years. I was doing okay in my real estate business and approaching my early goal of $1 million net worth when I discovered the value of sales skills; when I started using them, my income and my assets soared. It didn't take me long to realize these skills could be applied to any situation: buying and selling businesses, real estate, or products.

213

Look around at the successful people you know. Their job titles may or may not include the word "sales," but they know how to sell, and using their sales skills is reflexive. Shortly after Bill Clinton's first State of the Union Address, *Newsweek* magazine referred to the President as the First Salesman—and an important part of his, and any President's, job is to sell the American people on his programs.

The fact is that a solid understanding of sales techniques is essential if you're going to achieve financial independence—and sales is the ingredient that's missing from most wealth-building programs. Don't be alarmed; I'm not suggesting that you hit the street with a set of encyclopedias under your arm, knocking on every door until you make a sale. It's unfortunate, but too many people have preconceived notions of selling that are just plain wrong. Selling is not a slick, fast-talking presentation, nor is it tricking people into buying things they don't want, won't use, and can't afford. Selling does not have to be a pressure business, and the top salespeople rarely use pressure to complete a sale. Selling is simply helping someone do what he or she should do in a situation that can benefit you both. A great salesperson provides the positive leadership people need and want.

Think about all the things you do in the normal course of your life that would be easier with sales training. Think about all the new ideas you're getting for wealth building, and how much easier those will be to accomplish if you apply selling skills. Buying a house for no money down is selling. Getting a loan at a bank is selling. Convincing your spouse to support your dreams is selling. Convincing your boss to give you a raise is selling. In most successful businesses, the leaders have mastered the art of selling. In fact, I can't think of any personal or professional situation that wouldn't be enhanced by the understanding and application of sales techniques, right down to convincing an energetic toddler that he really does want to go to bed at bedtime.

Anytime you try to persuade someone to do what you want them to do, you're selling. The use of sales techniques gets people on your side; it makes them want to help you. A product doesn't have to change hands for selling to occur, and a successful sale isn't always a financial transaction. Just about any successful interaction between you and another human being requires sales skills.

You Don't Need Sales Skills—If You Want to Remain Broke, That Is

When the topic of sales comes up in my seminars, there's always someone in the crowd who says something like, "I'm not a salesperson. I couldn't sell a winter coat to an Eskimo."

That's usually a poor person talking. And it's a person who may end up poor not only financially but also in his personal and professional relationships.

Or sometimes I hear, "It takes someone special to be a salesperson, and I can't do that."

That's just plain not true. The techniques of positive communication are techniques that anyone can learn and develop. The only reason to think you can't is apathy. If you don't want to learn, if you're too lazy to practice, if you're not willing to do the work necessary to improve yourself and your status, then you *won't* develop the selling skills that will enhance all aspects of your life. It's not a question of *can't*. Anyone *can* but only a few *will*.

Selling requires communicating and understanding, and people who do this enrich their lives in ways far beyond their bank accounts. That good salespeople rank among the top 2 percent of income producers is not an accident, and it's also only one of many benefits their skills provide them. Top salespeople earn more than brain surgeons; they earn more than the President of the United States.

Think about it. Brain surgeons spend at least 12 years in school at a mind-boggling cost before they can begin to practice their profession. Then it's several more years before they reach their income potential, because it takes time for them to build up their business. (Would you want someone fresh out of school cutting open your skull?)

Salespeople, on the other hand, can learn the fundamental skills they need in a matter of days or weeks. By applying and fine-tuning those skills, they can reach the top of their profession in two years, with the potential to outearn any medical expert.

Brain surgeons also need some very expensive tools to perform their work. But as the surgeon operates with a scalpel, the salesperson operates with his tongue. And the skill with which each of these tools are used determines the outcome of the process.

How to Tell if You're a Born Salesperson

It's simple—you're not.

Of the estimated 5.5 billion people living on our planet today, not one was born a salesperson. Women give birth every day to sons and daughters, not to salespeople. Selling is a communications skill that you learn and develop, and it's something that all of us can learn and use in every aspect of our lives.

Though you're going to get the basics in this chapter, there are plenty of books and tapes about sales on the market, and I recommend that you add a number of them to your Mindfeed library. Consider attending a few live seminars; they have a totally different flavor than written or recorded material, and you'll learn something new from every sales trainer. The easiest way to teach and apply sales techniques is in a business context, but as you learn them and make them a part of your everyday habits, you'll find yourself applying them virtually all the time in all aspects of your life.

Why Do People Buy?

People buy based on emotion, and then look for logic and reason to justify their actions. It's up to you, the seller, to provide the excitement they need to make the buying decision, *and* the logic and reason they'll need afterward to feel completely satisfied.

People will buy when the following circumstances exist:

- They like you.
- They respect you.
- They can find some logic and reason to help them justify their decision.

If any one of these elements is missing, your chances for a successful sale are reduced by far more than one-third. But when someone likes you and respects you, and your presentation has logic and reason, you'll have a distinct advantage. The result, if you're prepared, is that you'll make the sale and both of you will win.

It sounds simple enough, but how do you do it? With a great presentation.

Presenting for Cash

There are four basic parts to an effective sales presentation. Though we'll be discussing them separately, when you actually use them you'll find they often blend and overlap. What's important is that you understand each step and how it's designed to lead to a successful conclusion.

I.D. Period. This is the time you get to know your prospect, identifying common interests and building rapport. This is also your opportunity to create the "like" that is necessary for a sale.

Begin by expressing a genuine interest in your prospect that is outside of your business purpose. Find out who they are and what they like to do by asking questions. If you're on their territory—either in their home or office—look around for clues to potential topics of discussion. Are there any trophies or plaques on display? Any models or collections? Books or magazines on specific topics? If you're in your office, on neutral territory, or on the telephone, just ask questions. Where are they from? How long have they lived where they live now? Do they have children? How do they spend their spare time?

People love to talk about themselves and their hobbies. It's critical, though, that you listen to them carefully and respond appropriately. If you're busy thinking about what you're going to say next instead of listening to them, they'll know it—and they'll know you're not being genuine. So be sincere, because it will show if you're not.

Another word of caution: Don't make the I.D. period seem like a test, with you firing off one question after another and the prospect providing the answers. Make it a conversation. This is not only the time to get to know them, it's the time for them to get to know you. Tell them things about yourself that will make them feel comfortable about doing business with you.

Presentation. Once you've established a mutual comfort level, you can move into a discussion of your product. This is the time to explain the benefits the prospect will receive by agreeing to your proposal. Don't bore him with a list of features; excite him by drawing a verbal picture of the specific advantages he'll receive from your product.

Your presentation should be thorough and answer as many questions as possible in advance. The formality will vary based on the situation, but keep it as conversational as possible and maintain a high energy level. Involve the prospect as much as you can. If you have a tangible product, let him touch it, feel it, try it out. If he expresses a strong interest in a specific aspect, capitalize on it.

You help the prospect like you in the I.D. stage, and you build respect during the presentation. This is when you demonstrate your product and your knowledge of the business or market. It's also the time to subtly feed in the logic and reason that will be necessary for the buyer to justify his decision.

Trial Close. This is the process of asking committing questions throughout your presentation. Using trial closes lets you gauge the effectiveness of your presentation as you go along, so you can make adjustments if necessary. Committing questions are designed to make sure the prospect is following your presentation, agrees with what you're saying, and is preparing to make a commitment. Even when I do a group presentation to 1,000 people, I involve them by asking questions and encouraging responses.

Committing questions are phrased to get "yes" answers; they are actually mini-closes so that when you get to the end of your presentation, the close itself is simply the final "yes." Committing questions lead the prospect into agreement with you; they get his head nodding in a positive way.

Examples of committing questions are:

- Would you agree?
- Does this make sense?
- Is that a fair statement?
- Do you like this part?

Pay attention to the subtle structure of a committing question. It's a closed question—that is, it's designed to draw a single response, either "yes" or "no," and not a lengthy answer. Don't say, "How do you feel about this?'' Instead say, ''Does this sound good to you?'' When the prospect says ''yes'' to a committing question, you can move on to the next part of your presentation. If he says ''no,'' then you can take the time to find out just where the sticking point is and deal with it.

Close. The close is the process of concluding your presentation by making the sale. The close shouldn't be a frightening experience, but it's where most salespeople fail, and it's usually because of the fear of rejection. If you don't close, you not only walk away without a sale, you're never sure why. But if you have done a few trial closes and asked committing questions along the way, the close should be a natural and logical conclusion to the presentation.

Part of conquering the fear of rejection is learning how to deal with rejection. The first step is to understand that rejection is normal; it's not personal, and you shouldn't take it personally. Just because a prospect can't afford to buy your product or turned down the offer you made to buy his property doesn't make you any less of a person. The prospect is rejecting a business deal, not you as an individual.

Having said that, let me add that closing is almost always a scary process. Especially when what you're selling is a bid on a property or a loan request, you're not only risking rejection, you're also risking not getting something that you want. And no matter how textbook perfect your presentation is, there will be times when you won't make the sale. But keep in mind that the only way to make money and finalize deals is by closing.

Your success ratio will increase significantly when you develop strong closing skills. The two basic techniques you'll use are the yes-or-no close and the assumptive/alternate-choice close.

The *yes-or-no close* is a question that is asked in a way in which the answer must be a ''yes'' or a ''no.'' It's similar to the committing questions you ask in your trial closes, but it's stronger and more definitive. After you ask the question, be quiet and give the prospect time to answer. He may need some time to think; don't distract him by starting to talk. Just wait confidently for the answer.

The *assumptive/alternative-choice close* is more subtle. You ask a question or offer the prospect a choice that assumes the deal is concluded. Some examples of this type of close are:

- Which color did you want, blue or red?
- Where will I be shipping this?
- Would you prefer to schedule the closing for the third or the fifth?
- How many did you want to order?

The Psychology of Effective Selling

I've said this already, but it's worth saying again: People buy based on emotion, and then look for logic and reason to justify their purchase. Your job is to provide both the emotion and the justification.

Excitement sells. Excitement is the primary emotion that prompts people to buy. It's up to you to generate the excitement that will lead to a sale.

Keep your voice up and the tone varied. Don't shout, of course, but make sure your prospect doesn't have to strain to hear you. Changing your tone increases the interest the prospect has in what you're saying. Think about how you react when someone talks to you in a dull monotone; don't do the same thing. Another way to generate excitement is to tell stories. Share examples of how other people have benefited from doing business with you. Use vivid, visual words so your prospect can see himself doing the same. That's what I do in my seminars, and what I've done in this book. In telling stories about myself, my family, and my students, I'm helping you see what *you* can do if you follow my methods. When you're face-to-face with a prospect, support your words with hand gestures and other body language that help keep the level of enthusiasm up.

When your prospect is excited, *then* provide the logic and reason he needs for buying.

Essential Basic Skills

Just as the brain surgeon's primary tool is a scalpel, yours is your ability to communicate. You don't need an extraordinary vocabulary, but you do need a strong command of the language. Your grammar doesn't have to be letter perfect, but it should be correct most of the

time. Most important, your speech should be clear and your pronun-
ciation accurate.

Practice your presentation into a tape recorder and give yourself a
ruthless critique. You've got to eliminate any mumbling or slurring; if
people can't understand you, they won't be able to get the information
necessary to make a purchase. Using consistently poor grammar and
mispronouncing words cast a strong shadow on your credibility.

Use Mindfeed to help in this area if you need it. There are plenty of
adult-oriented vocabulary-building courses on the market that you can
purchase and use at your own pace. This won't be the most exciting
part of your wealth-building program, but it will be a valuable one
because it will increase your self-confidence and your success ratio.

Another important tool is product and business knowledge. You
need to know everything you can about your product, and about the
competition. If a prospect does ask a question you don't know, never
try to fake it; tell him he's raised an interesting point and you'll have
to check on it and get back with the answer. Then make a note and
do it.

Read trade publications, check out the competition's products, and
study everything you can get your hands on about your own business.
The payoff is more than worth it.

Objections Are Just Questions That Lead to Money

The term "objection" is sales-training jargon. It doesn't necessarily
mean the prospect is objecting to something; usually it just means that
he needs more information. Objections generally come in the form of
questions, but sometimes they will be statements. Objections offer the
greatest opportunity in the sales process because they are the steps that
lead you closer to a deal. They are the signal that your prospect is
looking for the logic and reason that will justify a buying decision.
Ideally you want to answer all of your prospect's questions before he
can ask them; in reality, rarely will you go through an entire presentation without at least one objection, so don't let this frighten you.
Sometimes your committing questions will lead to objections, and
that's fine, because it gives you the chance to handle the issue and get
it out of the way early. When you hear an objection during the course
of your presentation, apply the following steps:

Restate and clarify the objection; if appropriate, determine why the issue is being raised. Rephrase what the prospect has said to make sure you understand it. Sometimes that simple step will eliminate the objection. At other times, you'll find that what the prospect said isn't what he really meant, and you won't waste time dealing with an objection that doesn't really exist. Just say, "So if I understand you correctly, you're saying that . . ." and then repeat the objection. Wait for him either to agree that you're accurate or to correct you. There will always be times when our brains and tongues don't quite seem to connect, and what comes out isn't what we meant to say at all. It happens to you, and it happens to prospects, too.

It's always a good idea to find out why the prospect has made the objection; that will help you determine the best response. For example, if you're making an offer on a property and you want the seller to hold the financing, he may say, "One of the problems with holding a mortgage is that it takes such a long time to foreclose." Is he implying that he thinks you may be risky? You need to find out. So say, "Are you concerned that you might have to foreclose on this mortgage?" He might be; then again, he might just be making a general comment.

Finding out why a prospect is asking a particular question is especially important if the answer to the question is negative or reveals a potential shortcoming in your proposal. For example, a prospect may ask if you provide 24-hour service, but you don't. Don't say, "I'm sorry, we don't." Ask, "Do you need 24-hour service?" You'll be relieved if he says, "Oh, no. I was just curious." And if he does need 24-hour service, you've bought yourself a little time to think about how to meet his needs within your parameters. You have to stay razor-sharp and be able to think on your feet.

Give the objection value. Let the prospect know you respect his concerns. Even if you think what he just said was the silliest thing you've ever heard, don't let it show. Try saying, "That's a good point, and I'm glad you brought it up because it gives me a chance to tell you about . . ."

Resolve the objection. Answer the question, make the explanation, or negotiate more if you have to. Does the product come in red? Either it does or it doesn't. How does that work? Show them. Can you make the terms better? Look for places you can compromise.

This approach should be used primarily for objections that come during the course of your presentation. Remember, objections during a presentation are a very good sign; it means the prospect is listening, is interested, and is looking for the information he needs to make a decision. The more objections you can handle during the presentation, the fewer you'll have to deal with at the close, and the more likely you'll be to make a sale.

When you hear an objection during your close, consider a slightly different approach. My favorite is to question the objection, and I do this by repeating what was said as a question. I don't change the words, I just repeat them with a different inflection in my voice. For example, if I'm making a low-money-down offer on a property, and the owner says, "I need more cash," I say, "You need more cash?" That forces him to justify his objection, and very often he starts to sell *himself* on my offer. The key is never to challenge the objection, but to turn it into a hot potato and toss it back in the tone of a question. Your prospect won't want to hold on to it, and by refusing to keep it yourself, you're forcing him to answer his own objection.

When you're closing, you must also isolate the objection to make sure it's the only one your prospect has. I don't want to negotiate on the down payment and then find out he's still not happy with my offer or the interest rate. You isolate the objection with a simple question; just ask, "If we can solve this issue, is there anything else that would keep us from doing business today?" If the prospect says no, then you simply resolve the objection and close the deal. If the prospect says yes, then find out what the other objections are and what you'll have to do to deal with them, one at a time.

Learn to Spot Smoke Screens

Often an objection the prospect may verbalize is not what is really bothering him. Pay close attention to what he doesn't say so you can spot smoke screens. Most smoke screens come in the form of price objections. In many cases, if the prospect says, "I can't afford it," he is really asking you to justify the price. Or he may be saying, "Solve my money problem and I'll buy," which means you may need to help with financing issues.

At other times, a prospect may voice a variety of objections because he really doesn't have the money, but doesn't want to admit it. When you've offered a reasonable resolution that he won't accept, or he starts to repeat objections, there's an excellent chance the real issue is money. If you think this might be the situation, tackle it head-on. Be gentle and tactful; say something like, "Mr. Prospect, it's been my experience that when people say the kinds of things you've said, what they're really trying to tell me is they feel they may not have the funds for this kind of an investment. Very often I'm able to help them, but I can do it only if I understand their true feelings and circumstances. So, Mr. Prospect, if you had the funds in ready cash, would you place your order today?"

If your product is good and your deal is fair, but the prospect continues to make objections, it's always the money—no matter what else he says. And when he doesn't have the money and there's no way you can help him with financing or guide him to a lending source, there's nothing else you can do. Don't blame yourself; just move on.

Other smoke screens are phrases like "I want to think about it" or "I never make a decision the same day." When you hear statements like this, dig for the real objection. Try saying something like, "I understand that this is an important decision, and you don't want to make it hastily. Is there any point in particular that you need to think about?" Then treat that point like an objection, answer it, and close again.

Negotiating Win-Win Deals

All too often we view negotiating as a war: deal making between adversaries where if one wins, then the other must lose. But effective negotiating produces win-win situations, where everyone walks away satisfied. True negotiations are built on persuasion, not power. And when you think about it, win-win negotiations do more than just make everyone feel good; they are tremendously practical. When people come away from a deal with you feeling like winners, they'll be back for more. If at the same time you've managed to get what you wanted, you'll be glad to see them again, instead of ducking them in shame.

Win-win negotiations begin and end with active listening. Pay careful attention to what your prospect is saying, and repeat it if necessary.

You might say, "So if I understand you, Jim, you need delivery within five days of placing your order. Is that correct?" Or, "Let me make sure I have the numbers correct, Diane. You want $5,000 in cash and you're willing to consider holding a second mortgage. Is that right?"

Compare what they want with what you can do. If it matches, chances are you've got a deal. If it doesn't, you must begin the give-and-take process of negotiating, adding a point here, taking away there, until you both have an agreement you're happy with. Remember, you can't beat your prospect into submission; persuade gently with questions that allow the answers (or the yes decision) to be his or her idea.

The One Time It Pays to Be Negative

One of the most dynamic and powerful sales tools is called negative selling, or reverse selling. Essentially, it's when you dare the prospect not to buy, and it can take you from closing one deal out of ten to five deals out of ten.

The way I demonstrate this technique in my seminars is to offer to sell a $12 gold pen to a student for $2. The student accepts the deal, I hold the pen out, but as soon as he reaches for it, I pull it back. He'll reach further until he realizes what I've done. Then I say, "I'm not sure I want to sell this to you, after all." I think for a few seconds, and then hold it out again. He reaches again, and I pull back again. Repeating the routine proves my point, which is that people want what they can't have. They're reaching for the pen because I'm pulling it away. Try this yourself to see how it works. You don't even have to include the selling part; just ask someone to hold a pen, and withdraw it when he reaches for it. He'll keep reaching as you pull back.

When you apply this technique to a true sales situation, you must use it in a subtle and sophisticated manner. If you botch it, you'll appear clumsy and manipulative, so practice extensively before you use it with a real prospect.

Negative selling builds a sense of urgency because of the implication that the prospect may not be allowed to purchase what you have to offer. Remember the banking paradox—bankers only want to lend money to people who don't need it. When you use negative selling, what you're projecting is that you don't *need* the sale; you would certainly enjoy doing business with the prospect, but it's no big deal if you don't. Negative selling is always maintaining a positive posture, never begging for the business. You don't need them, and you don't need their deal. Act as if you have plenty of other deals in the works— and if you've been following my advice, that will be true.

In fact, negative selling is an ideal technique to use when you're applying for a loan. The approach I use is to let the banker know I'm shopping and get him to sell me on using his bank. I say something like, "I was referred to you because you offer certain types of loans (I name them), and I wanted to see what types of interest rates and terms you have. I've put together a package that I've showed to a few lenders, and before I make a final decision, I'd like to see what you can do."

If I have made an offer on a property and the owner wants to stall for time, I use negative selling this way: "I understand that this is a big decision for you. By the same token, I'm sure you understand that I'm an investor and businessperson. I have a number of offers in right now, and there are two that have been accepted that I'm very interested in. There are some benefits your deal has that the others don't, but there are also some advantages the other deals have that yours doesn't. I would definitely like to move forward on this, but I have to make a decision in the next couple of days on where I'm going to allocate my money. When will you be in a position to make a decision?"

Add a New Word to Your Vocabulary: SINALOA

SINALOA is an acronym for "safety in numbers and the law of averages," which are two important aspects of selling. Sales is a numbers game, and you must have noes to get to the yeses. It works like this: Let's say a ten-year-old boy is selling plastic combs door to door for $1 each. What's going to happen? Some people won't be home, some won't be interested, some will have enough combs—and some will buy. If that boy knocks on enough doors and says, "Would you like to buy a comb for $1?" he'll sell some combs. And if he applies some sales techniques, like a bright smile, an energetic tone, and a presentation that includes some benefits, he'll sell more. It's a matter of making enough presentations (safety in numbers) to find enough people who will buy (the law of averages).

If I showed you ten envelopes and told you eight of them were empty, but one had $50 in it, and one had $1,000, and to get that $1,000 you just had to keep picking envelopes until you picked the right one, would you do it? Of course you would. It's the same with sales.

The law of averages is something a lot of people don't understand, and it has caused many an investor, business owner, or salesperson to quit before he reached his goal. If your presentation is good and your offer fair, and if there is logic and reason to what you're doing, the law of averages says you'll make sales. If you're not making sales, take a critical look at your presentation or your offer and see if there's something that needs changing. Keep working on your technique until you find something that is successful. If you keep trying, the law of averages says you will achieve success.

Once that happens, you'll develop a ratio of results. You'll know how many sales calls it takes to get a sale. You'll know how many offers you need to put in on properties to have one accepted. You won't make the mistake so many people do of quitting when you're almost there.

In baseball, a batting average of .300 is great. It could earn a player a multi-million-dollar contract and a place in the Hall of Fame. But do you understand what it means? It means that the player gets a hit only three times out of ten when he's up at bat. It means that 70 percent of the time, he's out. There's a story about Babe Ruth that I like. It seems that each time he struck out, he headed back to the dugout with a big smile on his face. Why was he so happy? Because with each strikeout, he knew he was that much closer to his next home run.

The best of the best understand the law of averages. They know it's a numbers game. We don't expect professional athletes to win every game, and you shouldn't expect that as a professional salesperson you'll make every sale. Just remember that each time you strike out, you're that much closer to your next home run. So keep playing.

Presenting an Offer to a Seller

Because I feel so strongly about real estate being a part of your wealth-building program, I want to specifically address how to use sales skills when buying property. Remember, people expect to negotiate on real estate deals, and there are plenty of angles to consider: the price, the points, closing costs, financing, down payment, etc.

I begin by establishing my own credibility during the identification period. I get to know the owners, and I let them get to know me. I want them to like me because when someone likes you, they feel a sense of obligation to listen to your presentation. When I get ready to present my offer, I want the owners to consider the entire offer before making a decision.

After we've gone through the I.D. period and I've inspected the property, I set up an appointment to make my offer, which is, of course, a sales presentation. I put my entire offer and any support documentation (such as estimates for improvements) in writing. If I'm dealing with a couple, I make a complete copy of the offer for each of them. By the way, I always talk to both the husband and the wife.

When I make a presentation to a couple, I always try to seat the wife between me and the husband so she is included in the conversation. Many times, whether you're a man or a woman, you'll assume the man makes the decision. In most cases, he really doesn't. The wife may not say anything during the presentation, but she'll have plenty to say after you leave. And if you ignore her, you won't have a deal. So always arrange the seating so you talk to both husband and wife.

I hand them the offer and explain it step by step. If I'm asking them to hold all or part of the mortgage, I tell them how much money they'll receive over the life of the loan so they can see how much they'll really make. For example, if I want them to hold a $20,000 second mortgage for 15 years at 9 percent, I tell them they'll receive a monthly payment of $202.85, which totals $36,513—or $16,513 more than the amount they would have received in cash. (Note: This is the exact opposite of the approach you take when you're offering to discount a mortgage.)

If my offer price is lower than their asking price, I explain why. I rarely, if ever, low-ball for the sake of low-balling. If the property needs work, or if comparable properties in the neighborhood are appraised at a lower amount, I tell them. I point out that as an investor, it makes sense for me to buy the property only if I can make a profit on it, and that I've done my best to come up with a deal that will be advantageous to us both.

Once I explain the details of the offer, I shut up. I give them time to digest the deal and to think of any questions they may have—and they usually have at least one or two. Once they start asking questions, then I start closing.

Practice, Practice, Practice

Like any skill worth having, sales skills aren't something you can learn once and then forget about. Just as performers and athletes practice every day to stay in peak condition, you must practice your selling skills.

Visualize each selling situation in advance. Walk it through in your mind, anticipating what the prospect will say, what the objections might be, and how you'll handle them. See yourself making the close and walking away with a successful deal. This will give you an edge few salespeople bother to take.

At the end of each presentation, regardless of its outcome, do a "curbside" critique. As soon as you leave the prospect, go over the presentation in your mind. What worked, what didn't? If you made the sale, what clinched it for you? If you didn't, why not? Do this with every presentation so you know what you're doing right and what you need to improve.

Keep your Mindfeed going and battle that old programming. You *can* be a super salesperson; you *can* be one of the top 2 percent of income earners.

CHAPTER 18

Benefits of Business

Shallow men believe in luck, believe in circumstances: it was somebody's name, or he happened to be there at the time, or it was so then, and another day it would have been otherwise. Strong men believe in cause and effect.

—RALPH WALDO EMERSON

Though money is the most tangible benefit of being in business for yourself, and it's the one we tend to focus on the most, there are many others. We saw clearly during the 1980s what happens to people who are driven by greed. If your only reason for getting into business is to make money and get rich, you may well find everything working against you. If, on the other hand, you're getting into business because you like what you're going to do and you feel good about it, and if you focus on doing the business right, the money will come automatically.

Right now, for example, there is a nationwide shortage of low- and moderate-income housing. As a matter of fact, this type of housing has always been in short supply. So it naturally follows that low- and moderate-income housing has the lowest vacancy ratio of any type of property, which is a strong indicator that you can make money investing in low- and moderate-income rental property. But if you're going to be truly successful as a real estate investor, you've got to get into the business because you care about people, not just because you can make plenty of money. You've got to get into the business because you want to provide safe, decent, sanitary housing for people who can't afford higher-priced neighborhoods. If you do that, and if you focus on the challenge of being the best property owner you can be and apply the formulas for positive cash flow I've shared with you, the money will happen.

The same principle applies to any type of business. Choose one that has the potential to make money, then forget about the money and concentrate on doing the business right. If you get too wrapped up in counting pennies, you'll never get to the dollars. And you'll never have the opportunity to appreciate the many other reasons for getting into business.

Why People Are Starting Their Own Businesses

The only way you will achieve financial independence is to stop being dependent on someone else for a paycheck. The easiest, fastest, and most popular method for accomplishing this is to go into business for yourself, which is a primary reason we are seeing an explosion in the start-up of small businesses in the United States and around the world.

But there are other reasons for starting businesses. In my seminars, I see people driven to become entrepreneurs by a variety of forces. One is that the baby boomers are maturing, which means a greater number of older, more experienced workers. These people have the knowledge and ability to start successful businesses, and they are doing so in steadily increasing numbers. A related reason is the streamlining of large corporations. As big companies eliminate the unnecessary layers of workers accumulated during the 1980s, large numbers of middle managers are finding themselves unemployed with no job prospects at all. The go-getters are taking the skills they learned in the corporate world and using them to start their own businesses. After all, looking for a job is hard work. Why not invest that effort in a business of your own instead of someone else's?

Another growing group of entrepreneurs is made up of women who, instead of fighting discrimination in the corporate world, invest their efforts in creating their own companies where there is no limit to what they can accomplish and learn. And the group that appeals to me most are the workers who go into business for themselves because they're tired of the corporate rat race and the demands that come with it. They see their own company as an opportunity to build a lifestyle of their choice.

Even more exciting these days is that small business no longer lives in the shadow of doom, gloom, and economic disaster. Small business start-ups are on the rise; small business failures are on the decline; and small business successes are producing more millionaires than ever before in our history.

Starting your own business has never been easier than it is today. You can begin from scratch, buy an existing company, or take advantage of a wide variety of franchise opportunities with an equally wide variety of terms. You don't necessarily have to have a lot of capital. Technological advances have made it possible for more people than ever before to start and build highly successful companies, often in a spare room in their homes with a relatively small investment. A telephone and a fax machine are all you need to operate on a global scale these days; add a computer, and your options are virtually unlimited.

One reality you can't ignore is that it takes time to build profitability in a company. But you can start part-time while you continue to work at a regular job that pays the bills. Once your business is off the ground and generating income, you can expand to a full-time operation and quit your job. Or you may want to work only part-time and spend the rest of your time doing something else; your own business lets you make that choice. And if you don't want to work at all, just build your business to the point where the employees run it for you—then sit back, relax, and enjoy the profits.

When you own your own business, you're not locked into someone else's schedule. You set the hours you're going to work and decide when you're going to take off. Do you want to come in late on Monday and leave early on Friday? No problem, it's your decision. Want to take a few days off and go on a cruise with your spouse? Again, no problem, it's your choice. On the other hand, if you want to get an edge on the competition or make more money by working longer hours, you can do that, too. And when you work longer hours in your own business, you get to keep all the profits—not just the pittance of a time-and-a-half overtime rate.

Because I often travel on weekends to conduct seminars, I frequently work seven days a week. But when I'm home during the week, I have the freedom to leave the office early to play tennis, or even take a whole day off because my kids are out of school and I may want to do something with them. Also, I take a month off at Christmas and another month off in the summer, and I go on four or five weeklong vacations during the year. The point is that it's my business and I set my own schedule. This is the advantage of having businesses that generate passive income, whether they are real estate or something else. My businesses make money for me whether I'm in the office or not.

Chances are you'll work longer and harder as a business owner than you ever did as an employee, but you'll do it on *your* terms. You'll make your own choices about when and where to invest time and energy, and when and where to sacrifice. You'll be able to balance your life according to your own priorities instead of someone else's— and when you are working, you can run your business the way you want to, not the way someone else thinks you should.

For example, have you ever had a boss or known anyone who had a boss who did everything wrong? And have you ever been in a situation where you knew that if the top people in the company would just listen to you, you could give them dozens of ideas to make the operation run more smoothly and be more profitable?

It's happened to all of us. Even as an ignorant kid working in the slaughterhouse, I saw plenty of ways the company could improve, but no one in management would listen to me, and I didn't see much point in trying too hard to get my message across. I have learned from that experience, and today I encourage my employees to participate in management decisions and to offer suggestions—but because it's my company, the final decision belongs to me.

Worldwide, creative workers are stifled by bosses and company structures that dictate how things will be done. But when you're the boss, you can move immediately to take advantage of opportunities as you see them and to correct problems quickly. When it's your business, you have the freedom to operate in the manner you know will be most effective and efficient. You have the freedom to make changes when necessary. And you have the freedom to make as much money as you want.

Financial Advantages That Go Beyond Cash

Whether it's part-time or full-time, your business will probably provide you with tremendous tax advantages. The way the U.S. Congress
has written the tax code has been a tremendous benefit to accountants
and publishing houses. The laws are so complicated that average
people can't understand them and must turn to professionals to prepare
their tax returns. And the laws change often enough that most tax-
advice manuals are out of date shortly after they are written. Even so,
the tax advantages of being in your own business are significant and
will likely remain so. A lot of the details may change, but one thing
the government has never done, and I don't think ever will do, is to
take away the right of a businessperson to deduct the cost of doing
business.

As a business owner, you are entitled to a host of tax deductions
generally unavailable to non–business owners. Just a few examples
are your automobile and the fuel to run it; your office, or, if you work
from your home, the cost of the mortgage or rent, utilities, furnishings, and maintenance of the portion of your house you use for business; your VCR if it's used to show training or other business-related
films; magazines and books (like this one); dinners and other forms of
entertainment with partners and customers (business must be discussed
at these events); and all or part of the cost of your vacations if you
arrange to conduct some business either along the way or at your
destination.

If you manage to come up with more deductions than income from
your business, you can use those deductions to reduce your tax liability on income from other sources—such as your job. Even part-time
businesses qualify for tax deductions, and you do not have to make a
large up-front investment to deduct your operating expenses. All you
have to do is keep careful records. It's also a good idea to establish a
relationship with an accountant who can guide your tax strategy in
accordance with changes in the laws.

Remember, just one rental property, even a single-family home,
constitutes owning a business. The same applies to a network marketing distributorship or any of hundreds of other profit-making activities you might do in your spare time. When you become a business
owner, you are qualified for all the same tax deductions any Fortune
500 company is entitled to take.

Your own business also provides a built-in hedge against inflation. During inflationary periods, employees are helpless to do anything but watch their purchasing power erode; they don't have the authority to give themselves a raise. As a business owner, when your costs go up you can increase prices to maintain profitability levels. Of course, you can't just arbitrarily raise prices; you have to consider your overall market, what your competition is doing, and how your customers will react, but the decision will be made *by* you, not *for* you.

If You Could Live Anywhere, Where Would It Be?

I realized fairly soon after getting into business for myself that I had a level of freedom employees don't have. Besides being able to establish my own working hours, I realized I didn't have to live in upstate New York and endure that region's bitter cold winters. My dream location was Florida, and because I had my own business, I was able to move there.

Maybe your dream location isn't where you are right now. Maybe you'd like to live in the tropics and enjoy year-round sunshine, beaches, and warm temperatures. Maybe you prefer the mountains with winter sports and summer hiking, the charm of a New England village, or even the excitement of a big city. When you own your own business, you can choose to live anywhere in the world you want. The key is to start a business now that you can move to your ideal spot in the near future. Or consider the idea of multiple locations, so you can move among them. All you have to do is stay alert to the opportunities that will cross your path every day.

Are You Driving a Car, or a Horse and Buggy?

That's a figurative question to get you thinking about the tools you use in your business. If you're going to get around efficiently in our modern-day world, you need modern-day transportation. If you're going to run a profitable business, you need the most up-to-date tools available. And the bare minimum in the way of tools is a computer.

Even if you are only investing in real estate, a computer will let you automate your records. You'll spend less time on record keeping and have a higher rate of accuracy. You can take advantage of programs that will help you analyze property and produce financial statements in a matter of minutes. Business paperwork that is professionally prepared labels you as a serious investor, and a computer makes it easy to create this image.

A computer also opens the door to literally hundreds of other businesses, such as the Mortgage Reduction System™. Many are home-based and can be started in your spare time. Just be sure you choose a business that is a business, not one that is a job.

Another essential piece of equipment is an answering device for your telephone. You can either purchase an answering machine or subscribe to a voice mail system, but your phone must be answered at all times. It's easy to think that if people have something important to say, they'll call back, but the reality is that that's not true. They may not have time to call back. Or they may decide to call someone else when they can't get you. So make sure your telephone is answered, and that you return calls promptly. Don't miss out on a great deal because you missed or ignored a message.

As a supplement to an answering machine, consider getting a cellular phone. Cellular phones are dropping in price, but the air time charges can still be fairly steep. Shop around for the best deal.

You might also have use for a fax machine, for almost instant transmission of documents around the world. An alternative to your own fax machine is a commercial fax service; plenty of business-related stores offer this. However, it's still more time-consuming than having a machine in your home or office. If you're spending more than $40 and three hours a month on faxes, it's time to invest in your own equipment.

The price tag on all of this exciting office technology is steadily dropping, and it allows you to project a successful, big-company image on a small-company budget. Also, having this type of equipment, which is relatively inexpensive, makes you *feel* important, it makes you *feel* like a real businessperson with a purpose. These tools will constantly remind you to dig for opportunities. When you look the part, you will act the part; when you act the part, you become the part.

What Do You Really Want to Do?

What would you do if money weren't an issue? How would you spend your time if you didn't have to concern yourself with paying bills?

I don't mean what you'd like to do on your vacation—I like to snow ski in the winter, but I wouldn't want to do it all the time—but what would you do with the majority of your waking hours if you didn't have to earn a living? Whatever this is, look for a business idea related to it.

Test your idea for feasibility and profitability by creating a business plan. I know many people think a trip to the dentist is more fun than writing a business plan, but this basic step is critical to your success. Before you start, you need a vision of what your business is going to look like:

- Are you going to buy an existing business or a franchise, or start a totally new company?
- Who is your market?
- How will you communicate with your market?
- Will your product or service be affordable in that market?
- Will your product or service sell in that market?
- What is your profit margin?
- How much start-up capital do you need?
- Who will be your suppliers?
- What sort of licenses/permits do you need?
- Who are your competitors and how are they likely to react to your entry into the market?
- Do you have an adequate labor pool?
- What are your short- and long-term income and expense projections?
- What is the growth potential?
- What is your estimated return on investment?

Writing a business plan lets you evaluate your business idea in much the same way that you would evaluate a property by inspecting it and then calculating the rents and expenses. If you put together a realistic business plan and show a return on your invested cash of 20 to 30 percent or higher, you've got the potential for a successful company. If the profitability potential isn't there, look for ways to adjust your plan, or look for a different business. There are plenty of them out there.

No paycheck is more secure than the one you write to yourself. Whether you start a new business, buy an existing operation, or purchase a franchise, one of the quickest paths to financial independence is through owning a business.

CHAPTER 19

Illuminate Your Fears

Obstacles are the scary things you see when you take your eyes off your goals.

—Russ Whitney

Let me guess how you feel now. There's a part of you that's fired up with excitement because you can truly see a future of adventure and financial freedom. You know you don't have all the answers yet, but you have plenty of ideas and you can't wait to start putting some of them into action. Then there's the part of you that's afraid. It's a fear that may be in the form of skepticism about your ability to put your ideas into action. So let's address those fears and see how to get them out of the way so you can move toward your financial goals.

The methods I'm sharing with you *work*. I've used every single one of them, over and over, and I know they work consistently. I've taught hundreds of people to do the same thing, and they've been successful, too. Many of these techniques are not new; people have been using them for decades. But you don't have to be a Wall Street broker or a financial whiz kid to apply these same principles and build your own wealth.

Remember, different circumstances require different techniques, and you must be able to evaluate many situations and make the right decisions about how to handle them. Sometimes deals will fall through for reasons beyond your control; when that happens, you just go on to the next one. But if you use my methods, and you use them consistently, you will build wealth and make steady headway toward your goals.

What about your ability? Believe me, you do have it. My techniques and strategies are not difficult, nor do they take any special degree of intelligence to apply. They *do* require commitment, and you are demonstrating the foundation of your commitment right now by educating yourself on how to build wealth.

Wealth building is a lot like cooking: Just about anybody can do it. If you can read and follow instructions in a recipe, you can cook. You may not ever be the greatest chef in the world, but you can prepare meals that taste good. If you follow the strategies explained in this book, you will build wealth. Your net worth may not surpass J. Paul Getty's or H. Ross Perot's, but you *can* become a millionaire and enjoy financial security and independence.

Ron Watcke of Troy, Michigan, began using my methods in 1985. In seven years, he purchased 18 income-producing properties (11 single-family homes, four duplexes, a triplex, a six-unit, and an eight-unit) with a total market value exceeding $1.5 million and an annual positive cash flow of more than $60,000. Ron's 19-year-old son, Mike, has also gone into the real estate business. He owns a duplex and an eight-unit building, and is on his way to becoming a millionaire. Ron's other son, 16-year-old Tim, also has closed on a property.

In just four months, partners Jill Hinderer and Larry Jackson of Aurora, Colorado, bought properties valued at almost $500,000 that are all generating positive cash flows. When they started, Larry didn't have particularly good credit, and neither of their jobs paid well enough to let them build up significant savings. Like me, Jill is a high school dropout; she's become a half-millionaire at 22, and her goal is to become a millionaire at a younger age than I did.

The first property John Belden of Atlanta purchased using my techniques was a foreclosed house. The only cash he needed was closing costs; he immediately leased the house at a monthly profit of $300 and then sold it to the tenant for $10,000 more than he paid. His goal is to purchase one property a month.

At 24, Michael Keiter of Westminster, Colorado, used my techniques to buy a 16-unit apartment building and several single-family residences. When he started, he was $400,000 in debt and had no credit. The apartment building was purchased with no money down and has a positive cash flow of $950 a month.

When Roy Torgeirson moved to Florida from Norway, he was looking for both a pleasant climate and economic opportunity. He bought a restaurant that failed. He tried several businesses and jobs—including selling vacuum cleaners door to door—before he read my first book on real estate investing. A year later, he owned 36 apartments, four houses, an office building, and some lots; those properties total well over $1 million in value and produce enough cash flow to support Roy and his family in comfort.

Arthur Arnold was a truck mechanic working long hours for mediocre pay when he decided to use my techniques to build a significant financial net worth with real estate. During the course of his purchases, he became an expert in 203(k) loans (a federal loan guarantee program). I helped him write a book that will probably earn more than $200,000 in royalties this year alone. Arthur is still investing in real estate, but he's now also an author and public speaker.

Guy Cozzi of Greenwich, Connecticut, used real estate to build enough capital to create a home-inspection business. He makes more than $100,000 a year working part-time, and he's developed a training course to teach his business to others.

Heidi Dickman was on welfare and looking for a way out when she came to one of my seminars and joined my Bird Dog Program. A very short time later, she found a 24-unit apartment building for $385,000. I put up the cash and she's managing the property, which will net around $20,000 a year. Heidi predicts this will be only the first in a long series of profitable real estate deals; as I write this, she's in the process of negotiating the purchase of a $750,000 property.

Illuminate the Fear by Turning the Light On

When you were a child and imagined horrible monsters under the bed or in the closet, your parents helped you deal with your fear by turning the light on and showing you that the monsters didn't actually exist. What they did was illuminate your fear. Many adults are being held back by fears that are no more real than imaginary monsters—fears that would go away if a light was turned on.

One of the scariest things I've done in my life was buy my first piece of rental property. My wife and I both had knots in our stomachs about the deal. But we knew that if we were ever going to get anywhere in life, we had to make the decision. We had to try.

We made the decision and it worked.

But what was even more scary than the first property was the second and third. The first one worked, but what if the second one didn't? Were we getting greedy? Were we making a mistake that would wipe out everything we'd gained on the first property? In spite of our fears, we made the decision. It worked. And we didn't have to face the fear of failure again—until we had to make our first half-million-dollar decision.

We looked at the numbers, and all those same fears and doubts came rushing back. But we knew that if we didn't make a decision, we couldn't move forward. We would never make any more financial progress. So we made the decision and it worked. We had overcome the fear of failure one more time. And we didn't have to face it again until our first million-dollar decision.

My point is that these fears will crop up, no matter what you are or what you're doing. They are natural and normal, but you can't let them cripple you. If you're going to get somewhere in life, you have to make decisions, and you make decisions by evaluating the logic and reason of the situation.

When we began buying rental property, my father-in-law would ask me things like, "What are you going to do if all the tenants move out? What are you going to do if all the furnaces break down?" Sure, those are scary ideas, but when I thought it through, I realized they were no more than the adult equivalent of a child's imaginary monsters. People have been renting properties in America for more than 200 years. Just because I buy one, does that mean all the tenants will move out? Of course not, that's ridiculous.

The same thing applies to businesses. Maybe you've been thinking about buying a retail or convenience store that's been operating successfully for years. Will the customers stop coming in just because you bought it? Of course not. If you're worried that they will, you need to realize you're experiencing the very natural fear of failure. Understand it, overcome it, and know that good things come only to those who seek them out. The reality is that you will always be a little afraid when you step out into new territory. That's okay. Just don't let the fear stop you from moving forward and taking action.

One of my students told me she really liked the rooming house idea and could see where the need existed in her community. She could handle purchasing the property and arranging any necessary rehabilitation. What was stopping her, she said, was concern about management and maintenance. Who would mop the floors? Who would clean the bathrooms? And how would the rents be collected?

In Chapter Eight I explained the mechanics of running a rooming house, so you have these answers. I could have done that with this particular student; I could have just answered her questions. But in talking with her, I wanted to help her realize that these were silly fears, not real ones. So I asked her if she inherited a rooming house today, if all of a sudden it was hers with no effort at all on her part to acquire it, and if she knew it would make her $1,000 a month on a very part-time basis, would she figure out the details of running it? Would she figure out what to do if a window broke and how to keep the common areas clean? Would she manage to collect the rents?

Of course she would. She was a little embarrassed when she looked at the picture from that perspective and realized that maybe she was using her fear as an excuse to avoid action, and maybe even sabotaging herself without realizing it.

When you see an opportunity but feel the fear of failure creeping up on you, you must ask yourself better questions. If you focus on the negatives, you'll stay trapped in the negatives. Don't worry about what will happen if all the tenants move out; instead, develop a plan to advertise and show your units to keep your occupancy rate as close to 100 percent as possible. Don't look at cleaning apartments between tenants or maintaining the common areas of a rooming house as oversized obstacles; just figure out a way to get the necessary work done.

Much of our fear comes from the conditioning we received as kids. Most of us had too many role models telling us that it was okay not to achieve anything significant with our lives—or, worse, telling us that we probably wouldn't be able to do it if we tried.

Most parents would be shocked to realize they were doing this. Here's how it usually happens: A child brings home a bad grade and the parent, in an effort to be comforting, says, "It's okay, we really didn't expect you to do any better than this." The parent will usually add, "You'll do better next time," but do you think the child hears that part? Of course not. He's too busy processing the fact that *underachieving is acceptable*. Conversely, when that same child does something exceptional, the parent will say, "Don't get a swelled head from it." The parent may be trying to help the child avoid becoming conceited, but the result is a message that says achievements aren't anything to strive for or be proud of.

Naturally we carry this negative conditioning into our adult lives, and when we are introduced to the abundant financial opportunities that are available, there is a major collision in our brains. We get a mixed message that results in a huge lack of confidence. We're afraid we're going to fail, so we may never even try. We literally self-sabotage. Believe you can become wealthy by putting my techniques and strategies into action and see how fast that belief becomes a reality.

I encourage you to take a close look at yourself. Study your feelings about wealth and about your present situation. Deep down, are you afraid of success? Are you afraid of becoming wealthy? If you are, use the knowledge you're gaining, your newfound confidence and common sense, and my faith in you to turn the light on your fears. Once you do, your life will become more manageable and less stressful, because you'll start to control your life instead of it controlling you.

Develop Money-Making, Problem-Solving Skills

Dealing with your fears doesn't mean you won't have problems. Though sometimes the simple process of illuminating a fear will eliminate it, there will be times when you will have to handle a problem. Problems are a part of life. We have big problems and little problems. We have problems that matter and problems that don't. We have problems that are easy to handle, and problems that are more difficult. And that's why you need problem-solving skills.

Occasionally you're going to run into problems on your way to becoming wealthy. That's okay, because once you solve them, you'll get paid—and that can be some pretty healthy motivation. The key is not to allow problems to overwhelm you. Don't try to swallow the elephant whole; eat it bite by bite. When you think you have a problem, apply these simple steps:

ILLUMINATE THE PROBLEM—Focus directly on the source of the problem and make sure it truly is a problem, and not simply a groundless fear. Then decide how important it really is and how much attention it requires. Too many people get all wrapped up in the little things, and never get around to handling the truly important things. Don't do that. Refuse to invest your valuable time "majoring in minors." Attack the major things first.

DEFINE THE PROBLEM—Make sure you have a clear understanding of what the problem really is. Many times the real problem is hiding behind a variety of symptoms. Our computer company sells a lot of computer systems at our seminars. A while back, I noticed our cancellation ratio had risen dramatically. We expect an occasional cancellation, since there is always someone who wants the system but can't get it financed; we refer to that as our funding ratio. But the percentage of people who committed to invest in a computer and then canceled their order had gone beyond the expected and understood number. And while that sounds like a problem, the real problem was not the cancellations themselves, but why they were being made.

IDENTIFY THE CAUSE—Once you understand the problem, track down the root cause. In our computer business, we examined all the possibilities for the cancellations. Was there something wrong with the computer or the software? Was it too complicated to learn? Was there a service we should have been providing that we weren't?

Ah-ha! There was absolutely nothing wrong with our products; the customers loved them, they worked great. But the people who were canceling their orders felt as if they weren't getting enough immediate support from the company to give them the comfort level they needed on such a big purchase. All along we had been thinking that providing the technical support after the system had been delivered was enough. But we realized our customers needed to have their purchase decisions reinforced *before* they took delivery of their computers so they wouldn't let time and their fears make them doubt the wisdom of their decision.

DETERMINE HOW TO CORRECT THE CAUSE—In many cases, simply understanding the cause will highlight the solution; other cases may take some additional study and thought. Either way, the next step is to decide how best to correct the problem. We implemented some simple but critical customer service programs that included a telephone call two days after the order was placed, a follow-up letter, and another telephone call after that.

DEVELOP A STRATEGY FOR THE CORRECTION—Plan how you will accomplish the correction. If different people will be involved, make sure each person knows what they are responsible for and when they must do it. In our computer business, we wrote new customer service guidelines and set up training sessions for all our staff.

TAKE ACTION—You know what you're going to do; now, do it.

FOLLOW UP TO MAKE SURE THE PROBLEM HAS BEEN CORRECTED—Check back in an appropriate period of time to make sure your correction has had the desired effect. In our case, we were able to see results almost immediately. Our funding ratio improved immediately and cancellations dropped to near zero. We could have wasted a lot of energy and effort tinkering with the computer itself, but by taking the time to define the real problem we were able to develop a permanent solution.

I once bought an apartment building that had what I considered to be excessive water consumption. The tenants weren't unusually clean, but the building did have a number of leaky faucets. New washers in the faucet fixtures solved the problem. The problem-solving process looked like this:

Define the problem: Excessive water consumption resulting in high utility costs.

Identify the cause: Leaky faucets in several apartments.

Determine how to correct the cause: Replace washers in leaking faucets.

Develop a strategy for the correction: Maintenance worker will purchase necessary parts and replace washers within two working days.

Take action: Work is done.

Follow up: Review of the next utility bill indicates water consumption has dropped to an acceptable level.

Let me emphasize to you that when I saw the high water bill, I didn't get overwhelmed and say things like, "Oh, boy, I knew this rental property would be a hassle." I just identified the problem, took it a bite at a time, got it corrected, and made money. And fixing those drippy faucets in an income-producing property I owned was a lot easier than struggling to pay bills on the low hourly wage I earned at the slaughterhouse.

After you have consciously applied the problem-solving process a few times, you'll be so comfortable with it that it will become automatic. With a systematic approach to problems, you'll never be overwhelmed, no matter how complicated they may appear on the surface.

Don't Sweat the Small Stuff

If it isn't important, don't worry about it.

The Benefits of Making Wrong Decisions

I could quote you a whole string of cute and catchy clichés about the concept of failure, but you've probably heard them all already. Notice I used the word "concept," because that's all failure is. Failure is a state of mind. It's not real; it's just an attitude and way of thinking that you have the power either to accept or reject.

Now, I'm not going to guarantee that you will never have a brief setback on your way to wealth; in fact, I can almost guarantee that you will. But learning from your mistakes will make you stronger, more capable, and eventually wealthier.

A bad decision is better than no decision at all. Indecision is the greatest thief of opportunity. Indecision will rob your bank account and your peace of mind. Indecision will steal from you daily.

Think about this: You may be worrying about making the right decision on a wealth-building strategy, but what will it cost you if you do nothing at all? You'll stay where you are, worrying about paying bills and getting deeper in debt. No matter what kinds of problems you have, they'll be easier to manage with money in the bank. I know that wealth is not a cure-all, but it will remove some of the stress from your life and give you the freedom to handle your nonfinancial issues.

While you sit on the fence not making a decision, the clock keeps ticking. Another second of your life is used up with every tick of the clock. Don't sit on that fence wondering what will happen if you get off on the wrong side—just get off! If you find you've chosen the wrong side, you can always climb back over the fence. Remember this: Wrong decisions give you the experience you need to make better decisions the next time.

CHAPTER 20

Get Started Building Your Personal Fortune

Reach high, for stars lie hidden in your soul.
Dream deep, for every dream precedes a goal.

—PAMELA VAULL STARR

Now that you're at the beginning of your own path to financial freedom and wealth, you're excited, you're motivated, and you can't wait to get started. You have learned how to find seed money and grow it into serious capital. You know how to make money in real estate, and how to watch for and benefit from other business opportunities. You know, too, that you've probably been the victim of bad programming. Most, if not all, of the people in your life up until now have told you that you can't be wealthy. Your parents, teachers, other role models, and even your peers have sent you the message that wealth is beyond you, that financial success is for others, that whatever you try to do to break out of your mediocre mold won't work.

It's not true! You *can* be wealthy, you *can* be successful, and you *can* make a difference in this world.

You can reverse the negative programming you've received over the years with the Mindfeed process. You're already off to a good start, but you must prepare now if you are to maintain the momentum you've built. Remember, it's not the how-to or even the want-to that will get you wealthy—it's the will-do. And the will-do is the most

249

challenging part of wealth building, because it is so easily sabotaged by negativity.

Fight back by setting aside time every day for Mindfeed. Reread this book and look for positive messages. Collect books and tapes by people who have something worthwhile to share. Study wealthy people. Learn their habits and techniques, and make those habits and techniques your own. Reject negativity. Wealthy people don't have time to be negative. The winners of this world consciously look for the good and avoid the bad, and Mindfeed is the tool you can use to make yourself a winner.

Make Yourself Uncomfortable

At my seminars, when I ask for a show of hands from the people who want to be successful, every single hand in the room is waving. But when I ask how many people are willing to do what it takes to be successful, at least half of the hands go down. Those people don't have the mind-set for wealth.

What is a wealth mind-set? It's the ability and willingness to identify, focus on, and take action on a wealth-building vehicle. It's staying open to new ideas and new opportunities. It's flexibility and creativity. It's doing what it takes so you can enjoy the rewards.

The single thing that prevents more people from becoming wealthy is their comfort zone. If you're comfortable, if you're getting by, if your house is okay, your car runs, and you're earning enough to pay your bills every month, it may be hard for you to find the motivation to develop the wealth mind-set.

Human beings are, for the most part, creatures of habit. Are you comfortable with your habits of getting up, going to work every day, coming home and watching television every evening, maybe fitting in a little hobby or community work on the side? If you are, you may feel you have no reason to change. As long as you are satisfied with your life, your life will never be anything different than it is.

But let's say you lost your job, or your spouse or one of your parents became seriously ill, and you needed money. Would that make you uncomfortable enough to change your habits? Would you be uncomfortable enough to develop a wealth-building mind-set?

Here's something else to think about. You may be comfortable today, with heat in the winter, air-conditioning in the summer, and plenty to eat, but what's going to happen when you retire? According to the U.S. Census Bureau, eight out of ten Americans will retire at or below the poverty level—and, believe me, *that's not comfortable!* And as our life spans get longer, that means more years of poverty and penny-pinching because we spent our working years being comfortable instead of building financial security.

Getting uncomfortable may be easier for people who are truly miserable, people who are like I was at the age of 20, with little education, a dead-end job, and a family to support. But you must have at least a small sense of discomfort if, deep down, you know that you can have more material things, that your bank balance can be larger, that you can build a future that is truly secure and not based on the economy or the whims of the market.

Let's build on that feeling of being uncomfortable, because that's the feeling that will drive you out of your present rut and propel you toward wealth and financial independence. And you know where to start. You have to get disgusted. You have to make a decision to change. You have to visualize that change becoming a reality. And you must take the action necessary to make it happen.

Try Something

Once you're feeling uncomfortable, you must do something. Don't wait until you've read 10 or 20 or even 200 more books, or gone to 10 or 20 more seminars, or listened to more tapes. If you wait, you'll end up with all the information you need, you'll be very smart, but you'll still be broke. You must keep reading, listening, and learning, but you must take action at the same time. Action will build your personal fortune one step at a time. Then all of a sudden one day you'll look up and be stunned by the magnitude of what all those little actions have done for you.

If I said to you that you must go out and buy an income-producing property with positive cash flow within 60 days or you would die, do you think you could do it? Of course you could. And if you could do one within 60 days, do you think you could do a second one within the following 30 days? The answer, again, is yes.

Of course, the motivation in this example is extreme, but if you read this book and don't do anything to change your financial circumstances, I believe there is a small part of you, deep inside, that will die. One little bit at a time, your dreams will wither and die because you never did anything to keep them alive.

It is the time between this moment, right now, and your first action that is critical. Anticipation builds anxiety, and anxiety builds fear. Think about it. When you're at the doctor's office and you find out you need a shot, the anticipation of the needle going in is usually much worse than the injection itself. The longer you wait to take action, the more boogeymen your mind will conjure up.

Action overcomes anxiety and fear. Action gives you the opportunity to see what you can really do, to see if you really have what it takes to make your dreams and wishes come true. Action will make you wealthy.

So try something—anything. And if the first thing you try doesn't work, try something else.

From there it's just a matter of duplication. If you can do it once, you've got what it takes to be rich. Because if you can do it once, you can do it again, and again, until you build your own personal fortune.

Upgrade or Quit

Once you've had a taste of success, once you've made some money in business or real estate, then you can decide if you want more. Did you enjoy yourself, does it feel good, is this something you want to do again? Or did you hate it, did it make you think that living from paycheck to paycheck and retiring in poverty is okay?

We know that money makes money, and success breeds success. I believe that if you have just one financial achievement under your belt, you'll want more, and you'll get more.

If you inherited a business, would you learn how to run it? If you won a million dollars in a lottery, would you learn how to manage that money? If you were given a rental property, would you learn how to maintain it and keep it producing positive cash flow? I believe you would. And you know you would. And since we both know that you can do what it takes, what's stopping you?

The only possible thing it could be is fear. One way to take care of that fear is to give yourself permission to quit. The catch is that you can't quit until you have one success.

Think about it: One success, and then you can quit.

Or you can keep going, which is what I believe you will do. Because that one success will prove what I've been telling you, and it will give you the confidence to keep going.

So just do one small deal. One little duplex. One part-time, home-based business. Do it right, according to the formulas I've given you. Savor the taste of success. Revel in the freedom to control your own life. And make your own decisions about your future.

Find a Niche

Finding a niche allows you to focus your energies on one or two profitable ideas. It gives you the opportunity to learn all you need to know about them and to sharpen your skills in those areas so you can maximize your opportunities.

In real estate, for example, you'll find that certain techniques work better in some parts of the country than others. I've seen several students become specialists in government grants and rehabilitating low-income housing. You'll find that the older, larger cities have more government grant monies than rural areas or newer communities.

Along the same lines, both college towns and inner cities are usually excellent opportunities for rooming houses. Remember, one or two rooming houses can mean financial independence for you. The experience you'll gain by making those one or two investments will make the rest easy, because you'll have all your renovation and management systems in place.

In urban areas, you may concentrate on apartment houses. In the suburbs, your focus may be on single-family homes. Just find a niche that you're comfortable with, that you can become an expert at, and make it work for you.

In other businesses, the same strategy applies. Find a well-defined area where you can become an expert. Identify a need that isn't being met and figure out a way to meet it. Then create an operation that can run with or without you.

When you see an opportunity, latch on to it and work it for all it's worth. It could be the tidal wave you ride to success and wealth.

Courage and Guts

Courage is the ability to face the unknown, to take something you don't know about, figure it out, and get it done. We draw courage both from within ourselves and from outside sources.

When you've made your plans and started to put them into action, and things don't go quite as you thought they would, it takes guts to keep going. It's much easier to admit your failure and go back to nestle in the comfort of the ordinary masses. They'll take you back, too, because quitting makes you one of them. They'll pat you on the shoulder, give you a few "I told you so's," and reaffirm their own conviction that wealth is beyond them.

It takes guts to face the rejection and torment you'll get from the 95 Percenters in your life. It takes guts to keep going after you've encountered a few setbacks. It takes guts to be different, to become wealthy.

You might be full of great plans right now, and get shot down on your first few telephone calls. Or you might start out with a few great successes, and hit a dry spell just when you think you're on a roll. And you might think that the whole thing won't work, that you can't get wealthy. You might think that going to work and drawing a paycheck is a whole lot easier than this get-rich business.

But if you have guts, you'll get over that and get back on track.

Jerk Yourself Out of the Routine

Your first step to building wealth is to change your routine right now. Jerk yourself out of your comfortable rut, the humdrum pattern you've gotten used to. Get up an hour earlier. If you usually get up at six o'clock, set your alarm for five. Go to bed a little earlier if necessary. You don't need to watch the late-night news; there's nothing on that broadcast that you won't hear or read about tomorrow. If you eat meals at a certain time, eat at a different time. Do something different!

Set up an area in your home to serve as your office. If you have a spare room, great; if you don't, set aside a corner where you can put a desk, a chair, and a telephone. Make this designated area a place where you do business and nothing else. The kids don't play there, you don't watch television there. This is your space for serious time, serious thinking, and serious action.

In your office, begin building your Mindfeed library. Arrange your business reference material so you have easy access to it. Put this book in a prominent spot so you can refer back to it. And if you didn't use a marker to highlight what you thought were important points as you read, go back through this book and do it now—and do it with every Mindfeed book you read from now on.

Spend time at your desk early every morning before you have to head off to your job. Get the newspaper and start reading the classified ads. Make some phone calls to prospect on property or other business opportunities. You don't have to commit yourself, but do something different and learn how wealth-building activities feel. Call a few real estate agents. Tell them you're looking for cosmetically distressed low- and moderate-income properties with owner financing, and that you have money to put down. Let them get to work for you finding properties you can use to build your wealth. Then go take a look; get used to inspecting real estate. You don't have to commit to anything, you don't have to buy. But if you take this action enough times, you just might find a great deal, so be prepared for that.

Wake 'em Up Early and Make 'em Say Thanks

Start making your calls early, as early as 7:00 A.M. You may think calling people at this time of the morning will upset them or make them angry. But think about this. If you're spending good money to run an ad to sell a piece of property or a business, and someone calls you at 7:00 in the morning because he might want to buy it, are you going to be upset? Of course not. You'd welcome the call—and you might even feel just a little bit guilty or embarrassed that you weren't up earlier so you could answer the phone in a sharp, crisp voice. Making calls early in the morning puts you at an advantage, not a disadvantage.

When you make calls this early, you won't reach a lot of answering machines. But if you do get an answering machine or for some reason you can't reach the right person, set aside a time in the evening when you know you'll be home to take calls; when you leave your message, let the seller know when to call you back. That lets you concentrate your business into designated hours so you'll be more productive.

Plan the rest of your day and evening to get the most out of the time you have. Turn off the television; successful people don't spend much time in front of the TV. Take charge of your life. Break up your old routine at all costs; that was the routine of mediocrity. You now want to establish a routine of wealth.

Set Personal Fortune Goals

You hear about goals all the time, and I've even mentioned the importance of goals several places in this book. What's interesting about goals is that most people think they have them. They want to be rich, or they want to own a fancy car or a big house. They think about it, they fantasize about it, and they might even tell a few people about it—and so they think they have goals. But those aren't goals, they're dreams.

When you just think and wish and talk, it's a dream.

But when you write it down and commit to it, it's a goal.

That's right, you commit by writing your goals down, giving them deadlines, and figuring out a plan to achieve them.

And it isn't easy. So once you've got your office set up, make goal setting a priority. You need goals to give you direction, to help you plan each day to bring you closer to your own personal fortune, to make your life richer both personally and professionally.

As you set financial goals, it's also important to remember that money is a result, not a cause. If your cause is right and if you do your business correctly, you will make money. Set action goals—that is, things you can do that will produce the financial results you want. For example, if you buy income-producing property, and you do it with the formulas I've given you, you'll make money. If you buy a business, and if you research it thoroughly and run it wisely, you'll make money.

So make your goals things you can literally do and check off when they're complete. Not "I want to be rich," but "I want to own ten income-producing properties" or "I want to start my own business by a specific date, and I will take the following actions every day (list them) to achieve this goal."

Your goals must have a life of their own. When you see the words you've written, you need to see more than just ink and paper. You need to be able to see that goal coming to pass; you need to be able to see a future that is far better than today.

Develop both short- and long-term goals. Where do you want to be in five years? In three? In one? What will your bank account and investment portfolio look like? What will your business look like? Most important, what will *you* look like? Set your goals high enough so you have to stretch to reach them, but not so high that they are unattainable.

In my early days of investing, I set a goal of buying 100 rental units in one year. That sounds like a lot, especially if you've never invested in real estate or don't have much cash, but it's very realistic and attainable. I know today that it was a realistic goal, because I did it.

Now, I understand why the phrase "buy 100 rental units this year" can seem overwhelming to most people. If I had set that goal and done nothing else, it probably would have been overwhelming to me, too. But after I decided that my one-year goal was 100 units, I asked myself what I had to do in the first six months. To do 100 units a year, I only had to buy 50 in six months. That's still a large number. So I broke it down to three months, and I only had to buy 25 units. That's just eight units a month, or one little duplex a week.

Just one duplex a week means you can meet a goal of 100 units in a year. Just one eight-unit rooming house means you've met your monthly goal. A 24-unit apartment building means you've almost met your three-month goal. It doesn't sound so difficult when you look at it from that point of view.

The year I set this goal, I ended up with 123 units. There were times when I went weeks without buying any property, but then I'd find a property ideal for a ten-unit rooming house conversion, or a great eight-unit apartment building. At the end of the year, I'd met my goals—and the money was rolling in.

Once you have your goals clearly spelled out and broken down into manageable increments, you then must decide what you have to do to accomplish them. Those are your daily tasks, and they, too, need to be written down, given a deadline, and checked off when they're completed. For example, your daily tasks might look like this:

1. Get up at 5:30 A.M.
2. Make as many calls from the classified ads as possible (at least ten).
3. Have fliers printed.
4. Tell at least five people that I am investing in real estate and looking for properties.
5. Talk to at least two real estate agents.

A fundamental part of goal setting is time management. Time is what puts everyone on a level playing field. It's a nonrenewable resource; when it's gone, it's gone, and you can't get it back. I have 24 hours in my day—no more and no less than you do in yours. It's what you choose to do during those hours that will keep you broke or make you a fortune.

Day Planning

If you don't have a good day-planner, you need to get one. Use it to write down your daily tasks and appointments, then check things off as you accomplish them. Carry your planner with you everywhere, and use it for both personal and business items. Your daughter's music recital is just as important as inspecting a piece of property, and you want to be sure you don't let those events overlap. Keeping more than one calendar is cause for confusion, so don't do it. And if you have your day-planner with you all the time, you'll never forget something because it didn't get written down in the right place.

You can spend a lot of money on a calendar system, or you can keep track of your appointments and tasks in a spiral-bound notebook. The method doesn't matter; the key is to use a system that works easily for you. Many time-management programs are too complicated to be truly effective. What's important in a day-planner is that each day's page has space to record appointments, things you need to do, and follow-up notes. I personally use a day-planner sold by WLG, Inc. It has a rich leather binder with a zipper, the pages are arranged so you can easily keep track of tasks and appointments, and it has a section for yearly and monthly goals. For ordering information, call (800) 741-7877. Whatever system you select, make sure it's one you can manage and control, not one that controls you and takes all day to use.

Every year, I set aside time in December to plan my goals for the coming year. I write them down, then break them into monthly and weekly goals. Then I note what I need to do day by day in my day-planner. I encourage you to do the same. Start with long-range goals, then break them down into manageable monthly and daily goals. Write them down in your day-planner; put the yearly goals in the back, and the monthly and daily items throughout the calendar where they belong.

Writing down goals and making "to do" lists is only part of effective goal setting. I also use my day-planner to record notes about what I've accomplished so I can make adjustments if necessary. In effect, you have to keep score; if you don't, how will you know where you stand? You wouldn't go into a championship basketball game without keeping score, and you couldn't hold a successful charity fund-raiser without tracking how much money you collect.

So set goals and keep score. Know whether you're winning or losing the game of life.

Keep Your Eyes Open

You must put your goals in writing, but they should never be written in stone. You can adjust them up or down, or in a different direction entirely. Once you get going on your wealth-building plan, more things are going to come your way than you ever thought about, and you need to be prepared to take advantage of them.

You might run into someone selling a small apartment building who is also selling a business you could be interested in. You might meet a contractor who knows about a new government grant program you can take advantage of if you change your strategy just a little. When you're playing the wealth game, opportunities will happen to you, so don't be surprised when the source is unexpected. Keep your eyes open, and be prepared to take advantage of anything that comes along.

Pay particular attention to the cycles of the economy we discussed in Chapter Six. Remember, when the economy is slow and prices are down, it's a good time to buy and arrange seller financing. When the economy picks up, go back to those sellers and arrange for discounts on their mortgages. Consider selling the property or business when you can get top dollar for them.

You don't need a degree in economics to watch for economic cycles. Pay attention to the news (but keep your guard up against too much negativity). Track property prices. Listen to your instincts. You'll know when the time is right to buy and to sell.

The Fuel for Wealth

Energy is the fuel for wealth, so develop productive habits that keep you energized. That means talking in an enthusiastic tone, standing up straight, and smiling. It means staying in shape with proper diet and exercise. You don't have to jog 30 miles or lose 50 pounds by next week, but you should set some goals to improve your physical condition to increase your energy level.

If you maintain a positive energy level, you never have to be depressed. Have you ever seen an energetic depressed person? Of course not. That doesn't mean you won't ever have problems; some days will always be better than others. But why is it that when some people get depressed, they stay down for an hour, and others stay down for three months?

How long you are depressed is your decision. It's up to you. When you get tired of it, you'll do something to get out of it. So take a walk. Eat a nutritious meal. Get some fresh air. Laugh out loud. Do whatever it takes to keep your energy level up, because energy beats depression. Energy gives you hope to visualize your dreams. And energy is your fuel for wealth.

What to Do Saturday Night or Sunday Morning

Most of us associate Monday morning with going back to work, back to the grind, back to the salt mines. We talk about the Monday-morning blahs. You might find it hard to begin your wealth-building program on a day that has such a bad reputation. But don't wait to start getting wealthy—do it now! Whatever time or day it is right now, make your plan and put it into action. Get out of your rut. Make every day a great day, because now you're working for yourself and your financial future. You're going to do the things that the 95 Percenters can't or won't do. You're an achiever, so get excited about it.

Go back through this book and focus on the one or two wealth-building techniques you're going to try first. Though I have used every technique explained in this book, I didn't apply them all at once. That would have been impossible, and I wouldn't be where I am today if I had tried. You shouldn't try to do it all at once, either. Just choose one or two ideas and make some plans to accomplish those things. Put your plans into motion, make them work, and then go on to something else. If you take a systematic approach, you will see results—and you'll see them quickly.

Come Back for Your Wealth Workout

Recently I was talking to the man who runs the health club where I work out, and he gave me a statistic I think is ridiculous. He said that 40 percent of the people who join the health club never come back for their first workout. Think about that! These people pay hundreds of dollars and never get any benefit at all from their investment. They don't even try it and decide they don't like it. They don't do anything at all!

Reading this book through the first time is the equivalent of signing up at a health club. To really get any benefit from your investment of time and money, you must come back for your workout. Because this is the workout of wealth.

Self-Help Resources

Note: Every effort was made to gather current information on public and private sources for you to use in developing your wealth-building program. However, it's possible that some of the addresses and telephone numbers have changed since this list was compiled. If you are unable to reach the office listed with the information I have provided, please call directory assistance in that city and ask for the correct number, or call me at (813) 542-8999 and I'll do what I can to help.

Federal Money Programs

Small Business Administration
Loan Policy and Procedures Branch
409 3rd Street, S.W.
Washington, DC 20416
(202) 205-6570

Contact for loans and loan guarantees for small business; loans to small businesses owned by Vietnam-era and disabled veterans; loans to small businesses owned by low-income persons; management and technical assistance for businesses located in areas of high unemployment. Type and amount of funds vary with programs.

Small Business Administration
Office of Women's Business Ownership
409 3rd Street, S.W., 6th Floor
Washington, DC 20416
(202) 205-6673

Contact for loans and information promoting small businesses owned and controlled by women.

Service Corps of Retired Executives Association (SCORE)
National SCORE Office
409 3rd Street, S.W., Suite 5900
Washington, DC 20024-3212
(202) 205-6762
(800) 634-0245

Contact to utilize the management experience of retired and active business executives who counsel and train potential and existing small businesses. You may be referred to a local SCORE contact.

Multifamily Housing Processing Division
Farmers Home Administration (FHA)
Department of Agriculture
14th & Independence Avenue, S.W.
Washington, DC 20250
(202) 720-4323

Contact for loan guarantees and rental assistance programs for rental housing in rural areas.

Economic Development Administration
Public Affairs Office
Room H7824, Herbert C. Hoover Building
Department of Commerce
Washington, DC 20230
(202) 482-5113

Contact for loans for businesses that create or retain permanent jobs and plants in redevelopment areas.

Office of Program Development
Room 5096, Minority Business Agency
Department of Commerce
14th & Constitution Avenue, N.W.
Washington, DC 20230
(202) 482-3237

Contact for business-development services for minority firms and individuals.

Office of Insured Multifamily Housing Development
Policy and Procedures
Department of Housing and Urban Development
Washington, DC 20410
(202) 708-2556

Contact for loan guarantees to provide quality rental housing for low- and moderate-income families, middle-income families, and the elderly or disabled. Also for loan guarantees to provide quality rental housing in urban-renewal areas, code-enforcement areas, and other areas designated for overall revitalization.

Title I Insurance Division
Department of Health and Human Services
451 7th Street, S.W.
Washington, DC 20410
(202) 708-2880
(800) 733-4663

Contact for loan guarantees for home-improvement loans.

Office of Urban Rehabilitation
Community Planning and Development
Department of Housing and Urban Development (HUD)
451 7th Street, S.W.
Washington, DC 20410
(202) 708-2685

Contact for grants for rental housing units for lower-income families.

Office of Elderly and Assisted Housing
Rental Assistance Division
Department of Housing and Urban Development
Washington, DC 20410
(202) 708-0477

Contact for information on Section 8 rental-assistance program.

This is only a partial list of the federal funds available to investors, entrepreneurs, and small business. For a complete listing, see the *Catalog of Federal Domestic Assistance,* published by the U.S. Government Printing Office in Washington, D.C. Contact:

Superintendent of Documents
Government Printing Office
Washington, DC 20402
(202) 783-3238

State Money Programs

Contact your state housing authority, your department of community affairs, and your local economic development office. Ask for a listing of all state grant programs; most states publish a catalog with this information.

RTC Headquarters

Resolution Trust Corporation
801 17th Street, N.W.
Washington, DC 20434-0001
(202) 416-6900

Credit Bureaus

TRW Information Services
12606 Greenville Avenue
Dallas, TX 75243
(800) 422-4879

CSC Credit Services, Inc.
P. O. Box 674422
Houston, TX 77267-4422
(713) 878-1990

Equifax, Inc.
P. O. Box 740241
Atlanta, GA 30374-0241
(800) 685-1111

Nonprofit Credit Assistance

National Foundation for Consumer Credit
8611 2nd Avenue, Suite 100
Silver Spring, MD 20910
(301) 589-5600

For Information about Biweekly Mortgage Programs

Mortgage Reduction System/EquityCorp.
4818 Coronado Parkway
Cape Coral, Florida 33904
(800) 741-7877

For Information about Russ Whitney's Bird Dog Program

Bird Dog Program
4818 Coronado Parkway
Cape Coral, Florida 33904
(800) 741-7877

For Information about Programs Offered Through the Whitney Leadership Group

Russ Whitney
Whitney Leadership Group, Inc.
4818 Coronado Parkway
Cape Coral, Florida 33904
(800) 741-7877

Acknowledgments

To note everyone who in some way made a contribution to this book would be a book in itself and an impossible list to compile. There are, however, some special people who deserve recognition:

Ingrid, my wife of 17 years, who has worked tirelessly as my personal and professional partner in our various endeavors, cared for our children, and been patient and supportive with my whims.

Thea and Russell, my children and true legacy, who help me see the world through a fresh perspective.

The late Russell Walter Whitney (1931–1970), my father, who was my foundation.

The staff of the Whitney Leadership Group, who share my commitment to helping others improve their lives, especially the people who work in our customer-service department and our dozens of business consultants who work in person and on the phones helping our students achieve their dreams.

Our longtime executives and administrative support staff, particularly John Kane, chief executive of our computer and software-development company; Scott Gleckel, president of the Whitney Leadership Group; Debra Patsones, vice president of customer relations; Cindy Barajas, controller of Whitney Leadership Group; Don Abbott, president of our television production company in charge of corporate communications; Shelley Crant-Baggot, my administrative assistant; Kathy Smith, Kathy Gomez, Scott Deane, and all the people who work for and with more than a dozen companies I own in the United States and abroad. Special thanks to William Ramirez, president of my manufacturing and construction companies in Latin and Central America.

Our hundreds of thousands of students, many of whom have been the source of the stories and illustrations in this book; they provide daily affirmation of my efforts.

My editor, Fred Hills, for his willingness to take on this project; and my literary agent, Michael Baybak, for his support during its creation.

269

Jacquelyn Denalli, who provided valuable editorial assistance and was so patient when the writing turned to rewriting. Great job, Jackie!

Finally, all of those people who told me all of these years that it cannot be done. You have pushed me to give you hope.

My thanks to all of you.

Index